SOUL LIGHTNING

SOUL LIGHTNING

✦

AWAKENING SOUL CONSCIOUSNESS

Aminah Raheem, Ph.D.

iUniverse, Inc.
New York Lincoln Shanghai

SOUL LIGHTNING:
AWAKENING SOUL CONSCIOUSNESS

iUniverse books may be ordered through booksellers or by contacting:

iUniverse
2021 Pine Lake Road, Suite 100
Lincoln, NE 68512
www.iuniverse.com
1-800-Authors (1-800-288-4677)

ISBN-13: 978-0-595-34811-4 (pbk)
ISBN-13: 978-0-595-79540-6 (ebk)
ISBN-10: 0-595-34811-4 (pbk)
ISBN-10: 0-595-79540-4 (ebk)

Printed in the United States of America

Dedicated to:

My soul mate and husband, Fritz Frederick Smith

and

My family of soul allies: Paulina Stomel, Philip Lindstrom, Rosalind Crew and William Henry Crew

Contents

Acknowledgements

I am blessed with many soul friends, colleagues and students who have supported and encouraged my work, including this book, over the past two decades. I thank my husband and soul mate, Fritz Frederick Smith, always a constant source of love, kindness, wisdom, and masterful treatments, who listened to chapters, encouraged me in the creative process and lifted my spirits when they lagged. My family, soul allies all, are ever close to me and my work.

I am especially grateful to my daughter Paulina, son-in-law Lauren, and son William Henry, for supporting my writing sabbatical; that time out made 2005 publication possible. I thank my son Philip, his wife Mara, and my daughter Rosalind for their ongoing love, encouragement and creative feedback.

Hal Zina Bennett, a master developmental editor and faithful friend, provided feedback, creative guidance and praiseworthy patience in helping me clarify and polish the original manuscript. Thank you, Hal, for being ever available with your valuable experience and compassionate heart.

The process of composing this book was greatly assisted by my writing group in Borrego Springs. Thank you, Barbara, Mary, Victor, Deborah and Charlie for your careful listening and insightful editorial comments during all those meetings.

I thank Dawn Robbins who provided invaluable service as a proof reader that went far beyond proofing. Her keen ear, eagle eye and enthusiastic response always cheered me on.

Lauren Stomel, a master of graphic design, interrupted his intense production schedule to create the cover. Thank you, Lauren, for your time, talent and love and for being part of the process. I also thank Cathy Miller for her first drafts of the cover.

I am deeply grateful to Susan Grant, Cathy Miller and all the creators of *The Birthday Party* which warmed my heart and whole life, and also helped support the sabbatical.

I thank the Process and Basic Acupressure Faculty and students for their dedication to our work and for reading and commenting on parts of the book, giving their permission to describe some of their experiences and enthusiastically supporting the process.

Finally acknowledgements of support, love and loyalty are only complete when I thank my Process Partner, Laura, long time soul ally, who was always available to read and give creative feedback.

Section I: Introduction

I was struck by the term "soul lightning" when I realized one day that our awakening to soul consciousness is often initiated by an abrupt, high voltage charge that disrupts our entire being, even as it illuminates our souls. Just as lightning brilliantly floods the entire landscape with a blinding flash that lasts but a split second, so it is that soul lightnings can instantly awaken us to our Divine essence.

While the book tells of soul lightnings in my personal journey and the life work that developed from it, it also tells about lightning strikes to others that I have witnessed and how those strikes affected them. From the beginning I have visualized the book as a way of shedding light on what can occur when we awaken from the cocoon of conditioning that has clouded our clear inner light of wisdom and love for centuries.

When I wrote my first book, *Soul Return: Integrating Body, Psyche and Spirit,* I believed it was necessary to clear the various layers of armoring in the body/mind before the soul was accessible. But I began to observe a remarkable *light-en-ing* process in my students—a speedy progression that was penetrating through the traumas and dramas of personal history to expose the center of light within them. It seemed as if once people were pointed toward the possibility of returning to soul they were able to do it without the aid of long-term therapy, if they followed their own process faithfully.

I was observing how people could find soul strength and guidance long before all their "issues" were cleared. I saw how they moved forward, faster and more expansively than I could have imagined. They had either found, or were working swiftly toward, their own soul wisdom and purpose. They were clearer, healthier, happier and more creative than ever before. They found deep satisfaction in their own nature and truth and were fulfilling their destinies. And as they claimed their own soul light-en-ing process they were similarly helping others, for most of them began to serve the world in positive ways.

At the same time there were others who seemed to get stuck in an endless recycling of past issues that had plagued them all their lives, never quite finding their way. I observed this especially in people who had done a lot of psychotherapy that didn't reference the body or the soul. They tended to become mired in a depressive processing muddle, cycling around and around in the traumas of their childhoods, unable to engage fully in the life they were living *now.*

Long ago, when I was a graduate student in psychology, I had a strong intuition about the inadequacy of psychotherapy alone to liberate the whole human being. Now I was beginning to observe empirically the fallacy of encapsulating a human being into that five—to six-year period of fundamental conditioning that Freud said would shape us for life. I was beginning to see that the programming of those first years was only a very small part of a more vast intelligence that contains centuries of ancestral strands, a multitude of past lives and an eternal soul blueprint.

Although I had been observing a soul lightening process in people in my spiritual practice for many years, I had assumed it could only happen with the extra grace of a spiritual practice. Now I was observing it in the ordinary world. I was beginning to see the filmy shape of soul destiny and it looked like the gold at the end of the rainbow.

So this book is also about healing, finishing the past and creating a new life from the fabric of our own souls. It is about returning to the soul and to the unity and love inherent in all life. About a radical awakening in human consciousness, soul lightning, that is already happening as we move inexorably toward massive change. Amid the many ills and catastrophes in our world today, this is good news.

The book also describes the remarkable teachers, places and events that illuminated soul paths. And it tells how we can embrace the power of soul lightning for our own good. I have done my best to tell these experiences truthfully.

This is the book you're holding now. I hope it stimulates memories of soul lightning in your own life and helps you seize them with fervor.

1

The Rainmaker

An ancient Chinese story about a village emergency and a Taoist Master is a timely metaphor for our present world struggle. The story requires understanding of two simple but key words and concepts from the Chinese Taoist tradition: Tao and Taoist master.

TAO means the One, the Allness of everything that is—all at once. TAO is the Origin Spirit, the fullness and emptiness, the beginningless and endless substance from which all else arises. We come from it and return to it. A western translation for the TAO would be God, the Divine, Great Creative Order or any number of other Names for That which is nameless.

A Taoist master is one who follows the Way of the Tao: in other words he seeks to be, and live, in harmony with Divine Order, All that Is.

The story goes that a Chinese village found itself in a big mess one year. All was in chaos. There had been a drought for a long time, and crops weren't bearing. People were starving, frightened and at odds with one another. They started hoarding and quarreling.

Finally an elder spoke up.

"Stop! Listen! We need outside help, higher help. There's a famous Taoist Master who, it is said, can make rain. Let's call him in."

So the Taoist master was sent for and arrived at the village. He took a long look around, walked among the people and talked with them. Then he asked for a private place where he could be alone for awhile.

The people provided him with a little hut. He went into it and shut the door. He didn't come out that day or the next, or the next.

You can imagine how the people were baffled. They grew restless, hung around and wrung their hands. They waited, grumbling. They had expected some kind of ritual or prayer at least but this "savior" they hoped would make rain just stayed in the hut, without a word. Still they waited. And eventually surrendered to the inevitable.

Then, on the fifth day it started to rain and rain and rain.

After awhile the Taoist master came out of the house. The people cried:

"What happened to you? We asked you here to make rain and all you did was hole up in our hut."

The Taoist master replied:

"When I first arrived in your village, the people, the environment, everything was so out of Tao that I had to withdraw to a quiet private place where I could get myself back into Tao before anything was possible. Now it's raining."

Today we live in a global village and we are in a big mess. Droughts and all kinds of other disasters, natural and of our own making, plague us. We are quarreling and hoarding, grasping for more and more material and frenetically creating our own destructions one upon another. We are out of harmony—with ourselves, our fellow humans and nature. We desperately need to find our way back to the One Spirit of creation. To respect ourselves and one another as all part of that One radiant, abundant, unifying Spirit.

I have been pondering our world situation for a long time and trying to find ways to contribute to health and well being for more people and our planet, beyond individual therapy. After facing death at twenty-nine I made a vow to God to serve Divine Order the best I could for the rest of my life. I decided at that time that one of the best ways for me to serve life in this world was to help individuals wake up to become healthy and whole because healthy individuals could create healthy societies. Toward this purpose I studied many methods of healing and bodywork, completed a Ph.D. in transpersonal psychology, and post graduate work in Process Work.

I continued to learn for twenty-five years as I practiced body/mind therapy with individuals. I also worked as a helper, a kind of counselor, in my spiritual practice of Subud. That practice had given me a direct and sustaining experience of my own soul and its wisdom. Therefore all the time I was studying about the body and the personality that develops through early life I always knew first hand that people are more than their minds, feelings or bodies.

During study and practice I learned several major keys to help people free themselves from traumas and misguidings of the past. From psychology I learned how the past, particularly early conditioning, is held in both our conscious and unconscious minds and shapes our personalities, sometimes for an entire lifetime. Through bodywork, I experienced and observed how that past, our personal history, is stored as palpable information within our bodies, and I learned ways to release damaging history directly from the tissues.

Sometimes these traumas of the past could be released without the client's awareness of their content or any processing about them. At other times traumas needed to be brought to consciousness and understood. Then the client could make conscious, free choices about their beliefs and behaviors instead of being driven by unconscious forces.

In Process Work I learned how to simultaneously process mental and emotional information that arose from both the conscious and unconscious minds. This was an invaluable skill when unconscious information and emotions were released from the body. Yet through all these studies and their applications I remembered the importance of the soul in my own life and others I observed.

As I worked with people I gradually designed a holistic way to work with the body, mind, emotions and soul simultaneously. It was empirical and tested, on myself and then others in a busy practice. Although

I facilitated clients in processing through the layers of inherited physical, emotional and mental trappings that impeded their whole development, the main aim of this work was always to help people uncover the sound guidance that every individual has at a soul level. I wrote about that approach in *Soul Return, Integrating Body, Psyche and Spirit*, published in 1991. Even before its publication I had started teaching my work around the U.S. and in Europe.

I started to write a sequel to *Soul Return,* to explain more exactly how the lofty aspirations of spiritual development needed to be grounded through the physical body and the personality. I described how personal history is imprinted in body tissue and how to update obstructive patterns through conscious work with the body. I wrote more exactly about the energy systems of the body as the integrating factor between body, mind, emotions and soul and how to work through them to reach the soul. Principally I was trying to substantiate how to attune to Spirit, and follow it, to find the peace and happiness we all crave.

Finally I had a book's worth of manuscript that spelled out the particulars of holistic psycho-spiritual work. It was a decent text but the book just wouldn't gel; something didn't click. That book still sits in the closet.

Then one day as I was fussing with myself about how to proceed a new book was born. *SOUL LIGHTNING!* flashed across my consciousness. That's it, said my inner soul voice. Tell about soul lightning.

Now at the time I didn't understand what that meant. But my body, heart and soul knew right off the bat. I felt electrified, stunned and wide awake all in the same moment. Dannion Brinkley's story flooded my mind, the true story he tells so well in *Saved by the Light*,[1] a book I highly recommend.

---

1. Brinkley, Dannion. *Saved by the Light.* New York, HarperCollinsPublishers, 1994.

In his book Brinkley explains how one lightning bolt flashed through the telephone line he was talking on and killed him. He was clinically dead for twenty-five minutes, until he was miraculously resuscitated. During those minutes Brinkley "lived" through a remarkable near-death experience that has informed his life ever since. As he left his body he traveled through a dark tunnel and finally into a brilliant light where he was greeted by Beings of Light who offered him complete love, forgiveness and understanding. Then they led him through many stronger-than-life experiences that clarified the life he had lived. He was also shown his own future, and the possible futures of our planet, events that *could* happen on earth.

Finally Brinkley was instructed about the life he was to commence upon his return. As his book title indicates, he says he was saved during this near-death experience because he was shown a vast Universal vision of life and purpose, beyond the ordinary tangles of this world. He saw the holiness of life and the power of love to transform what had been spoiled.

Brinkley's experience transformed the life he had been living and gave him a life mission of world service beyond anything he could have imagined before. He reported that his old life was broken and shaken beyond comprehension. He came back to a life in which the past had been burned away.

His body didn't fare so well; the experience was physically devastating. Even though he was resuscitated, most of his nervous system was seared, his skin charred, several organs torn up and his brain and consciousness re-arranged. There was a long recovery period. It was relentless, painful, and disorienting.

But eventually Brinkley was able to integrate and ground what he had experienced in that Other Dimension through a more-or-less recovered body. Now he travels around the world telling about his personal transformation because the teachings he received during his death-by-lightning were for all of humanity, not just himself. At last report 95 of the 117 future events he was shown have already come true. His book is riveting and it deconstructs much of what we think we know about consciousness.

I had also been studying other accounts of people who had experienced near-death experiences in recent years. Almost all of them reported spiritual awakenings. Their lives had been quickened and irrevocably changed. As they examined and integrated the effects of their deaths, each experienced a greater commitment to meaning and purpose in their lives, and they never feared death again.

Near-death survivors experienced not only the illusion of death but also the eternality of life. Many psychological afflictions were cured in one flash: despair, boredom, superficiality of a materially oriented life, rampant violence that focuses on destroying life, lack of joy, the overwhelm of many seemingly insoluble global problems. Instead they came away from the lightning strike of near-death with a serenity that lifted them out of these prevalent mires. They saw through the shutters of this world into a great benevolence and order of the Universe. They had seen eternity for a short moment.

In one sense all of these people did die. The old self they had lived came to an end. Although they still functioned externally as they had before, the foundation of that old self had been burned up and eventually just fell away. A rebirth into a deeper self, an inner lightening of the soul, became more important than the personality of the past. They also experienced the interrelationship of all life, the Unity of the Great Creative flow. They had been returned from the edge of death with a perspective and purpose that were to make their "new" lives much richer. Life after near-death was more precious, more meaningful.

It took awhile, and more soul searching, as I contemplated just how to write about soul lightning. I remembered something I had read about Peruvian shamen who trek high up into the Andes mountains in search of lightning because it strikes there frequently. They believe that if you survive lightning it can bring enlightenment.

Then I remembered how lightning first appeared in my life, the story I tell in Chapter 2. I began to recall all those lightning strikes I had experienced in my own soul journey and those I had witnessed in friends, students, and clients. Then I gradually realized that I had been on the trail of lightning all of this life without ever actually defining it until recently.

In this book I tell about how I tracked the zigzag course of lightning through my and other people's lives. I asked, "What were those events, people and phenomena that lighted up my soul and helped me see the grander design of the Universe?" Gradually I remembered and gathered stories about the lightning strikes of awakening that I had witnessed. About the strokes of Heaven that came, unexpected and unbidden, in a burst of light and shock so great that soul consciousness was aroused and the landscape of life changed in a flash. About the deaths caused by that light and the new life that grew out of it.

Section II: Early Soul Signs

2

The Beginning—Lightning in the Saucer

Lightning first struck our family when I was only eleven or twelve years old. I understand now that it seared an essential life teaching through my whole body-being. But of course I couldn't possibly understand then that lightning was a soul sign to guide my destiny and purpose later on.

It happened like this: My mother, my two little sisters and I were alone in a mountain cabin for the summer while Daddy worked in the valley. It was just a simple little cottage, dilapidated but cozy, with a big oak tree leaning into the roof.

One afternoon the four of us were sitting at the kitchen table finishing lunch. I remember exactly where we were, my littlest sister, still a baby, beside mother in a high chair and the other sister, just four, next to me.

A storm was slithering down from the higher mountains. Gigantic summer boiling thunderheads were pushing a big creeping shadow across the land. We could hear thunder beginning to rumble in the distance.

As the sky grew darker Mother reached up and turned on the light just above the table. It was a single unshaded bulb at the end of a cord attached to the ceiling. I remember that she pulled a little chain at the top of the light bulb. It felt comforting when the light shone on the table into the darkening room.

Mother said something motherly, like "Oh, an exciting storm coming our way."

I didn't know what she meant but I felt scared as the sky darkened and gusts of wind pushed at the door. I wiggled around in my chair and looked at mother for some kind of assurance. Something like, don't worry, it will be OK. But she jumped up to put a chair in front of the door to keep it from blowing open. We could hear the big oak tree creaking as it pushed harder into the roof. It seemed like it would crash through any minute. Mother listened, her ear upturned, as thunder rolled, closer and faster between rumblings.

Then rain pelted the roof in raspy hits. The wind blew a cold spray through the flimsy door jam. I ducked as it splashed my legs. Little sister's eyes flew wide open and she leaned into me. Soon we could hear rivulets whishing down the hillside near the cabin. If it kept up I knew water would be flooding into the cabin floor.

A flash of lightning streaked past the window.

Then a boom of thunder shook the flimsy cabin.

Little sister whimpered. I put my arm around her. Although I was only eleven I felt responsible, along with mother, for the younger ones while Daddy was away. My mind scurried after him and his steady, skilled strength. I was scared myself but aware of the responsibility for little sisters, I was double scared. Usually I loved summer storms with their great mountain foamy clouds and distant thunder. But this one suddenly felt too big and we were too little. I wasn't at all sure Mother could deal with what was happening.

Mother picked up the baby and held her close to her body. In retrospect I am quite sure she must have been terrified herself. I remember looking to her for direction.

She started to say something, perhaps to give assurance, when a deafening crack of lightning hit the roof right over our heads. Then a pinging sound like a bullet whining. A brilliant flash of light. And a gigantic jolt pounded the cabin.

We had been struck!

It must have happened in a split second after the hit but what we saw next dragged through my consciousness in slow motion like a stretched-out, time-lapse movie…

The hanging lightbulb just over our heads…
severs from its cord with a hissing burn-flash.
The bulb hits the table right in front of us
It lands in the center of a saucer…
I watch, spellbound,
As the bulb rocks back and forth in the saucer
before it just settles there
at full stop
completely intact.

We sat frozen for a few moments in that scene. Everything went silent. A singed smell hung in the air. The baby clung to Mother. Little sister held to my waist without a sound. Mother's eyes were wide with fear and wonder. She knew full well, which I only sensed instinctively at the time, that we had been very close to extinction in that moment and that it was a miracle we were alive.

Then there was the visible, incontestable fact of the lightbulb.

"Well look at that!" Mother said, her eyes fixed on the fragile lightbulb in the saucer.

I too looked at it in wonderment. Why hadn't it broken? How had it missed any one of us as it fell so directly over our heads? Why hadn't we ourselves been struck down by the lightning bolt that severed the light cord directly over our heads?

It was an amazing mystery even Mother couldn't explain. I remember that she told Daddy about it later as she showed him the lightbulb. He took it in his hand and looked at it for a long time, turning it over and over. Then he just shook his head. I didn't know if he even believed her.

We never talked about it after that. There was something mighty and magic about that event that required saving it away, buried in a pocket of my secret unknowing. *The lightning bolt that burned an indelible image across the fabric of my life.*

Sometimes it came back to me, nudged at my consciousness and posed unanswerable questions: How was it possible for the electrical cord to sever completely and the paper-thin light bulb not to break, not even crack? There was no answer in contemporary physics. How did we escape harm, not even one little burn? Neither medicine nor philosophy have provided an answer for that.

Much later in life I wondered if there could be a pattern of destiny in it: why did this happen to the four of us and not Daddy? What was this single strike from heaven, awesome and terrifying that could shake the earth, crack into our home and still leave the most fragile of structures, a lightbulb, intact? Why did it come back to me again and again, this strange luminescent memory, when it had faded from our family's history? These questions defied all analysis. Where could I find the answers?

I pondered these things occasionally, searching for a meaning that would help me. I didn't find it until *Soul Lightning!* flashed across my mind. It is only recently that I began to comprehend the message.

Although I have never told anyone about it until now, that was the lightning strike that marked a destiny design into my life. And the one that started this book.

3

The Light and Dark of the World

Light Behind the World

Big Light had appeared in my life even before lightning in the saucer but I didn't relate the two until many years later. It showed up as a radiant glow behind the world that lit the whole landscape much brighter than day.

I must have been about four or five years old when it happened because my real father was already dead. He was run over by a train not long after my fourth birthday. Mother was in the car with him when the train hit it but she was thrown free. In her body, that is. I believe some parts of her were trapped in that death scene for the rest of her life.

Father's violent death registered deep within my psyche even though I was with a baby sitter at the time. I know about this because of an experience I had in India more than fifty years later when the impact of his death hit me in a full-body way.

At that childhood time father's sudden death was still hovering over mother and our lives as a great heavy sorrow. The house felt coated with it, somber and silent. Mother was listless, in deep confused grief. She never laughed nor smiled. Our ranch home on the Sonora desert, once a happy and endlessly fascinating playground, had become a funereal wasteland. I felt smothered in that thick blanket of unspoken pain and helplessness. To me it was as if both parents had died. I felt abandoned, alone and forgotten in the tidal waves of grief that continued to wash over mother, grandmother and anyone else who came near us.

So one evening when I wandered off barefoot into the twilight desert mother didn't notice. The further I got from the house the better I felt. I was free out there, peaceful, away from the grief-soaked house.

I just walked along noticing the rocks, the afterglow of sunset on the mountains in the distance, little creatures—desert rats, chipmunks and rabbits scurrying between scrub brush. I kept going, on and on, right up a "mountain" to my child's eyes although it was simply a small ridge above the desert floor. There was nothing in my mind but wonder.

Suddenly everything—the sky, the brush, the mountains—lit up in an intense glow. It was as if a gigantic floodlight shone out from the center of the universe, penetrating everything everywhere. The light was so bright it seemed to erase the world. Mountains glowed gold, bushes turned translucent, even rocks sparkled. Everything was intensely alive.

I stopped, stunned by the incandescent beauty of the light. At the same time an intense feeling of allrightness began to envelop me. How to describe this feeling in words? It was expansive, all pervasive and it filled me with comfort and love bigger than anything I had ever experienced. I no longer felt alone, I felt *accompanied.* In a burst of clear knowing, I could *feel* that my father was alive and near, protecting and caring for me. In the same instant I *knew,* or remembered, many things at once: That I was a part of all this wonder surrounding me. That all of It was pure love. That It had never abandoned me, or anyone. That It had always been right here. And that all of It was One Thing.

I have no idea whether that instant light lasted for a few seconds or long minutes but its effect has endured all my life, shining behind all the tangled dramas and traumas, like a clear beacon. It first showed me that a Great Loving Radiance shines behind the world all the time. In adulthood when I read about mystical experiences I understood what had happened to me. I would come to realize that it was that Radiance that gave me a first impression of enlightenment.

When the light subsided that evening it was suddenly night. Only stars shone in a black sky. I ran all the way home in the dark, not afraid but still infused with a mighty bliss. When I reached the house I wanted to give That comfort to Mother, to spread It everywhere, to tell her that everything was all right, that there was no need for grief, that father was right here, that he loved us and looked out for us and that we were all One in a Great Thing. But of course I didn't have the words for all that.

So I sat down quietly and waited for her to notice Something. But Mother didn't notice the love nor see the light that I still carried. She couldn't seem to feel any of That through the thick veil of her sorrow. Instead she looked at my feet.

"What happened to your feet!" she exclaimed.

Then I saw the cactus stickers all over my bare feet. I hadn't felt them go in at all and they weren't stinging as they usually did.

They stung a lot when she pulled them out though.

Dark in the World

It was about the same time that the darkness of this world also visited me. It came in a nightmare with a force far beyond my five-year-old self to handle. It wasn't until mid-life that I became aware of its soul implications.

In the dream I was alone in our family cemetery at night. It was pouring rain so hard that the earth was beginning to slide beneath me. I was cold and wet and my feet were slipping in the mud.

My father's grave was open, close to where I stood. He was trying to rise out of that great black hole. His body was already decaying. Only the top of it was partly intact; the bottom beneath his waist was decomposing, exposing the skeleton. The rain was pouring down over him and the grave was filling up with mud. He had a tortured look in his eyes. He reached his arms out to me, imploring. Although he didn't speak he seemed to be calling desperately for help, before it was too late and he was completely decayed.

I was at once horrified—the sight alone was hideous—and paralyzed in terror. Could he pull me into the grave with him? At the same time I felt that I *must do something* to help him but I was entirely powerless. I knew I was too little and anyway didn't know how. I stood there, frozen in place.

Then I woke up, shaking in panic. I ran from my bed to get my mother but when I found her I was too frightened and dumbstruck to tell her about the dream. Instead I just followed her around, holding on to her skirt, trying to get some comfort and guidance for something that was beyond understanding or solace.

The dream happened only once but it burned a permanent imprint into my mind that was always hovering in the background. Throughout childhood and early adulthood it felt like a curse that I must never divulge for fear that its power could spill out into my or others' lives. I never told anyone about it until midlife.

The nightmare also alerted me very early to the power of dreams, an understanding that has always figured prominently in my personal process. During hard times I have often relied more on dreams than waking life to give me guidance about where to go next.

Many years later, when I studied psychology, I learned about the connection between dreams and life and how to interpret their meaning. I thought about the nightmare and tried to analyze it from a psychological perspective. It seemed to defy those guidelines however; I couldn't decipher its meaning. Any interpretations I gave it felt contrived.

After graduate school in psychology I studied Process Work with Arnold Mindell at his Process Work Institute in Switzerland. There I learned about the connection between dramatic childhood dreams and soul destiny. C.G. Jung, the great depth psychologist, first identified the relationship. He discovered that very often a strong childhood dream revealed an important pattern of destiny. He said that his exploration of patients' earliest dreams had often revealed talents and propensities, symbols or designs that had shown deeply meaningful directions for the whole life. Arnold Mindell told me he had verified Jung's discovery many times with his own clients and students.

I was fascinated by this concept and everything else we were learning about Mindell's brilliant Process Work method. We were finding out how to follow the signals of the unconscious to discover what was really going on beneath the surface of the ego and personality. How to process through the tensions and supposed obstructions in our lives so that we could probe the cocoon of conditioning. I loved gaining these tools. They helped me and my clients to penetrate beneath pretenses and to track what was trying to unfold from the growth shoots of the unconscious. They helped us cut through the tangles of personal history more rapidly and truthfully. Many personal mysteries became clear that I hadn't been able to unravel through my psychological training.

We also learned how to process dreams in a more holistic way than I had learned before. That is, we tracked beyond associations and symbolic interpretations to the inner dream-maker and the very roots of the dream within our bodies.

I decided to revisit the early nightmare and explore it with a Process Work approach. A colleague and good friend assisted me in acting it out. He directed me in the steps of the nightmare and encouraged me to feel the dream as if it "were happening right now."

First I re-experienced the cemetery, the rain, and the mud sliding down. I felt helpless in the face of that onslaught. Then he told me to become the grave. It was bottomless, a great vortex pulling me down. Then my colleague said to become my father in his half-decomposed state, reaching out to me. When I became Father an indescribable desperation gripped me as I grasped for the tiny child who was my only hope. Then I was asked to become the child. I was again that terrified little girl, wanting desperately to help, but paralyzed in fear and helplessness. I felt the child's impossible dilemma.

Through the body-felt enactment of the nightmare I began to experience a depth of knowing in body and emotions that I had never fathomed through mental analysis. That hologramic reproduction made the dream's meaning available to adult consciousness. By the end of that process I was exhilarated as many implications began to dawn in consciousness.

For example, I became aware that this nightmare had directed much of my life's work. I realized how my interests and training had led me to try to help people rise out of the death trap of unconsciousness. I had been trying to awaken myself and others to the vital life beyond the cocoon, the grave of conditioning.

The dream was actually part of my soul destiny encoding.

This understanding brought emotional release and purpose about the nightmare. Its original trauma had transformed into a gift that brought strength for my soul purpose.

But even after the relief of penetrating the nightmare I continued to ponder about some unknown aspect related to my personal father. Was he only a symbol of humankind or fathers in general? Or was there something particular about him that I needed to respond to? After all, it was *his* desperate plea for help. His tortured eyes continued to pull me, toward what?

Something else happened in Switzerland shortly after the dream enactment that had bearing on my personal father. It became part of the unfolding destiny pattern that would take another ten years to understand and resolve.

My Process Partner and soul friend Laura and I left the intensive Process Work training in Zurich one weekend for a break in the Alps. We traveled to the top of Mt. Pilatus, one of the most spectacular peaks. It was winter, cold and the mountain was thick with snow. A surreal landscape, all white except for the few black brush strokes of wintered trees, and still as death.

We found the only lodging on the mountain, a small alpine hostel, all but buried in snow. It was closed for the season but the owners took pity on our situation—two women traveling alone near sunset—and opened a tiny bedroom for us. The bed coverings, which we would call comforters here but which look like giant pillows there, were ballooning up from the beds. Already chilled to the bone, and tired from hiking, we dived under them as soon as possible and into welcome sleep.

But rest wasn't allowed. We kept being waked as the comforters sidled, seemingly of their own volition, off the beds and onto the floor. A blast of unheated air wrenched us awake. We grabbed the comforters back as quickly as possible, nestled down again and returned to sleep—only to be awakened within an hour by the same inexplicable phenomenon.

Finally one of us sat straight up, despite the searing cold, and practically shouted,

"What's going on?"

We talked it over. Was the place haunted? Were there really little people up here in the Alps as so many claimed? Should we wake up the owner to get help? Our conclusions were no, no and no. Finally we agreed to pray and ask if there was anything significant we were supposed to be getting from this exhausting experience. Sleepily, after the prayer, we once again crawled under the comforters, and slept.

I was awakened suddenly from a deep sleep and sat right up as if I had been shot. A voice said, "Pray for the redemption of the father."

What? Although I had read and heard the word I didn't actually have an experience of what redemption meant, except in terms of grocery store coupons, and I was sure this was not the meaning.

Laura woke up abruptly. I told her what I had heard.

"But I don't really understand what redemption means, nor for what father. Does it mean our teacher? Who is the father? Is it Arny, as the father of this community? Does it mean the fathers of the world?

Certainly they need it but it said father, not fathers. I don't think it would be my personal father. He would have known less about redemption than I do. What does redemption mean anyway?" I asked Laura, knowing that as a minister's daughter, she could shed some light on it.

"Well, in the Christian sense it means that one is rescued from sin and error, saved, as in salvation."

We couldn't figure it out but we prayed anyway, for the father, whoever he was, or fathers in general.

There was yet another dimension to the nightmare, beyond psychology and what I knew so far. A final completion to come that could only be discovered in a powerful spiritual field. In India, many years later this soul destiny dream was finally revealed and fully resolved. I tell about Father's redemption in Chapter 24.

Now I understand that these early soul signs showed me about the light and dark of this world. They defined two polarities that all humans contend with here. They were irreconcilable then and for many years to come. As a child I didn't have the skill to sustain the light and was too terrified to enter the dark. Certainly I was helpless to bring light into the grave.

These polarities would thread through my life, weaving a tapestry of soul design. It would take most of my life to decipher that design and bridge the worlds of light and dark. Eventually I would learn how to track the threads of light and also enter the dark consciously in order to discover its hidden meanings and teachings without getting lost in them. Then to finally discover the safe sure path of the soul.

After working with many clients and students I am confident now that the soul gives all of us early soul signs like this. They can help open awareness to our true nature and purpose. And then we can learn to follow the light of the soul through the thickets of life.

Section III: Being Lost and Found

4

The Ten Thousand Things

Ancient Chinese Taoism said that all creation originated from the One, the Tao, and that all creation is infused with It forevermore. The One divided Itself into two—yin and yang—and they became the polarity which expressed through everything—heaven and earth, dark and light, female and male, hot and cold, dry and wet, etc. Yin and yang further divided to create the five primordial elements from which all else arose.

Humans were created with the polarity of yin and yang within them and they had a special task related to those two. The ancient Taoists had a clear and simple idea about the right function of a human being. They taught that humans had the distinction of functioning as a bridge between the two realms of Heaven and Earth. Divine order flowed down from Heaven through them to manifest Itself into Earth. Humans were given the capacity, and responsibility, to maintain the symmetry and harmony of the One between the Two. It was their job to sense how to preserve the Divine Creation on Earth in a balanced way so that all beings could be united in the Tao and thus live in harmony, with themselves, others and nature.

But humans were also invested with the ability to create for themselves independently, what we call free will. So they began to create various useful objects that multiplied and morphed into more and more things until finally they had created the Ten Thousand Things. It was understood then by the sages that this talent for creating carried a risk with it. Humans could become so entangled in the ten thousand things of their own creation that they could eventually drift away from the One.

As we see today.

My early life on the desert was filled with the wonder of the One. Our family lived in harmony with It. The desert was a God-filled field, with its vast landscape, sky, sun, stillness, and raw untended nature. Not that we knew anything about religion or church, there was none out there in the wilderness. Anyway, we didn't need one since God was with us all the time.

Father's cousin and best friend, Dick Robbins, had come to mother's rescue after my Father's death, to tend the cattle on the ranch and help her reconstruct the pieces of our lives. Within a short time he married mother, to my delight; I loved him and he was always a wonderful stepfather to me. My sisters Annie and Nancy came along shortly thereafter. We were a loving family unit, with simple means and simple tastes. We cared for each other and lived in harmony with nature, much as the Indians did who once lived on the very ground where our ranch was located.

But eventually mother, my sisters and I had to move into town where we could properly attend school when I was in my early teens. The transition was full of shocks. The noise, commotion, and crowdedness of town contrasted sharply with the silence, solitude and vast space I was used to. Nevertheless I tried hard to adjust to, even succeed in, school and the town-culture we moved to. Yet I always felt like an alien, displaced in a crazy world.

As I grew up I was socialized as everyone else is, that is, educated, and taught how to cope in the world as it was and generally do my best to fit in. I studied, worked, married and had three exquisite babies. But there was always an unfulfilled longing for something brighter—true love, happiness or meaning. And I was always searching for it, first through academia, then travel and independent study of philosophies and religions. Yet the search yielded only confusion and disillusionment. The ten thousand things were piling up around me.

Part of the search included an important marker, however. I studied international relations and European literature at the International Peoples' College in Elsinore, Denmark. In 1955 my first daughter, Paulina, and I traveled there with a group of graduate students seeking new ways to help a war-scarred world. We were eager and idealistic.

The school gave us an entirely different slant on life than the privileged one we had known in the U.S. It was established after World War I by a true visionary, Peter Manniche, in an effort to prevent the kind of war Europe had just lived through. He had traveled all over Europe collecting money to establish a school that would bring people together from different cultures, religions and races so they could know one another personally and learn to cooperate for the good of all.

Professor Manniche was still living during the term we spent there and I had the privilege of attending classes in his living room where he explained to us how important it was to learn to live and work together. Although already in his 80s and even after the world had once more been ravaged in the same ways he had tried to prevent, he was full of spirit, enthusiasm and passion for fostering understanding and cooperation. His spirit remained in my heart.

At the school we met people, customs and languages from around the world that were entirely strange to our sheltered selves. Europe was still wounded, physically and psychologically from World War II. We got to observe first-hand the deprivation and lingering trauma of the land and people. It was my first exposure to wide world conditions and suffering. It was thought-provoking and sobering. I wondered why humankind has continued to make war over and over, with enemies that later became friends and then enemies again. I started studying Gandhi and other traditions of non-violence and hoped to go to India one day to study them firsthand. I wanted to help in some way, as Peter Manniche had done and was still doing.

That year was a big education for my daughter and me and has figured prominently in both our destinies; each of us have tried to help those less fortunate than ourselves ever since. As she said to me recently, "the best possible thing is to make a supreme difference in peoples' lives."

When we returned from Europe I dived into the American Way once more. I was so grateful for our great potentials of abundance, high values and vital spirit in the U.S., and fueled by the possibilities for international cooperation we had experienced at the International Peoples' College, I thought we privileged Americans could help turn things around for the world.

But the realities of life, living and working in poverty with three small children, soon obscured my high hopes. Just surviving took everything I had. Then one day while I was working, and pregnant with the third child, our 18-month old son Philip was severely burned in an accident at the baby sitter's. It almost killed him. He lay across my chest in a coma for days and his full recovery took years.

While that horrible trauma was still going on, with terrible pain to him, hospitalization and surgery, my daughter Paulina was burned by a sparkler at a 4th of July picnic. I watched it happen in slow motion without being able to reach her in time. There was something so incongruous, so ludicrous, so *unjust* about it that in that very moment something just cracked within me. My youthful dreams of love and bright futures started to disintegrate.

Not long after that, when John F. Kennedy and Martin Luther King were assassinated, my hopes for non-violence and a better world simply collapsed. I thought, they murder all higher souls in this world.

It seemed then that ever since we left the desert my life had been on a runaway downhill grade and I couldn't find the brakes. One disaster after another beset us. I had tried to be responsible, gain acceptance and fit into life as I encountered it. But instead I was simply drowning in it. Whereas my life had begun in union with the One it was now lost in the ten thousand things.

5

Just When You're Lost the Teacher Appears: Bapak

In 1959 when I first heard about Mohammad Subuh Sumohadiwijojo, called Bapak (for Father) by his followers, I was put off by the claim that a man could give transmissions from the Divine. Bapak was described to me as just that. At the time I was young, untempered and ignorant, especially about spiritual traditions. I thought of myself as an intellectual atheist. My experiences of churches, when we first moved from the desert into town, were depressing. The hypocrisy I met there, the discrepancy between teachings and behavior, contributed to my early cynicism.

Therefore, when I heard people speak of Bapak in superlatives I dismissed their glowing reports as the delusions of true believers.

Even so, by that time I was desperate.

Despite the advantages of a good family, an education and three beautiful children, I was disillusioned with life as I had met it and lost to it. My search for truth and meaning beneath the mundane had seemingly led only down blind alleys. Although I had found tiny glimmers of light in Gandhi, Zen Buddhism, Edgar Cayce, metaphysics and the Gurdjieff teachings they weren't nearly enough to sustain me. But I remember one firm decision I made during these searches. I think I was about eighteen when I concluded that the only thing I could see worth pursuing in this life was enlightenment. Perhaps, at some transcendental level, that decision started opening a path for me then, but I didn't sense any immediate signs of it yet.

By the time I was twenty-five, I couldn't find any light at all. The radiance of the early childhood soul signs had faded almost completely.

It was lost to me, buried someplace in my unconscious. And I was lost, to myself and any purpose for life. Already sound asleep, hypnotized and buried in the morass of material reality, I was at a dead-end in my life, any hope for clarity and sanity dashed to dust.

To cover despair, I cloaked myself in a bored existentialism. But underneath that I thought, if this is all there is, if the world is as insane as it seems, devoid of meaning, I don't really want to live. The only thing that kept me from suicide was the responsibility for my three beautiful children.

Just at this time my poet friend, Bill Dodge, came to visit bringing news of a "spiritual exercise" that had saved him from the kind of despair I was living. Because I was so desperate I listened with a mild, albeit cynical, interest. Bill told me about Bapak and his Transmissions, and described something called the *latihan*, an Indonesian word for "spiritual exercise." He had been doing this "exercise" for several months and he said it had literally snatched him from the brink of suicide. Not only that, he said, he had also found himself again and returned to writing poetry.

Latihan, he explained, was not a religion, but the spiritual practice of Subud. It had been given to Bapak by God as a gift for humankind and God had asked Bapak to pass it on.

Though I didn't really believe what Bill told me, I did believe in him as a good friend. So on the basis of trust in him, and my own mounting despair, I decided to try this spiritual exercise.

But only as an experiment. I said to myself, I'll give it six months and then if nothing happens I can quit.

I had already practiced the *latihan* for a couple of months when we heard that Bapak was coming to California. Although my experiences in *latihan* were strong enough to keep me attending—I felt its electric power in my body and my mind and feelings had lightened, I was even willing to continue living for awhile—I wasn't ready to embrace a "guru," particularly a man.

When I heard all the excitement about seeing Bapak from my Subud "brothers and sisters," my reaction was, so what if he's a spiritual teacher? He's still just a man. Who does he think he is anyway, to assume he could give directions about how Western people, especially me, should live in this world? I'm not ready to believe or follow any ordinary man into the unknown.

Reluctantly, I went to see and hear Bapak anyway. My friends were going, I'd tag along. But objections and resentments toward him remained active in my mind.

When we arrived at the large conference hall there were several hundred people waiting for Bapak. I was judgmental about the pushing crowd and didn't identify with its fervor.

Then I saw him. It's very hard to describe that first impression in words. He showed up through the crowd as a wide still space. Time stopped. The world stopped. Suddenly everything else simply faded away. The pushing and chatter ceased. There was a clear light in the room, full of stillness and soft power.

This indescribable presence walked slowly through the crowd. He moved with easy grace. He didn't look unusual in his conservative western suit, quite ordinary in fact. But there was a feeling in the space around him that transfixed me, more like a gentle pour of light from the pitcher of Heaven than lightning.

That moment is etched in my memory to this day.

He sat down and started to talk to us. He said the same things I had already read—"Brothers and Sisters, there is only one Almighty God…right livelihood…surrendering to God's will" etc. But his words floated out over us like soft beams of sunrise. For over an hour they streamed, the voice melodious, soothing. A deep calm settled in.

Afterwards I only remembered one thing he said: "I am not a spiritual teacher because it is not necessary for you to accept or believe anything I say. The truth lies within you. In time you will receive it for yourselves through the *latihan*."

My experience that evening was quite outside my ability to capture with words. A feeling of being Home, letting go into wholeness. Peacefulness. Sanity. Calmness. Being cared for at the deepest level. A sense of the mind expanding out of its cage. A Knowing unlike intellectual understandings.

All these impressions at once stunned me. My mind splattered. Like being hit by an earthquake out of the blue. It wasn't what I saw or heard that evening that made a lifetime impression. It was an experience of Spirit beyond the ordinary senses. I had only one thought; he isn't just a man.

In the years ahead, I would learn much more about Bapak, partly explaining why he wasn't "just a man."

Here is part of the story of the extraordinary man who initiated my spiritual journey.

God asked Bapak if he would devote the rest of his life to serve the Divine Will when he was only thirty-two years old.

At that time in 1933, Bapak had never traveled beyond the region of his tiny Indonesian village. He already had a family with four children to support and he was a dedicated provider. His education was minimal; he made a simple living as an accountant. Although he was perfectly content with his life, his premonition in childhood that he would die by the age of thirty-three haunted him. He had prepared himself the best he could for that possibility by seeking spiritual teachers and disciplines even as he maintained a normal life as a householder.

When God made His request Bapak had no idea what serving the Divine Will would mean. That he would be snatched from the role of householder and thrust into the world as a spiritual leader, that it would require leaving his job, losing his family and being ridiculed by his people. Nor could he yet realize that it would be the end of his life as he had known it.

Years later Bapak told us about his experience when we were crammed together in a makeshift auditorium on the banks of the Shenandoah River in Virginia. Bapak said he had questioned God from the start: would he have the strength to carry out this mission? And God answered:

"If you have complete faith and trust in Me, be willing to be My slave, My soldier, then go on. I will always be with you."

He sang a prayer with the story to demonstrate how he had responded to God:

"So Bapak said yes to God
and promised to give his life, body and soul
completely into God's hands
and obey anything that God would command
to the slightest, smallest thing."

His voice was sweet and melodious like an innocent child's. Bapak had said yes and kept his word. I remember that the sincerity and purity in his voice touched my heart so deeply that I started to cry on the spot. I rummaged around in my purse for a handkerchief; the woman next to me handed me one. As I looked up to thank her I saw tears running down her cheeks as well.

I don't remember Bapak mentioning much at all about what happened in his life before his illumination. It was as if that event blinded out most of what came before. I knew from reading that he had been born in a small town in Java, Indonesia, to devout Muslim parents of simple means, that he was sick at birth and not expected to live. He did tell us of the "stranger" who showed up shortly after his birth to advise the parents that since their child was so ill his name should be changed right away. He should be given a name more in harmony with his nature and time of birth: Mohammad (for the prophet, also born in June) and Subuh (the name of Islamic dawn prayers, taking place at the time of his birth). The parents accepted this advice and changed the name. The baby recovered.

Afterward the stranger disappeared and never returned. Bapak told us that this stranger was an ancestor who had come back into this world for a short period to help him when he was too young to help himself.

Bapak also told us about his early premonition that he would die at a young age. And how he prepared for death by seeking various spiritual teachers and methods. But none of the teachers he met would accept him; one explained that Bapak would receive his own teaching directly from God. Although he was raised as a strict Muslim, Bapak was also familiar with the Sufi tradition, well known in Indonesia, in which great masters dropped all dogma in favor of direct contact with God.

Bapak grew up, married young, had children and took on adult responsibilities. His interest in spiritual matters waned in those early years as a householder. He became a very hard-working high achiever among his contemporaries.

Then in 1925, when Bapak was just twenty-four years old, Divine Lightning struck him. We were fortunate to hear this story just a few times and each time it seemed both preposterous and utterly real as it came from his mouth. This is how he told it:

One night around midnight, Bapak went for a walk to cool off from the sweltering heat within his house. Suddenly he was enveloped in "brilliant light, which came from above." Bapak said the light was so bright he "felt as though the whole of Semarang, (his town) was illuminated."[1]

---

1. It has been recorded for posterity in *The History of Subud*. H. Longcroft. History of Subud, Vol. 1. Houston, Texas, Al-Baz Publishing, Inc., 1993.

He looked up to see where this great illumination was coming from. Astonished, he saw a "radiant ball of light which looked like the sun in the daytime." This "sun" was coming toward him very rapidly. Then it fell into his head, and entered his whole body. His body started to tremble and his heart shook within his chest. He thought he was having a heart attack. (In fact, Bapak said that when he *did* have a heart attack years later, it reminded him of that experience.)

Bapak remembered the prophecy of an early death and thought that his time had surely come. Wanting to prepare himself, he walked home as fast as he could, and lay down to die. He said he crossed his hands on his chest and surrendered his life "completely to the power of God," thinking it was his end.

Then suddenly his whole body was filled with brilliant light…"like illuminated electric wires…from his toes to right inside his head."

While I heard this story I remembered instruction in the Chinese classic, *The Secret of the Golden Flower,* which says:

> "When the light circulates, the energies of the whole body appear before its throne…Therefore, you only have to make the light circulate; that is the deepest and most wonderful secret."[2]

Yet without preparation, formal instruction or personal intention Bapak was experiencing this circulation of light on his own bed in a remote village of Indonesia.

Bapak's mother had also seen what she called a "sun" descending out of the sky that night. She worried about what was happening to her son, but she also remembered her intuition before his birth that he would be "special."

---

2. Wilhelm, R. The Secret of the Golden Flower, p. 22, 1962.

The light of that night ignited a lightening process within Bapak, which continued, steadily and intensely, for about a thousand nights. He barely slept during all that time. The energies, action and process of the *latihan* were being born, grounded on earth through Bapak's body and consciousness.

During those first thousand nights Bapak received many revelations and prophecies. For example, he was told there would be another world war and that after it Indonesia would gain independence from Holland. That development seemed impossible since the Dutch had occupied Indonesia for three hundred years and had no intention of giving it up. Bapak was also told that he would travel around the world many times to pass the *latihan* on to others. These revelations were being shown to him some fifteen years and more before they actually happened. They were unimaginable at the time.

Although Bapak reported only a small part of what was happening to him, what he did tell seemed preposterous to his relatives who feared he was going crazy. Many turned away from him, especially after he received the message that he should stop working as an accountant and devote all his time to his mission. "Bapak turned to God to ask for strength and a strong faith, otherwise he felt he would go mad," said one of his friends.

How would he take care of his children? Bapak asked God. He was told that God would always be with him and that he and his family would be provided whatever they needed.

Some of Bapak's friends who had been with him in various spiritual searches in the past reported that he became noticeably different from the seeker they had known. He was no longer looking for a spiritual path. He seemed wiser, with an inner knowledge. For example, when he met people he could look right through them. "He knew their content-saw their heart," one of his companions reported.

Noticeable changes began to happen in the people around him as well. His friends were affected by the energy of the *latihan*. Some of them asked Bapak to formally transmit it to them, which he did, after explanations of how its action had affected him.

The initial transmission of the *latihan* was called an "opening." Anyone could be "opened" if they asked Bapak although he was told from the beginning not to proselytize or advertise in any way. As Bapak stood with a person and entered into the *latihan* state that person would automatically receive the energetic transmission. After the opening a person repeatedly practiced the *latihan* with others who had received it until the action was well established within him. Eventually he would be able to practice it confidently, even alone.

The process of the *latihan* changed people over time, in both subtle and dramatic ways.

Some of these changes were not recognizable at the time but over the long term they could be clearly seen as major reorientations to life. For example, when Bapak was asked about the validity of astrology and its implications about a predetermined life, he replied in a fascinating way:

"Before someone is opened I can see his whole fate extending out before him. Fate is the inevitable playing out of the conditioning and circumstances of a person's birth and I can see it all. But after that same person is opened in Subud I can't see what will happen to him anymore. The true destiny of his soul, beyond conditioning, is then possible."

As the *latihan* progressed within Bapak he was purified, he said, and prepared for his world mission. By the time he was thirty-three he had the clarity and strength to say yes to God's request to give the rest of his life to transmit the *latihan* to the world.

Divine revelations continued within Bapak from then on. They were sealed into his destiny when he gave his promise to God. He did not report many of these to us because, as he always emphasized, his mission was to pass on the *latihan,* rather than give spiritual teachings.

God had already given mankind all the religions and spiritual teachings he needed, Bapak explained. The *latihan* would enable him to follow and practice those teachings. And through our practice we could eventually reach our own understanding.

From 1925 to 1958 Bapak opened many people within Indonesia. A loose organization was formed to help people receive the *latihan*. Bapak said it should be named Subud to denote the action and purpose of people who practiced the *latihan*.

Subud is an acronym of three Sanskrit words: *Susila, Budhi* and *Dharma*, all of which are Javanese words of Sanskrit origin. *Susila* means surrender to God's will and righteous living according to the Divine plan as a true human being; *Budhi* denotes the Divine power within every person which makes it possible for him to know the Divine plan, and *Dharma* means right action from inner knowing.

In the beginning Subud was simply a growing spiritual organization in Indonesia, entirely unknown in other countries. Then in 1958, just as Bapak had predicted in 1936, a seeker from the West, Husein Rofe, came to Indonesia where he found Bapak and asked to experience the *latihan*. Rofe wrote a fascinating account of his own search and discovery of Subud in his book *The Path of Subud.*

Through Rofe, Bapak was invited first to England, then Europe and the U.S. From that one initial contact the *latihan* was finally seeded in seventy-two countries around the world. Eventually people from many cultures, ages and all religions—Christianity, Buddhism, Islam, Hinduism, Judaism, even those without a formal religion—came together to practice the *latihan*. For example, in the Middle East Muslims and Jews did the *latihan* together in sincere worship. I have often wondered if today's conflicts could have been altered if the *latihan* had spread more widely there.

From 1958 until his death in 1987 Bapak traveled around the world, transmitting the *latihan*. He gave every moment of his life to keep his promise to God, to pass on what he had received to all those who wanted it.

God was always with him.

People ask me, what did Bapak teach? What did he say? As in "the Word is God. If you can't put it into words it isn't real." Well, he said a lot of words, probably several billion since he traveled around the world giving talks from 1958 to 1987 as I've said.

I heard or read many of his talks. They were basically about the same things prophets have been saying throughout history. Bapak said that we didn't need new spiritual teachings or religions because God had already provided plenty of religions to teach righteous living. There were different forms for different kinds of people. But like the spokes of a wheel all religions lead to God at the center, he said. This was why Bapak was not a teacher, he explained, but simply a transmitter of a Way, the *latihan*, which God had given to help humans follow whichever religion was right for them. And this was why Christians, Jews, Muslims, Hindus, and Buddhists could all practice the *latihan* together in one room, all in accordance with their own religion.

He said things like God is Almighty, more powerful than any other force, omnipotent, omniscient and omnipresent. By surrendering to Almighty God in the *latihan,* he said, we would eventually come to a state of noble *humanhood*, which God intended for us in the first place.

Bapak said that in the present world, material (as in the *Ten Thousand Things*) had become so dominant that it literally ruled us through our attachments to it. Whereas we were meant to be the rightful rulers of material, things were now ruling us. Bapak said that we were meant to sit on the chair, not the chair on us, we should drive the car, not allow the car to drive us. Sometimes his language and way of speaking seemed strange to our Western ears. But now it seems to me that contemporary society demonstrates what Bapak was talking about very well.

He explained that our highest and most reliable part is the soul but that it was difficult for us to be aware of it because of impurities built up in our lives and those of our ancestors. Thus, as we did the *latihan* we would be purifying not only ourselves, but eventually our ancestors.

At that time the possibility of ancestor purification seemed fantastical and remote to me, surely unlikely. But after awhile a number of us became aware of curious patterns of thought and behavior that seemed more like a great grandmother than ourselves. These experiences would appear and then fade away, like a ghost walking through. Sometimes they were accompanied by dreams of an ancestor, or impressions of one, in our own *latihans*.

Now 50 years later many serious explorers of consciousness are discovering the ancestral connections that indigenous peoples have always remembered. Therapists and people committed to serious work on themselves are finding the threads of ancestral patterning within their own clearing process. They have also come to realize that as they clear themselves, they are also affecting their immediate forbears and layers of regressive patterning in the world field as well. Many of us are seeking, and have found, ways to free or update those patterns, for ourselves, our ancestors and the world.

Bapak said that persisting in the *latihan* would remove our obstacles over time. As passions were purified our souls would emerge, clear and shining. We would be freed of the fate we were born with, which was dictated by cultural and familial conditioning. The soul's truth within would begin to guide our daily lives and one day, Bapak said, the light of our souls would even go out ahead of us, illuminating and making way for the path of destiny. Our right work and purpose, in harmony with our own natures, would be revealed.

This, he said, was why we didn't have to accept anything he told us because eventually we would grasp the Truth from our own souls. In later study I learned that this principle of finding the truth within, the Divine Self, is actually a fundamental esoteric teaching of all religions and spiritual practices.

Yet we should always remember, Bapak admonished, that we are simply ordinary people, as he was an ordinary man. We should not see ourselves as special because we had the *latihan*, nor claim any unusual powers. Rather we should go about our lives and our work like everyone else and let the force of the *latihan* within us change whatever was not right within or around us. And eventually we would live in "true social democracy" where all peoples could live as brothers and sisters in harmony. Then they would share material equally and be served by it.

When yet another Middle Eastern crisis erupted in 1980 Bapak composed a prayer on his birthday to address it:

The duty of all mankind
Is to worship Almighty God
So that their hearts and minds
May be at Peace
So that in turn the world may become
Peaceful and calm for all mankind.
Therefore, worship Almighty God without delay
Let it not happen
That at the end of our lives we
Find ourselves far from God's Power
For this is God's Authority
Which can truly
Bring peace and serenity
To the life of man.

Bapak's vision was inspiring and most of us embraced it. After all, in the Subud community we were living it. In those early years Steve Allen, the well-known commentator and performer, recorded an interview with G.J. Bennett, a scientist and author of *Concerning Subud*[3] about how Subud could affect the world. Steve Allen had been opened in Subud so he could speak from experience with Bennett who was one

3. J.G. Bennett, Concerning Subud, published about 1959, now out of print as far as I know.

of the first Westerners to be opened. These two brilliant men offered their speculations about Subud's potential for bringing peace and equality to the world that were somewhat similar to Bapak's vision.

It was an inspiring conversation and convinced me at the time that the *latihan* could save this world from the chaos and destruction that seemed to engulf it even then. It was during the 1960s, the time of John F. Kennedy, Martin Luther King, civil rights marches and the optimism and innocence of flower children and hope for the world seemed feasible.

I held to the possibility that Subud could "help save the world" for at least two decades and even devoted my attention and work to contribute.

Recently I had a conversation with my son Philip, now a fine doctor and long-standing Subud member himself, about the fate of the world.

"What is your perspective, Mom, about whether the world will survive?"

I told him I had thought about it for years and that from a factual, logical point-of-view we seemed doomed but that I was aware of the lightning that had been grounding grace from higher dimensions to us since the end of the nineteenth century. Ramakrishna, Vivekenanda, Yogananda, Gandhi, Bapak, the many apparitions of Mother Mary, Martin Luther King, Sai Baba and many others had been blessed from higher dimensions to intervene for humans and to guide them into transcendent consciousness for over one hundred years. All these great teachers have embraced and taught to all religions, not just their own, without prejudice. And the higher energies they channeled had been distributed widely among us for all that time.

But whether there's enough grace and higher guidance yet to save the world can't be known by ordinary means. We humans have to do our part. Will enough of us heed the call to higher consciousness? Or will we continue to dawdle around in the lower levels of greed, terror, enmity, and hoarding of material? Will we destroy the entire planet in our own narcissistic quest?

I told Philip I couldn't see how it would come out. And that although I had once believed that Subud would save the world and that I could work toward that I no longer believed I could do anything more than surrender to Divine Will and do the best I can to follow the guidance I've been given while I'm here. That salvation depends on all of us together.

But I also reminded him that both Bapak and Sai Baba had predicted a "golden age" to come.

Bapak told us the same things over and over, with different words or examples, but basically they were the same messages. Even when the words were the same the talks were always different because Bapak delivered them with an alive vibration that carried much more than words. He was receiving, and transmitting, directly from Source as he spoke. Even after we had heard the messages many times through the years we never wanted to miss a talk.

Occasionally Bapak said very unusual things which seemed different from spiritual teachings we had heard. For example, he told us that as we purified we would attract higher souls as our children. Then when those children were born we should observe their true nature carefully and encourage it. While they were young it would be better not to instruct them in religion because they were still in a very receptive and formative stage. For that same reason, most of us had learned the opposite—to take our children to Sunday school as soon as possible. But Bapak said we should allow the soul to come forward and choose the religion that was right for it.

Bapak told us that we were probably able to find the *latihan* in this life because there had been a very holy person in our ancestry, as far as seven generations back.

He explained that we would come to understand past spiritual teachings directly through the practice of the *latihan*. He said that long ago, before recorded history even, we had organs of perception that allowed us to see directly into the truths of creation. They enabled us to understand and attune ourselves with the natural order of things. That was a time when we still knew the Universal language, *menusia,* he called it, of communicating with animals and plants, with all of life. But over time, he said, as we drifted away from the harmony of creation, these organs had covered over and eventually became vestigial, as they are now. Bapak said that through the *latihan* they would open up again and then we would be able to "receive" the truth of anything directly.

Beyond understanding ourselves we would also discover abilities to penetrate history or science through inner knowing. He said that scientists who were purified would then be able to *know* the workings of nature directly. Theoretical physicists at Los Alamos told us later that they did receive explanations of physics through the *latihan.* Once an internist told me that he often received an accurate diagnosis of a patient before the technical tests were returned.

Stories were often told of Bapak's direct knowledge of history and science. For instance his encounter with the Chairman of the Physiology Department at London University. This scientist was interested in studying yogis who could consciously control their bodies' automatic processes, such as breathing and heart rate. He had heard of instances when they had voluntarily been buried underground for several days. He wanted to find such adepts to test them scientifically.

In this context the Professor was introduced to Bapak. He and Bapak met for about two hours. When they came out of the conference the Professor was shaking his head. He said, "that man knows more about physiology than any person I've ever met." Of course Bapak had never studied physiology.

Bapak's son, a medical doctor, told how Bapak sometimes corrected the textbook teachings of cell biology he had learned in medical school in the 1950s. Bapak's corrections had to do with sub-atomic physics that had not yet become a part of the medical curriculum.

I have met, and read about, a number of remarkable people who can access information from other levels through extrasensory perception.

Things like seeing with x-ray vision inside the body, finding lost objects, reading past lives. But Bapak seemed to have the ability to tap into universal mind for direct information on any subject. I never met anyone else who had that faculty until we met Sai Baba.

Bapak usually spoke to us in the evenings. As we sat in the crowded room, tired after working all day, many heads would start to droop until finally they fell over onto chests in peaceful sleep. This made me irritated because I wanted everyone, especially my husband at the time, or close friends, to *get* it. The words were very important to me then. I wrote many of them down, thought about them and repeated them to others because in those days I thought getting the words was the same as getting the message. So as we sat in the talks I poked those around me to wake them up. They would glance up momentarily and then easily fall back to sleep.

One evening after Bapak had finished speaking, a bold person asked him why most of us went to sleep as he talked! Bapak nodded very seriously and replied that we shouldn't worry about that, it was good for us to sleep during the talks because then the message would go deeper, beyond our ordinary minds into our whole beings.

After that evening I focused less on the words and began to pay more attention to whole-being awareness. My view softened and widened and I noticed more subtle signs.

For example, when we were all gathered to greet Bapak, or see him off at the airport, small children often wiggled free of their parents' control and ran straight up to Bapak to touch him or speak to him. The lucky person who chauffeured Bapak in his car always looked transformed, healthier and happier and reported that he had extra energy for days afterwards.

Once my daughter Paulina, then a teenager, was asked to help clean Bapak's sleeping room. At the time she was in full blown adolescent rebellion. She felt rejected or judged by practically everyone while she was simultaneously angry, rejecting and judging of all adults. But during the days she was Bapak's cleaning girl she turned suddenly clear and peaceful. She said later, "while I was cleaning Bapak's room I felt good about myself and completely loved and accepted." That *feeling*, about being just right as herself, became a marker for her for many years to come.

I've told these personal stories to illustrate how powerfully Bapak affected us. We didn't need to talk personally with him or even have correspondence with him. His presence alone, as well as his guidance through the talks, kept us on the right path. One time he told us that after his death he would be even more available to us.

He recited to us his "plea to the One Almighty God" that he made every day.

O God, don't give your blessing to me alone.
No.
But to all mankind,
And to you who happen to be close to
Bapak right now,
Or to all Subud members,
So it is not only Bapak alone who can go to heaven, but all of you.

Through the years we came to value his visits as a period of New Year, when the old was cleared away, new clarity realized and the spirit uplifted. Our histories were marked according to these visits—"Oh, that was in 1967 when Bapak was in Virginia." "That was in 1983 when Bapak was in Santa Monica and Sara was born."

As I look back over those decades now I wonder how I would have coped with life on earth without the *latihan* and Bapak's example as a true human being. Actually I believe that given my beginnings and the direction I was going, I would be dead, alcoholic or insane by now without the *latihan*. I remember thinking once, during a painful relationship loss, that I knew one human being on earth who truly cared about the welfare of my soul, and that was Bapak.

Our lives were lighted up and made whole each time Bapak came. He was the spiritual father so many of us longed for in those chaotic days of the 1960s. But those days with Bapak taught us much more than just coping with life on earth. They also gave us sound guidance and modeling about how to follow our own soul truth which was connected to the Divine. They inspired us to find our true work and contribute to right human living for the good of all.

We imagined, but could not face, that those days would end one day.

Bapak first died in 1982.

The news of his heart attack spread around the world within hours. Telephones rang from New York to Quebec to Hamburg. We were in shock. We cried. We prayed for his life. How would we manage without our beloved spiritual leader, our anchor? There were so many questions left to ask. How could we do without his constant presence, his wisdom, his strength? How would it be to never see his beautiful face again?

We waited for news. Nothing good. It was a severe heart attack and Bapak was in the hospital, unconscious. He wasn't expected to live. We redoubled our prayers and waited more. I remember thinking at the time of how we had waited to hear news of John F. Kennedy after he was shot and still in the hospital. My heart sank at the comparison.

Then, within four or five days, the news phone-jetted around the globe: Bapak has opened his eyes! Maybe he could live after all. Our spirits lifted somewhat although we were advised that he certainly wasn't out of the woods.

As Bapak revived we expected him to be laid up for a long time. A Subud world congress was coming up within three months and we knew we would have to do without him.

But no! A month before the congress we received word that Bapak was coming! We couldn't believe it. Of course we were overjoyed and wanted to see him but at the same time we worried that he might be pushing too hard.

When he arrived at the congress Bapak looked frail. His typical meticulous business suit hung limply on his body. He had always been radiantly healthy and it was clear now that the heart attack had knocked him down. He walked much more slowly and leaned on the arm of his Granddaughter.

But his spirit was as electric as it had always been. When he started to talk, his voice seemed weak. Then, as he continued it came forward stronger and stronger until it had the same forceful tones we were used to. Our hearts rose up to meet him.

He told us the experience of his death:

"When I died during the heart attack I went far far beyond this world, beyond the sun and out into the galaxies. I traveled for a long time until finally I reached a place of great authority. When I got there they asked me 'Aren't you the one who is down there on earth trying to help the people?' When I said yes they told me that I would have to go back because my job wasn't complete. And this is how I am sitting here with you now, Brothers and Sisters."

Then Bapak laughed in the beautiful way he had of tilting his head back and letting the laughter roll out of his chest like great waves of music.

The last time I saw Bapak he had come once again to Los Angeles. Several hundred were gathered in the auditorium, waiting expectantly for him to arrive. I sat about twelve rows back from the stage so I could see Bapak clearly. I knew he had not regained his robust health but I was shocked and anxious to see his fragile aged body slowly walking up the aisle, as he leaned on the arm of his translator. Somehow I had never expected Bapak to age, to be subjected to the same wearing away of the body as the rest of us. But here he was, obviously an old man now, needing help to get up the stairs. I took a deep breath as he eased limply into his chair and noted the sinking feeling in my chest. Was this dear old man our golden hope for salvation?

Slowly Bapak leaned toward the microphone. His first words were weak and faltering, "Brothers and sisters…" The same gentle compassion in his voice but it was faint.

Then gradually there was more force. As the words built, "You know there is only one Almighty God…" his voice came clearer, the message strong. I sat transfixed as I watched him transform before my eyes. Bapak's face began to come alive with his message. He smiled, nodding his head this way and that to punctuate what he said. The fragile body began to light up; the hands gestured in those same graceful sweeps so familiar to us. My heart lifted, as I became completely engrossed in this spectacular display of bright spirit.

Suddenly Bapak was out of his chair, moving around the stage like a dancer. He showed us the liquid movements of a martial artist, an athlete. At one point I almost expected him to rise off the floor, he was so light.

A surge of happiness rippled through me. Yes! This was our Bapak, the fully alive human being, demonstrating to us in the last of his life the tremendous power and blessing to everyone when a human being is able to allow the Divine to flow through him, without obstruction or deflection.

At the end of his talk Bapak was again a fragile old man, helped from his chair and down the stairs. I remember how the tears rolled down my face as I watched him walk back down the aisle. Great waves of gratitude filled me up. Gratitude for his life, for his devotion to his mission, for the opportunity we had to be blessed by him.

Bapak died for the last time in 1987. He had become ill at his home in Indonesia with what seemed like pneumonia. The doctor said he should be taken to the hospital. His wife sat in the car beside him. She said he refused to lie down. Instead, he held onto the door pull to stay upright. But finally he leaned back into the seat and took a deep breath.

Then he said to her,

"It is complete. Pray for me." And he was gone.

Section IV: Openings

About Opening

When we have lost our spiritual birthright, and ourselves, an initiation or opening is required to pierce through the bindings that obscure who we actually are. All religions or spiritual practices have initiation ceremonies for being "born again" into spirit, such as baptism, confirmation, consecration, ordination, bat and bar mitzvahs, vision quests, or entering the inner sanctum.

What are openings? And why are they necessary for us to remember our origin?

As we grow up a cocoon of conditioning develops around our essential spirit. Shaped from patterns of our ancestry, nuclear family, education, culture and events, traumatic and otherwise, the cocoon is more or less fixed by early adulthood. It also defines our personality, the one we call "I," and our persona, the polished mask we present to the world.

Psychology has studied and described the personality for a century and has detailed how our consciousness is trapped in, and limited by, our conditioning. Gurdjieff called the personality the "false self." He taught that it covered the "real self" that needed to be awakened from its sleep. Otherwise, he said, we would remain wrapped for life in false assumptions and beliefs, never realizing the extraordinary possibilities of flight that lie unattainable within our folded wings.

In bodywork we call the multiple layers of physical conditioning "armor."[1] We have discovered that releasing the physical armor will often cause corresponding changes in consciousness.

Similarly, our souls are obscured by the mental and emotional patterns, or armor, of the personality. We unconsciously created the armor in the first place to protect ourselves and help us cope in the world. Psychology carefully describes these "defenses" and "coping mechanisms." But at some point in life that very protection inhibits our inner truth and vitality. We find ourselves thinking, feeling and behaving according to feedback from the world. We identify only with the personality. Eventually we become numb and mechanical, asleep. We seem to have lost our essential self in the process.

When we bow to the cocoon of conditioning, we are fixed in those programs, just as Bapak could see a person's fate stretched out ahead of them before they were opened. After the opening he could no longer see a clear patterning. Then there was an opportunity to exchange a pre-determined fate for a soul destiny.

Awakening from the cocoon of conditioning is not a simple task though. The cocoon has become familiar, comfortable and protective. If it eventually becomes uncomfortable, if our personality seems awkward or unacceptable in society, of course we can always change it. Almost a century of psychology has shown the possibilities of personality adjustment. It has taught us well how to cope, to adjust our behaviors, to better serve the adult self. For example, we can learn how to resolve and change early childhood conditioning through therapy or long-term self-reflection with adequate commitment.

But methods that focus only on the personality may substitute another conditioning for that of the parents. The new belief system, such as psychoanalysis or a particular philosophy or religion, can help

1. See Soul Return.

us move the pieces around within the personality. And a new system may help a person cope better with the stresses of the world, and even succeed, where parents have failed.

Many biographies and novels have focused on this theme—poor boy learns skills unheard of by the parents, seizes opportunities and becomes rich and famous. But this characteristically American dream often finds the hero unfulfilled in the end. He has missed something. His worldly successes have failed to touch some deeper meaning beyond the status and materials he has given his life to.

At present we are witnessing much of our culture enslaved to this lost dream. The result is what Mother Theresa called our "spiritual poverty," when she spoke in California. Unfortunately, for over a century psychology has principally ignored that spiritual dimension of our being. For example, Freud, the father of psychology, thought spirituality was illusion.

Fortunately there are time-proven ways to activate our spiritual possibilities, beyond the personality. Sages, saints and teachers throughout the ages have sought a deeper meaning in life, than familial or cultural conditioning. The Delphic Oracle commanded, "Know thyself." Jesus taught that "the kingdom of God lies within you." Many have found the kingdom, including Bapak and the others teachers I describe in this book. They found it by following their own unique awakening process to liberation.

An awakening process is usually gradual, initiated through individual resolve and followed by the repeated practice of going within, through prayer or spiritual practice. But often, particularly within the last few decades, awakening begins with a rupture, or "opening," in the cocoon of conditioning. This opening can be abrupt, sometimes unexpected, such as those described within this section.

For example, a severe "natural" impact, like lightning, death of a loved one or the onset of a serious illness, can crack the cocoon open. Usually a rapid soul awakening follows the impact. Abrupt openings are often frightening. We don't adjust to them easily. Often we would rather return to the supposed security and familiarity of the cocoon.

In my experience, true spiritual development and soul consciousness only become accessible after a person has been opened in one way or another. A stronger or higher force is required. It comes through sages and true holy people who have the skill and energy to transmit it. Bapak was an instrument of that higher force. Certainly the Bible is full of descriptions of Jesus' transmissions that changed lives forever. Muktananda imparted it to thousands of people. The Dalai Lama has traveled the world conducting Buddhist initiations that have undoubtedly helped open the world to its own soul.

Why and how do openings come about? I believe they happen as a result of a person's deep yearning. The yearning for God, the yearning to return to Source. To reclaim the Holy Spirit within each of us. To grasp true meaning and purpose in life.

The following section describes several openings, and subsequent awakening experiences, that not only penetrated the personality but also changed the direction of lives. Some caused permanent alteration. Some were seemingly temporary. All demonstrate the process of waking up, out of the sleep of conditioning and into the soul within.

6

Opening in Subud

When I was opened in Subud I knew nothing about traditions of initiation in religions or spiritual practices. I thought "opening" was simply a quaint interpretation of an Indonesian word. I certainly didn't understand about the energetic-spiritual transmission I would receive. My "opening" into the *latihan* of Subud irrevocably changed my life forever but I could never have imagined how radical that change would be.

I was only twenty-five and in despair about life already, as I've described, when Bill Dodge arrived unexpectedly from Los Angeles with his enthusiastic report about the "spiritual exercise" that had transformed his life. He had driven all the way to La Jolla to tell me about it. I listened cynically as he described how the *latihan* had cured his alcoholism and depression. Only a few months before he had been planning suicide.

He told me the unusual story of his effort.

Bill said he drove his old woody station wagon up to the tall beach cliffs over Big Sur, intending to drive it, with himself inside, over the edge. He got out of the station wagon to take a last look at the beauty of Big Sur. In those very moments a long-time friend, an artist, came walking along the cliff. The friend asked Bill what he was doing there. Bill replied honestly that he was planning to drive himself over the cliff. His friend said,

"Wait! Don't do it yet. I've just been "opened" into this new spiritual exercise and it has completely changed my life. I'm now back into my own creative stream after being dry for a long time. I'm loving life again. Why don't you try this thing before you drive over the cliff? Then if it doesn't work you can still kill yourself."

So Bill agreed to try the *latihan* of Subud. To his astonishment he found it to be all that his friend had promised and more. He was no longer interested at all in suicide and he wasn't drinking. He had driven all the way from Los Angeles to La Jolla, to share his experiences with me.

I wasn't excited about Bill's stories of rescue, healing and joy. They sounded like zealous fantasy in my depressed state.

"But what would you have to lose?" Bill asked, "since your life isn't working for you anyway?"

Bill left me the book, *Concerning Subud.* I read part of it but was intellectually critical of almost every page. I finally threw it across the room in disgust. It seemed like magical nonsense to me, the rationalist, the atheist. Nevertheless I couldn't entirely discount Bill's experience. He was a trusted friend who had introduced me to many helpful ideas in the past. I thought more about what he had told me. I began to wonder, what if there was something real to this *latihan*? Could it possibly help even me?

I reasoned that sampling Subud "as an experiment" couldn't hurt me. So being an empiricist, I agreed to try it. After all, I could always quit if nothing happened, free and clear, especially since no personal or financial commitments were required.

The only requirement to entering Subud was for a person to wait three months before being "opened." That time was a "probationary" period during which interested persons were asked to meet weekly with others who had already been opened. We could listen to their experiences and ask questions about the *latihan.* Then in the last month we could sit outside the *latihan* room so that we could hear and sense it. This period was designed to give ample opportunity for thinking it over seriously before submitting to the action.

During that waiting time many curious things happened, all of which kept the process interesting enough to pursue. A peaceful calm came over me for awhile. Daily life was easier. But the weekly meetings were distasteful. They were with several middle-aged women who had recently been opened. To me they seemed old and I thought we had nothing in common. I wanted to know about the philosophical foundations of Subud. They talked about the grace of God and surrendering to His Will, neither of which I could relate to.

One lady told me she had always wanted to understand the teachings of Jesus more deeply and had prayed for that in her opening. She said that since the opening she had many new insights about Jesus and felt satisfied that her prayer had been answered.

"You should think about what you want to pray for," she advised. I couldn't relate to that either. Nor did I find out until later that one wasn't supposed to ask for, nor expect, anything from Subud, but simply to surrender, without agenda, to God's will. Apparently this lady hadn't been properly instructed at the time.

After one such meeting a huge rebellion arose in me. Even though I wasn't a drinker, I bought a bottle of wine, locked myself in the bedroom and drank the whole thing. As I wobbled into drunkenness I kept repeating over and over to myself, "they'll never get me," which meant something like "I've already seen through the hypocrisy of churches, the blindness of cults and groups and they will never capture me."

Yet I continued with the waiting period and the meetings. Why? I'm not sure. Certainly it wasn't a rational decision.

As it turned out I didn't have to wait a full three months. One of the ladies called me and asked simply,

"Are you sure you want to be opened?"

When I said yes she explained that several Helpers in Subud were arriving from Los Angeles to open those few of us in Del Mar who were waiting. I thanked her but when I put the phone down I was seized by conflicting emotions. Did I really want to do this? Yes. No. Yes. What if it was all a hoax? What if nothing happened?

As the day approached for the opening I grew more agitated and anxious. Probably nothing would happen to me, I wasn't the right type. On the other hand what if something promising did happen? How would I deal with that?

A few days before the scheduled opening I thought of the lady's prayer advice. I resolved to ask to "wake up" through this process. This wish was based on my study of the Gurdjieff teachings, which stressed that humans were all asleep in a hypnotic trance of conditioning. According to Gurdjieff one needed to work very intensively to wake up to the actual reality of life in order to avoid extinction. He had devised an elaborate and complicated regime of exercises to help people "self remember." I had wanted to work with a Gurdjieff group to learn his consciousness exercises, but hadn't found one.

So when the day came for the opening I repeated over to myself a kind of prayer: "I want to wake up, I want to wake up."

Bill arrived to accompany me and my new friend Lisa whom I had met at the probationary meetings. She would also be opened that day. As I drove us to the opening I kept pushing the accelerator harder and harder until I was clearly speeding. Finally Bill said,

"Are you afraid God won't wait for you?"

I slowed down and grew thoughtful. What if God wasn't there? What if God was there? What if God actually *was*?

When we arrived at the appointed place we were asked to take off our shoes and gather for an introductory talk by one of the "helpers." This Helper, a gentle older man, explained that the *latihan* was a mysterious and powerful energy that God had given first to Bapak, with the instruction that it was to be passed on to anyone who sincerely asked for it. He said that we would receive this energy by standing in the presence of a Helper who had already received the *latihan.* The transmission would happen, through that Helper to us, just as it had originally passed from Bapak to others. Then the action would continue in us by itself through subsequent *latihans.*

I could feel an inner excitement growing as the man talked about the *latihan*. I admitted to myself that despite all my cynical questionings, I actually did want to experience this energy, that I looked forward to how it would work in me.

But then the Helper changed to a religious tone. He spoke for almost forty-five minutes about how important Christian values were, the power of Jesus, how he had come much closer to Jesus now since his opening, and on and on.

Being an avowed non-Christian at the time I was offended by this part of his talk. I thought I had been misled because all the initial information about Subud had stressed that the spiritual action of the *latihan* was not attached to any religious dogma. I was upset by the Christian talk.

At the end of it the women and men were instructed to go into two separate rooms for the opening. As we gathered with the women I walked over to one of the female Helpers and told her my concern—that I was not a Christian and couldn't subscribe to all the things the male Helper had said. She looked at me intently for a few seconds. Then she said,

"Subud isn't for everyone." Which left me completely on my own to go through with the opening or not.

I hesitated, irritated and confused. Then I walked to the door to take up my shoes and leave.

But as I stood there I couldn't pick them up. My hands simply wouldn't reach down for them. Instead I turned around and joined the other women waiting to be opened.

The Helper instructed us to remove our jewelry, close our eyes and sit quietly, allowing our minds and feelings to become still, until she asked us to stand up.

My mind wasn't still. I was wrestling with the Christian lecture and its contradiction with what I had been told about Subud, that it had no dogma and accepted followers of all religions. What about religion anyway? I didn't believe in it. Was I making a mistake? "Subud isn't for everyone" repeated over and over in my head. On and on my mind chattered. After perhaps fifteen minutes the Helper said,

"Please stand." There were four of us to be opened and three Helpers. We stood together.

At the present time in Subud each candidate for opening is asked to declare her belief in God. Fortunately for me, Bapak had not yet given that instruction in those early days. I couldn't have honestly said it of course since I didn't even know then if I believed in God.

One of the Helpers read Bapak's opening words, which asked us not to use our self-willed desires and thoughts but to open our feelings and truly surrender to God. Then she said,

"Begin."

Remember that I had already decided on a six-months' trial before I made any real commitment to this action. So I didn't expect anything much to happen during the opening, and was prepared to wait through several experiences of the *latihan* without making a judgment.

Therefore I was astounded when my body started moving slowly of its own volition across the room. It came to a stop and my eyes automatically opened. Directly in front of me was a single red rose in a vase. As I looked at the rose, which seemed incredibly beautiful in that moment, a message filled me. It was a whole-being experience, not exactly in words, but in sensations and images. A kind of hologram explained to me everything I needed to know about my father, his life now, and my life. Translated into words, and therefore diluted, the message said something like this:

"Your father is alive, just as this rose lives. He loves you and watches out for you in certain ways. His death was beyond his control. It was fated. Your path is to live your life now. There is no need to seek after him because he is right here."

This knowing answered a lifelong longing and quest for my father. Much of my personal search for meaning up to that time had revolved around understanding why my father left me so early, how I could adjust to not having his paternal influence in my life, whether he had a life after death and if so, where he was now. Accompanying this profound message was a feeling of great peace and resolution. It went through my whole body, something far beyond my mind. And my mind at last became quiet.

When the Helper said, "finish," signaling the end of the *latihan*, I felt quite different than when I walked into the room. I was more at ease with myself and in an elevated state of awe and gratefulness. As we drove home I had very little to say, unusual for me at that time.

This is how I was opened into another dimension of life from what I had known before. It took years for me to really grasp what that opening would mean in my life and destiny. It was an experience, which I could neither deny nor explain at that time. And I didn't try. Bapak had said it was better not to think or talk about the *latihan* when we were outside of it.

Startling events happened shortly after the opening.

Just two weeks to the day Lisa and I were driving to Tijuana from La Jolla for a day of shopping. She was driving. We were talking and laughing, having a good time, as we approached the border crossing.

Suddenly I wanted an American snack before we entered Mexico. I asked Lisa to stop the car for a few moments. She pulled over to the side. Then I jumped out of the passenger seat and darted across the street, heading toward a store I'd spotted there. I'm sure I didn't really look at the four lanes of traffic behind me.

Wham! I was hit. I knew it was a car before I ever hit the pavement. I lay there on my back on the highway, stunned, frozen.

Then, like gunshot, several thoughts exploded in my mind at once. Am I dead now? No. Am I pregnant? I remembered how often I had been pregnant recently and realized that such a hit would surely harm the baby. No.

Then I became aware that I felt no pain. I was astounded and disoriented. No pain? How could that be? I must be dead, I thought again. Otherwise how could there be no pain, not even an ache?

Then a sudden revelation:

"I'm alive!

It's a miracle.

And it's Subud!"

These were the exact words that came to me. I can remember them now as if they happened this morning.

In those few seconds the driver of the car that had hit me jumped out and ran up, hysterical. He was waving his arms, shouting in Spanish, "I didn't see her! I didn't see her." It wasn't anger in his voice but desperate worry. Others had also gathered around, looking at me in horror. I'm sure they expected me to be dead.

I looked up at them in wonder. They looked so beautiful, these human beings concerned about another human.

I sat up, then stood up. There was no pain, no bleeding. I saw then that the car that had hit me was a large Buick. It had flipped me up in the air and then I'd slammed back down onto the pavement on my back. It was a miracle all right. How could I possibly be standing up, now walking, as if nothing had happened? The people backed away from me as if I was a ghost rising.

"*Que curioso, eh?*" (How curious, eh?) I watched them in wonder, filled with gratitude—for my life, their lives, all life.

I assured the Buick driver that I was OK. I apologized to him for running in front of his car and scaring him half to death.

Then Lisa and I drove on, dumbstruck by this experience.

"That guy had to be going at least thirty miles an hour," she said, "I'm astounded that car didn't kill you." She didn't even ask me a thing about how I had done something so stupid and I didn't offer. In fact we didn't say anything at all for the next two hours; we were both too stunned. I did say to myself though, "you had better pay attention."

The next morning my whole body ached as if I had been hit by a Buick. I worried then whether I had broken any bones or in other ways truly hurt myself but within just a few days I was quite normal.

Except for one mark. At the very base of my spine was a small red impression that looked exactly like a birthmark. The skin wasn't broken and there was no bruise. I showed it to Lisa.

"It looks like a birthmark," she confirmed.

That mark remained for many months.

Exactly two weeks after the car hit me I was walking across the street in La Jolla, in a crosswalk, after looking very carefully in both directions—I had learned my lesson about crossing without checking first. Suddenly, out of nowhere, a big black car came careening toward me. Instinctively I ran for my life. The car barely missed me as it zoomed past. It didn't even slow down.

This time I was shaking all over and almost fainted when I reached the sidewalk. A couple of people who saw the car speed past were shaking their heads in disbelief.

"Are you all right?" asked one. I said that I was but in fact I was scared out of my wits. I had to sit down for some time before I could walk, or even think.

I remembered the hit of the Buick and the euphoria afterward. There wasn't any this time. I was stunned and frightened. Paranoid even. "What's going on?" I asked myself.

An inner response was swift and severe: "You asked to wake up. Now you had better wake up!"

These were my initial experiences after being opened in Subud. Even though I now know that we don't pray for anything at an opening, and even though we surrender everything to God's will at each *latihan,* for me the opening and every *latihan* since has been a gradual waking up process. Waking out of sleep and awakening to the truth within. Through that opening, and the process of continuing *latihans,* I gradually became aware of my own soul and eventually reclaimed soul consciousness. The awareness of God's love and guidance that developed later was a bonus.

Since I was opened in Subud I have also witnessed openings of many other Subud sisters. Each one was different. Some people reported remarkable revelations from that first *latihan*, others tell of subtle but continuous changes in their lives ever since. There were also openings that didn't seem to register at the time, but Divine action is not readable by normal signs.

My opening started a lifelong path that continues through the Subud *latihan*. Yet through the years I have learned that people can be opened in other ways as well. Dramatic events, like those described in the following chapters, can also break the cocoon of conditioning and awaken the soul. Although these shocking experiences don't automatically assure opening, they can result in it.

7

Life After Opening

The Subud *latihan* has been my spiritual practice, and Bapak my spiritual teacher, since I was 25 years old. Many extraordinary experiences have happened to me and everyone else I know in Subud, both in the *latihan* and in life, all of which I attribute to Subud.

For instance, the life-long quest for understanding about my father's death was cleared up at a personal level. My life was miraculously saved twice, as were other Subud members' lives, especially during the Vietnam War. Not a single Subud person's life, American or Vietnamese, was lost in that horrendous event despite extremely hazardous missions.

The first year of practicing the *latihan* brought a euphoric state; I seemed to be filled with grace. My spirit lifted out of despair, my mind and emotions grew calmer. I developed good friends in Subud and we shared our deepening experiences; we were truly a brotherhood/sisterhood and all was well. We were inspired and strengthened.

And there were transcendent experiences. For instance, once, in an elevated state I was wondering why the *latihan* had been given now. I didn't expect it but an explanation came: "It is an experiment, to see if humankind can handle direct Divine energy and guidance, and put it into practice, without intermediary priests and teachers."

Another time I was pondering time, how the past and future actually related. And for a few moments I *experienced,* beyond thinking, that time is simultaneous, not linear at all as we think of it. I certainly didn't have the physics or math background to question or explain the experience but it stays with me as a multi-faceted truth.

Gradually and subtly my perception began to change in *latihan*. I experienced more of a witness state. That is, I could observe my mind chattering away in its usual mundane way while simultaneously I was aware of a much greater truth unfolding. It was accompanied by whole-being awareness, a state in which I could can see, hear, feel, move and vocalize in unity all at once. None of this experience was self-directed but moved from the mysterious force of the *latihan*.

About that time Jacob Needleman wrote *The New Religions*.* One chapter of the book was devoted to Subud which Needleman called "the farthest out and the deepest in"[1] of all the practices he had explored. In those first years most of my Subud friends were young mavericks. We thought Needleman's description was just right; we were delighted to find our own impressions described by a scholar. We felt we had been blessed with a dogma-free, truth-promising practice. It was definitely becoming a way of life for us.

Early in my Subud life I became obsessed with the idea of moving to Indonesia where I could be close to Bapak all the time. When he came to Los Angeles I requested a private interview with him so that I could tell him about my wish and ask his counsel.

Complex arrangements had to happen with a number of people to obtain this interview, and it was by no means assured. I waited with mixed eagerness and dread.

I was 150 miles away when the call came that an appointment had been set for me. I jumped into my VW van and drove like a maniac to make it.

I was extremely nervous as I waited my turn among many people. When I was called into the room with Bapak and his interpreter I lost all courage to ask what I really wanted to know, namely if I could have

1. Needleman, Jacob. *The New Religions*. E.P. Dutton & Co., inc. New York, 1970. (called by Theodore Roszak at the time, "The best survey of transplanted oriental mysticism in America that has yet been undertaken.")

his permission to come to Indonesia with my four children to live near him for awhile.

I sat there, literally dumbfounded.

Bapak waited patiently for me to speak. His presence was so still and vast that my impractical wish suddenly disintegrated; it seemed utterly absurd at that moment. I sifted through my mind to find something innocuous I could ask instead. Finally I came up with a true experience even though it seemed trivial to me at the time. I told Bapak about the colored lights that appeared in my hands during *latihan*. They rolled around in my palms—blues, purples, and yellows—sometimes quite bright, dimmer at other times. I asked for his clarification.

Bapak gave an explanation but I can't remember anything he said. Years later, when I learned to use my hands in healing, I thought of the colored light question but whether Bapak addressed it or not I don't know.

I thanked him and bumbled out of the room, relieved to be away from the exposure of my cowardice and mental meltdown. I headed straight for my van without saying a word to several friends who were standing around, looking at me expectantly. I got in the car and started to drive home.

Then there was a great wide space in time. No thought. Only a feeling of limitless expanse. Seeing, hearing, and feeling in a paranormal way all at once. Like being suspended somewhere off-world.

When I came out of this state, back into normal consciousness, I was shocked to realize that I had driven 30 miles in the opposite direction from home. I couldn't remember how or why I had taken that direction.

This sense of having been somewhere altogether extraordinary persisted for a number of days. I couldn't understand at all what had happened with my mind and I certainly couldn't put it into words.

Now, after many years of practicing the *latihan*, I would say that I received a dose of lightning directly into my soul that day from Bapak's extraordinary presence. It was the second enlightenment experience of my life, the first having occurred on the desert in the Great Loving Radiance.

Now I would explain my experience in terms of the spiritual channel, a term I invented later for my work to describe the higher perceptions possible in humans, a sensing not explained in communications theory. A multi-channeled awareness in higher consciousness that enables us to see, hear, and feel all at once at an extrasensory level beyond thinking. It is difficult to *describe* in words because it is beyond words but everyone has these *experiences.*

After the first blissful year in Subud we came to learn that opening was only the very beginning. The process became more demanding. We started to see our "demons" more often, the unfinished business and mistakes of the past, our "stuff" as it is called in psychology.

About this time I became pregnant with my fourth child, which was a complete shock and very unsettling. Our marriage was rocky, we were strapped financially and I was already pushed beyond my limits trying to raise three children and work at the same time for extra income.

I realized, without doubt, that I was pregnant during the only vacation my husband and I ever had. As we bounced along in a train headed for Mexico City I was so nauseous and upset that I could hardly take in the scenery. When we finally arrived in Mexico City all I could think about was finding a *latihan* to get myself in order.

I entered the hall that night sick and depressed. How on earth would I cope with this latest challenge? But shortly into the *latihan* I received a clear message:

"Nevermind. This baby is a boy and he is full of light (I actually saw a bright light). He is a great blessing and will shine brightly throughout your life." The depression lifted instantly and by the time *latihan* finished I was peaceful and happy.

Of course later, faced with the same reality in my earthly life, I again sank into doubt and worry. Nevertheless, the message was exactly correct and it strengthened my faith in receiving. My son William Henry has been a lighted blessing from the very beginning right up until this moment. It is partly because of his generosity that I was able to finish this book.

Within a short time the purifying action of the *latihan* became intense for some of us. Bapak had explained that we would be cleansed of old physical illness and spiritual mistakes. He said that during the purification process we could easily die forty-nine times, as layers of ignorance and wrongdoing were peeled away from us. We marveled at this. What did it mean?

But after awhile we began to experience parts of ourselves dying as one way of life or perspective dropped away completely to be replaced by a new state of consciousness. Former beliefs crumbled in the face of *latihan* experience. It was disorienting and hard to keep our bearings while early conditioning was being unraveled in the mind. A number of times I feared I would go crazy.

Old physical symptoms resurfaced, to eventually work through the body. When they happened we wondered whether to resort to medicines or wait it out. Incidentally, there is a corollary in physical healing. It is known as the "law of cure" within homeopathy and other natural healing methods. As therapy is administered old illnesses come to the surface to work themselves through the whole system.

Four years into Subud physical crisis hit me. I was diagnosed with cervical cancer, extent unknown. I felt stranded. The recommended treatment was complete hysterectomy then. I was 29 years old, by this time the single mother of four children, working for subsistence wage and completely perplexed about what to do. There were only hints of alternative treatment for cancer at that time; most of them sounded risky. I wondered if the *latihan* could cure me; I had witnessed several remarkable healings myself. But with four children to consider I feared relying on unproven routes.

The secret explanation to myself at the time for this crisis was that past sins had caught up with me. The process of *latihan* had exposed my youth as full of ramshackle havoc, like a car that had reeled out of control. I had pursued one relationship after another, seeking permanent love and meaningful life, neither materializing. The *latihan* had burned holes in the fabric of that old existence, exposing its false assumptions. It had set me on a serious course of corrections. Then, just when I felt I was beginning to get it together, to see a clearer path, this hit knocked me flat.

Looking back now I see that what I called "sins" then were no worse nor better than the mistakes and ignorance of most of my generation, living in the human condition of the mid-twentieth century. Measured by a higher order they were definitely soul failings. Admitting that was a wake-up call that brought me to the brink of a profound change.

But there wasn't much time for reflection or feeling sorry for myself. The chips were down. I needed soul guidance. I cabled Bapak, explained the whole situation, and asked for his counsel. He cabled back immediately:

"Bapak prays for a successful operation."

The choice was clear. Surgery was scheduled in ten days. Doctors wouldn't be able to tell how extensive the cancer had spread until surgery was performed.

During those ten days I faced death.

I put affairs in order as best I could and then took stock of my life. I analyzed my mistakes. Almost too much to face. I experienced a phenomenon then that I would learn about intellectually much later in life. The life review that happens automatically and inevitably as one faces death, is reported by many near-death survivors. In this experience one meets their full history head on in the most minute detail. Every action, event or relationship passes through consciousness. And the really difficult part is the "sins" against others, including those little hurts often overlooked. They hit the hardest and you wish desperately that you could somehow undo them. My life's review showed me that I had been far off the mark of a soul path too many times. In a flood of guilt I finally accepted that cancer, even death, was not unfair penalty for my "sins."

About the seventh night of this siege I gained clarity. I prayed accordingly: "Dear God, if it is necessary to forfeit this life for my past mistakes then I simply surrender it to You. But if this life can be saved then please guide me to use my talents to serve Your Will for the rest of it."

The night before surgery a close Subud sister came with me to the hospital. I confided my prayer to her and we prayed it again together. I went to the operating room the next morning with calm acceptance of my fate.

When I awoke from surgery the doctor, a compassionate woman, greeted me with a radiant smile.

"Good news! We didn't find a single cancer cell in the tissue we took to pathology."

With that message the second part of my life began. I had vowed to serve the Divine Will for the rest of life and from that moment on I followed it the best I could. Of course purification wasn't over and I made many mistakes, misjudgments and failures. I continued to fall off the path but the vow, and the *latihan*, acted as anchors to bring me back to center eventually.

The first action toward the vow was finding the right way to serve. How could I be the most effective with the talents I had? As I studied this task it seemed to me that I could help the most by seeking, and assisting others, toward individual health and enlightenment. Bapak had said that if there were only one hundred true human beings in the world at one time, which I translated as healthy and whole, the world could come to order.

Later I was prompted through the *latihan* to study psychology, then healing and bodywork. But those developments were yet beyond my imagination, as have been all major progressions in my life.

Questions left over from surgery could never be answered: Did Bapak's prayer cure me? Would the *latihan* have cured the cancer without surgery? Or was there no cancer in the first place?

Another question arose a couple of years later when I received a new name from Bapak.

From the beginning Bapak had given new names to Subud members who wanted them. He explained that he had the ability to hear the sound of a person's soul. He selected a name as close to that sound as he could find.

I found this practice distressing at first. How silly to change your birth name, I thought. For myself, I loved the name my mother had given me: Renee.

But sometime into the purification process I began to feel uncomfortable in myself, almost as if I was inhabiting the wrong body, or mind. Like wriggling around in a too-tight wet suit. Eventually I equated this discomfort with the realization that I was no longer the girl my mother had named.

I had started to say "Amana" over and over in the latihan. I thought perhaps it was my true name. I wrote to Bapak of this experience and asked him about the name.

He responded with an astounding report:

"Your name is Aminah. With it you have received a new soul."

Why did a new soul appear? Could Renee have died during the surgery and a new soul of Aminah taken her place? Were the two things even related?

No amount of speculation ever answered these questions either.

I have described how directly Bapak affected us all, how inspired and awakened we were when he came to see us. In his presence, every part of us—mind, body, feelings, soul itself—was quickened. Things started moving when we were within his field. Each year he came brought noticeable growth spurts and lasting inspiration.

Two major turning points in my life happened like that when I was close to Bapak.

In 1971 I spent a month in Indonesia at Bapak's home attending the Third Subud World Congress. I prepared for the most primitive and taxing circumstances from reports of Indonesia. But Bapak had arranged accommodations for us that were both primitive, and utterly wonderful. He had created an exotic and complete environment for us, his global family. Two-story bamboo-thatched dormitories had been constructed for the Congress. They provided small rooms for each person or couple. I spent some lovely hours in one of those rooms. I can still feel the soft air of the tropical night, smell the bamboo, and hear the creaking poles as we walked through the corridors. And most important, was the constant electric field of Spirit, with its peace, harmony and creativity. Everything we really needed—rooms, food, entertainment, medicines, even clothes, and *latihan*—was available.

That Congress had a long-term impact on my life. It showed me so many possibilities for individual and collective true human development. How healthy, happy and creative we could be. How old silly antagonisms of personality could dissolve. And especially how continual spiritual nourishment made everything else more manageable. These experiences informed me for the rest of my life.

The two events that happened during that time fundamentally inscribed my destiny and work.

The first was my only Subud "crisis." It was extremely instructive and soul strengthening.

Here's the background. We had known about, and observed, this phenomenon of "crisis" since the beginning of Subud. In England the medical community had even given it a diagnosis, the "Subud syndrome," which they used when someone was admitted to a psychiatric hospital. A crisis could come over a person gradually or suddenly. It usually presented a schizophrenic-type behavior in which people could hear voices, see beings that were invisible to others, be unresponsive to the ordinary responsibilities of life, sometimes leave their bodies and usually had to be tended like an invalid. I had heard that Bapak said this sometimes resulted when a person did too much *latihan.* They were trying to go too fast, he said. I had witnessed someone in that state and it scared me.

But the day it came over me there was no fear at all. Rather I experienced an expansive liberated state that was deeply interesting. It happened this way:

I had rushed into the ladies bathroom to get away from the incessant nagging of an abusive husband. I was crying uncontrollably, at my wit's end in coping with him.

A helper came over to comfort me. She put her hand on my shoulder, tilted her face down into my sobbing one and asked,

"What's wrong?"

The question was so unanswerable, and it called up such a volcano of irresolvable issues in my mind, that something snapped within me. Perhaps her question acted something like a Zen koan, deliberately designed to astound and confound the mind so completely that a person is forced out of it. I just flipped into another dimension where those "issues" were irrelevant.

I left this world.

Did I leave my body? Not exactly. I was perfectly aware of it but also simultaneously detached from it. I seemed to be seeing, hearing and feeling from a higher perspective. Although I was in my body I had no volition to move it. While still in it I found I could travel anywhere by simply focusing my attention on the place I wanted to visit. And all the time I was still sitting right where my body was parked, quite relaxed and aware of my surroundings.

For example, I could see into the women who began to gather around me in concern. That is, I could see their motives, their personality types and their feelings. I knew which ones were frightened of me, which had pity for me and which could accept me in what was happening. And none of these reactions mattered in the least to me. This was very different from my normal personality then, which would have been mortified by other peoples' distaste or fear.

Of course these helpers were only trying to help me. They were especially intent on bringing me out of the crisis. They reasoned with me, they comforted and cajoled. One even shouted in my ear,

"Come out of it!"

I had no reaction, nor interest, in anything they said or did however. I was entirely detached, absorbed in that other world that I found fascinating, minute by minute. I longed to remain still in that realm of higher perspective and freedom. I just wanted these well-meaning ladies to leave me alone. But I didn't even have enough interest to say that. I just stared past them.

Finally a helper I knew from California pushed through the crowd, came over to me and gently took my hand. She was a woman who had lots of drug experience before Subud.

"Come with me, Aminah," she said. "We're going outside to sit under the banyan tree."

And so I went with her easily and we sat under that tree for several hours. Some of the most engaging and sublime hours of my life. I am forever grateful to that woman, gone on to the other world now, who knew exactly how to simply be with me in that wonderful state. She didn't try to bring me out of it, find out anything about it or judge me for it. She was just present, with a quiet mind and compassionate heart. Thus I was supported to dwell in that realm for awhile, and be instructed and nourished by it.

We stayed there long enough for things to somehow come to a soul order in my life. It's beyond me just how that order came together. Certainly it had nothing to do with a mental analysis of my dilemmas. I can only report aspects of it. For example, I traveled freely in space and time. In this way I saw events going on within the Congress and then flew all the way to California to view my family there. I traveled to Bapak and Ibu, his wife. When I entered their chamber they looked up, unsurprised, and then welcomed me. Then they gave me spiritual instruction. Although I couldn't consciously remember the instruction later, something significant had happened with it; I felt assured and comforted.

Eventually, having received respect and protection for that free state of consciousness by the helper, I came out of it naturally. Apparently I had received what I needed. A "normal" state of consciousness returned. Like waking from a dream, I gradually became aware of what was happening in the reality immediately around me. I noticed then that my body had become quite cold in the darkening evening. I told the helper.

"Let's go get a jacket now," she said.

We got up and walked to my room. And that was the end of the crisis.

The aftermath of the crisis was hardly noticeable at the time. I couldn't understand what had happened and I didn't try. If someone asked where I had been all that time, I said truthfully that I didn't know. I only knew I had come to peace within myself and that my life would change.

Yet I know now that during those few hours I had moved into a higher state of consciousness beyond where I was living at that time. I had remained in the spiritual channel for an extended period. I was able to see a higher perspective and to move beyond denial and illusion to completely face the unhealthy conditions in my life at that time. The "crisis" was actually a temporary enlightenment, but one that I didn't know how to integrate and ground into ordinary reality at that time.

Although these realizations did not become fully conscious for some time, the foundations for radical change that would eventually manifest in life were laid that day.

The second soul lightning event occurred a week later. I believe now that the crisis prepared a receptive state of consciousness for its realization. It happened in perhaps thirty seconds during one of Bapak's talks but it set the course for my life work.

One day it was announced that Bapak would give a talk for teachers in the afternoon, a spontaneous offering not on the regular schedule. I heard the announcement although many didn't.

When I arrived for the talk few people were there. I sat on the marble floor where it was slightly cooler in the hot afternoon but I immediately felt drowsy and started to doze. I had to wiggle my toes and fingers to keep from nodding off.

Then suddenly I was intensely alert. Bapak was saying something like:

> ...Psychology then is the study of character, all those traits of the personality that have been built up through life from familial and cultural influences.
>
> **One day you will discover the psychology of the soul.**
>
> And that will be the true psychology that will help you understand a complete human being...

I have emphasized this one sentence because that is the way I heard it then. It jumped out of the other words and struck like an electric shock through my body, a bolt of lightning. It was thrilling. Yes, yes, this was it! This was what I had been struggling to define. This was my task! This soul truth filled me with an intense energy and interest. I was charged with it all that day and every time I remembered the sentence after that.

I have never heard another person speak or write about that sentence.

I was already a serious student and teacher of psychology at that time but I had experienced that the field didn't adequately address a whole person in either body or soul. This deficiency frustrated me in my work with young people but I hadn't yet found a way to integrate what I had learned about the body and what I knew about the soul from *latihan* in a definable way.

Bapak's prediction gave me guidance and courage to push beyond what I had learned in school and to follow soul guidance toward the discovery of my true work and purpose in the world. Eventually it became clear to me what was needed for healing and how to become whole. I would learn how healing had to go far beneath body or psyche symptoms to the very core of being.

Of course the conditioned ego-mind that had been professionally trained wasn't ready to back off that easily. It started a long debate with my soul. It commandeered a conversation that went something like this:

How can you do it? It hasn't been done, it's impossible.

The soul answered: your possibilities are limitless if you reclaim who you are.

The mind countered: Who do you think you are to attempt such a thing?

The soul responded: You are you.

What would be your credentials? The mind wanted to know.

The soul quietly showed me the expanded state of the crisis and its vast realm of comprehension.

This debate went on for many years, ad infinitum. Although it impeded and slowed down an easy development of my work, it didn't stop me from persisting with the soul task that I believe Bapak delivered to me that day.

8

Fritz' Opening with Muktananda

Dr. Fritz Frederick Smith is the Originator of Zero Balancing, a body-mind system that is a brilliant blend of western and eastern medicine. Zero Balancing has helped thousands gain greater health and well being through its elegant approach to body, mind and spirit. Dr. Smith's training and experience, in osteopathy, medicine, Rolfing and Chinese medicine, had prepared him well for the development of Zero Balancing. But his work actually coalesced in a remarkable spiritual experience. In the first class I had with him, and for many thereafter, he didn't once mention that occurrence.

I first met Fritz in a Zero Balancing class where his students were principally osteopaths, physical therapists and acupuncturists, who were attending there to refine their hands-on skills. Fritz was teaching us how to effectively balance energy and structure in the body, to alleviate clients' complaints, particularly back problems. As a psychology student I was less experienced than the others with hands-on work. My principle interest then was in the psychophysical aspects of symptoms. At that time I already realized that the soul psychology I was formulating would require direct work in the body. So I was studying various bodyworks and developing an approach to the whole person that included Bapak's guidance about the soul. I was interested in locating threads of history in the body and learning how to release them.

Fritz didn't directly address any of that. He spoke as a medical professional to other healthcare professionals. I would only find out much later that he knew a great deal about how personal history was imbedded in the body and how to release it at a very deep level. He looked and talked like a regular M.D. His anatomy instruction was detailed and clear and he spoke with authority about various medical conditions. His office resembled any other medical clinic although I noticed a bronze Buddha head and a colorful Tibetan thanka on the wall.

Yet from that first class I felt something special about his work and practice that was beyond his impressive medical credentials and knowledge. There was a mastery about the way he drew on the board and demonstrated his work with his hands that seized my attention. I was seeing and feeling something outside the words he said. There was an inner aliveness that drew me. Even though I had only planned to attend that one class I decided on the spot that I wanted to learn what this man embodied.

So it happened that I continued to study with Fritz for twenty-five years, right up to the present. I learned more than I can describe from him through the years, both directly and in observing him. He was teaching how to go beneath trauma to the essence of a person, to the soul in bone. What I was trying to accomplish in consciousness he was doing in the body. I am still learning from him. His work has become an integral part of mine and yet both works retain their individual signature.

During those years our relationship has evolved through many phases: from novice psychology student, to intern, to serious Zero Balancing teacher trainee, to co-therapist and finally collaborator and wife. Therefore I know him well and can say with authority that he is a remarkable human being. Inspiration, joy, discovery, love and co-creation have marked the evolution of this relationship, and it is still evolving. I continue to learn everyday from Fritz. I thank God everyday for him, a true mate and soul friend. But that's another story.

In this book I want to tell about the extraordinary opening Fritz received through Muktananda, the Indian sage who taught in the U.S.

in the 1970s and 1980s. Zero Balancing eventually developed from that opening.

Although my first Zero Balancing class was in 1978 I didn't hear this story, nor did anyone else, until about 1984, when Fritz told it to a few advanced students. When I heard it I thought he should tell the world. But he didn't speak of it publicly for another ten years. Now I know he was wise to withhold it until the world was ready. He has written about this experience in his new book, *The Alchemy of Touch*,[1] from which the following quotes are taken.

Fritz said he had practiced general medicine in a traditional way-—drugs, minor surgeries, baby deliveries, the works—for fifteen years before the first shock to his "straight" path occurred. As he tells it "I had gone from grammar school to high school, to college, medical school, internship, residency and into practice without looking left or right. I was very straight and didn't even know it."

Then a single event cracked his medical model. It happened when he saw an acupuncture demonstration by an English teacher of acupuncture, Dr. J.R. Worsley. At that time Fritz had barely heard of acupuncture and wasn't really interested. But when he received an invitation, with several other doctors, to attend the demonstration he went along. He says the diagnosis and treatment he witnessed that day, which he tells about in *The Alchemy of Touch*, deconstructed much of his medical belief system. Fritz said it just crumbled on the spot, and he said to himself, "I have to study with this man to find out what he knows."

So Fritz studied with Dr. Worsley for ten years and started to practice acupuncture in his medical office. The results were so effective that he finally decided to retire from general practice altogether in favor of hand manipulation and acupuncture only. By then he was a very different person from the young straight arrow medical student who had graduated third in his class. His mind, eyes, and hands had undergone an irrevocable transformation.

1. Smith, Fritz Frederick. *The Alchemy of Touch*.....Redwing Publications, 2005.

During his acupuncture training in England Fritz roomed with a doctor from California who had seemed fairly withdrawn, despondent even, when they first met. After a three-month break in the training, when he saw the doctor again, the man seemed very different to Fritz. As he tells it:

"When we got together again I looked at this doctor and realized something fundamental had happened to him, he was a very different person. His eyes were diamond clear. A veil that he had before had disappeared. I asked him what he had been doing and he told me he had been in India to see a holy man, Sai Baba. While he was there...he developed this inner clarity. The difference in him was so remarkable, that I remember saying to myself: 'I want some of that.'"

Shortly thereafter Muktananda came through California. Fritz was invited to do Darshan with him. Darshan is the Indian spiritual practice of sitting in the presence of a holy person to receive his or her blessings. Fritz realized that here was his opportunity to meet a holy man from India. Still, it was the early 1970s before eastern sages were much known, and Fritz was a respectable medical doctor. He wondered if it was appropriate for him to attend this foreign ceremony. So he asked for a sign to let him know: "Is this the right place for me to be? Is this the right thing to do?"

Darshan was quite a strange ceremony for Fritz. While Muktananda sat before the twenty or so people assembled, each person approached and then bowed down to him.

Fritz said that bowing down to another human being was "totally contrary to my early Episcopal training. It seemed wrong, improper and bizarre. It was only through an act of will that I forced my body to bow before Muktananda."

Muktananda received hats as gifts from people. He would wear the hat for awhile and then pass it on to someone in the audience. Fritz willed himself to approach Muktananda and bow to him. When he rose to leave, Muktananda called him back and put the hat he was wearing on Fritz' head. It was the only hat he gave away that day. Fritz took it as the sign he had asked for.

After that first encounter, and the sign, Fritz started studying with Muktananda. When he heard of a month's retreat in Northern California, where Muktananda would be giving teachings, he decided to attend.

It was during this retreat that the remarkable opening happened. Fritz describes the experience in *The Alchemy of Touch*: as follows:

> "That week changed my life. On my last day I had to leave early. I knew I would need to leave in the middle of meditation that morning. So I made sure I sat on the aisle...When I had to go I bowed to Muktananda (which by this time was easy and joyful), got up, and went to (get) my shoes. I was in the aisle and Muktananda was sitting about one hundred feet from me at the other end of the aisle. I (put) my shoes on, and turned to bow to him one more time.
>
> "Suddenly a bolt of lightning shot across the room from him to me, and hit me on the top of the head! I was totally stunned, and jerked up in a daze, not expecting anything like this. I then realized that it was a very auspicious moment, so I bowed down again, and a second bolt came...To this day I can still see that first bolt which was 100 feet long."

Nor was that lightning bolt the end of it. Fritz told how that powerful energy hit set a process in motion in his life "which was unbelievable." Strange things began to happen to him. When he stood still he could feel the earth begin to shake, like an earthquake. Since the shaking didn't happen when he moved, he kept walking around. He thought he might be going crazy.

This strange process continued for two weeks. Fritz became exhausted, from fear and too much walking.

Like many openings, this one permanently altered Fritz' life. He would never be the same dutiful student, respectable doctor, good guy golfer that he had been. From that time on Fritz was on an uncharted journey of new discoveries and service beyond his medical training or ego.

The opening continued and it brought many gifts. One of them eventually affected the world. It was Zero Balancing. He explains:

> "During those heightened two weeks an event occurred which was probably the most important thing that happened during that time. One night I was in the hot tub. It was big enough to stand in, with water up to the shoulders and you could do a kind of a dervish movement without touching the sides. I was doing this slowly when all of a sudden, information began to pour into the top of my head. For about one minute it was like a funnel in the top of my head, and information just poured in. It was about energy, and how energy and structure interrelated and interacted in the human body."

Fritz said that his mind seemed to come apart, disassemble and then re-form, with this new information. As he tells it,

> "From that day on, I have known how energy works. Much in Zero Balancing has come from that experience, and thirty years later I am still recalling things I received that night.
>
> I was given a huge piece of information that evening that totally changed my life, and has made this whole teaching of Zero Balancing possible. The exciting thing is that the information can be taught...it can be transmitted."

And transmitted it has been. By Fritz and many other Zero Balancing teachers he has trained, who have in turn taught thousands of health care professionals who subsequently delivered Zero Balancing sessions to countless clients around the world.

Zero Balancing is therefore much more than a synthesis or summary of all that Fritz has studied—the mechanics, medicine or osteopathy of the twentieth century. Certainly he was a well-cultivated vessel to receive this information because of his previous education and experience. But the soul of Zero Balancing came from his opening into grace that brought forth an extraordinary revelation. One that would result in an instrument of world healing.

The transcendent lightning that was given to one man in a few moments thus blesses the world.

9

Lightning Bolt Through the Spine

Some openings come unbidden. But as the Hebrew saying goes, "Bidden or not bidden, God is present." Whether we consciously seek an opening or not, are prepared for it or not, it brings long-lasting spiritual effects, as in the following examples.

Laura and I have been Process Partners for over twenty years. During that time we have studied, taught, worked and traveled together through many healings and learnings. And we have become true soul friends. She said that when she first saw me she fell backwards in time, reliving, in a few seconds, many times and places we had previously met. In this life we did so many trainings and journeys together, in California, Colorado, Switzerland and Egypt that we knew each other's histories backwards and forwards. Along the way we came to know of our openings, and have shared our journeys of awakening.

What I will tell here is about the destiny-marking trauma that happened to Laura when she was just thirteen years old. The trauma that was also an opening and teaching.

When she first mentioned this story, early in our developing relationship, it was so shocking that my mind went into temporary denial; how could this possibly be true? Over time, as we came to know each other well, she finally told me the whole of it, when I had the strength to take it in. And through the years, as I witnessed her working through the trauma, to deeper and deeper layers, each time suffering all over again and healing one more part, I came to accept that this terrible event was also part of her destiny. It was both the most horrible wound and the deepest soul sign in her very unusual life.

This is what happened:

Laura and five classmates were walking on the beach near their homes on the island of Kiawa where they had played all during childhood. At that time the island was a private gated community, owned by the people who lived there. No hunters were allowed. Guns were illegal. Laura had spent many hours and days, playing and exploring in that safe haven. The rolling sand dunes, the gentle lapping surf, the occasional clump of grass along the shores, had always provided the most idyllic playground for carefree young spirits.

Laura said Kiawa was the only place her overly-protective minister father would allow her to roam freely. She wasn't exactly in his good graces at the time. She had already rebelled rather forcefully against him and the church where he preached. At twelve she had refused to attend church every Sunday, as her father required. She was questioning everything about church life; she had seen too many hypocritical discrepancies between doctrine and behavior. In fact, she felt the doctrine of the church kept her from a personal relationship with God.

But this was a special day and religious questions were far from her mind. It was Laura's first "date." She and two friends, Liz and Sharon, (not their real names) had invited three boys they liked to come to the beach with them. As they walked together along the dunes they talked and laughed self consciously, as teenagers do, shy and exhilarated at the same time.

Suddenly there were popping sounds in the distance. They stopped to listen.

"Firecrackers," said one confidently. They knew that sometimes people set them off on the island. They walked on.

Shortly they came across a perfect white seagull lying in the sand. They could see it was dead although there wasn't a visible mark on it. Laura felt sad about the bird but she didn't want to touch it. They paused for a few minutes, looking at it, wondering what had happened and then walked on.

Suddenly there was a second loud cracking sound. This time Liz screamed. Laura turned around to see blood spurting from Liz' shoulder. She reached out to catch her friend. The doctors said later that the gesture saved her life because otherwise the next bullet would have pierced her heart.

Another loud sound. A searing pain exploded across Laura's chest. She said it felt like she was on fire inside. At first she thought she had been hit by a firecracker. But then she realized she had been shot. The impact to her body was like an earthquake. Blood rushed out over her sweater. It was a nightmare scene. Seashells, sand and little pieces of shot flew up all around them. Laura said that her mind and body exploded instantly and simultaneously in a blast of questions, impressions, feelings. She was terrified, horrified. She, and the others, would die. Why, why would anyone shoot them? Who could save them? Who could hear them?

Liz was still screaming and quickly soaking with blood. Her boyfriend was holding her up. Laura's boyfriend stood back, his face paralyzed with terror. They all looked around wildly, trying to locate the shooter.

The pain in Laura's chest was sharp, searing, throbbing. She could feel herself growing dizzy and faint. Her knees started to buckle under her. She began to fall. Then, she said, she felt consciousness slipping from her. She felt that if she went down that would be the end. Somehow she knew she had to remain standing.

"They're coming, they're coming!" screamed Laura's boyfriend, looking back over his shoulder. And he ran for cover into the dunes. Laura saw him run but she couldn't follow. It took every ounce of strength she had to stay upright. She looked back in the direction he was watching and frantically tried to see the men her boyfriend saw, but could see no one. In her mind's eye though she saw hooded figures in long black cloaks, as if she were reliving a memory. Did she call out for help then? She couldn't remember.

Suddenly a golden shaft of light shot straight up through Laura's spine. It bolted far into the sky and then straight back down into the ground. It was electrifying. "It felt like a steel rod in my spine," she said. Her body shot upright again and she felt life strength surging through her. She could move.

In that instant Laura knew the light was from God. There was not a shadow of doubt in her mind. She says that after that moment she never doubted God's protection in her life.

When Laura told me of this single lightning moment that marked her whole life I was reminded of the prophecy from Mother Mary at Medjugorje. The Mother said there would come one instant when everyone in the world would know of God. She told that just one spiritual sign would appear on the hill near Medjugorje for all the world to see, and that in that instant, everyone everywhere would know that God existed. A sign that would be "beyond destruction by mortal man."

When Laura saw that shaft of light and felt God's presence she started intoning "God, God, God"...over and over again. She repeated it all the way, as she and the others struggled to walk toward her house. Her companions said later that she started to fall down five times but each time somehow held herself up, all the while saying "God, God, God."

Everything went into slow motion then. All she could see was the blood pouring down her sweater. Again she felt that if she fell she would die. She thought to herself, "nobody shoots anybody in the heart without meaning to kill them. We have to keep moving."

They heard a car coming. Was it the shooters coming after them? They were terrified—hoping against hope for help. Maybe their parents had heard the shooting and the screams. A jeep slowed down as it came to them. Laura saw two unfamiliar and ominous-looking men staring at them. They looked drunk. One of them was the "darkest looking man" she had ever seen. She expected the worst. The jeep drove on by.

"Then a miracle happened," she said. She has no idea how long it was before another jeep drove up, but this one stopped and three people jumped out to help them. Two were doctors, one a woman. She remembers that they put the kids in the jeep and drove toward her home. She remembers that the woman doctor said to her, "You're going to be all right, sweetheart." That was the first, and only, human comfort she received during the entire episode.

After that her memory became hazy.

Next she recalled a part when her father was driving her and Liz to the hospital. He told her later that he was terrified at the time but what she remembers is that he yelled at her, "You look like you're going to die!" She thought then, "he can't be with me now."

That was the last thing she remembered until she woke up on a hospital gurney. She was struggling desperately as a nurse was trying to put a large hypodermic needle into the wound. Someone said, "if you don't let us do this now it will hurt much worse later."

Then doctors were probing at the hole in her chest. One almost shouted in his agitation, "Where is the bullet? Where the hell is it?"

In that moment Laura remembered in a flash that a giant angel had come to her just as the shot rang. It had put its hand over her heart. Laura knew then, as the doctors continued to work frantically, that the angel had deflected the bullet and saved her life. But she also knew she couldn't tell them that.

The doctors never found a bullet in her chest. Its trail was there but somehow it had exited. They were confounded; there was no good explanation. Perhaps it hit a rib and veered back out, they speculated. Laura didn't tell what really happened for many years.

The first time I heard this full story I was shocked, horrified, and outraged. I asked her many questions in rapid fire. What happened then? Who shot you? Why? Did the police go after him/them? What happened to the first jeep? Where did the second one come from? What did your parents say, do? How long did it take to recover? And so on.

The more she told me the more confused and outraged I became. It seemed that whoever shot her was never found, that the police investigation was thwarted, literally called off by the police chief. A year and a half later that same chief was prosecuted for his involvement in a drug ring.

Periodically Laura returned to her home in Kiawa for family and community gatherings. Often after one of these trips I asked her if anything had been discovered about the sniper in her town and if the event was ever discussed. Always she shook her head. The motive and identity of the assailants have remained a mystery to this day.

And to this day no one in her town ever talks of the incident.

As for the last question, how long did it take to recover, the final answer is, almost a lifetime.

The wound in her chest was "superficial" according to the police report. What that means is that the bullet wasn't found and that after examination at the hospital Laura was discharged. But the wound took a long time to heal. The breast tissue where the bullet had hit kept pulling open. For a thirteen-year-old, whose breasts were just beginning to develop, it was a constantly painful and humiliating experience. Yet officially, her life wasn't threatened. In the body, that is.

Of course her psyche was life-threatened. Imagine being shot as an innocent 13-year old by some unknown assailant in your own private world. Consider how that experience would influence your feelings of safety and comfort in life, how it would affect your relationship with anyone you didn't know very well, even think about how you would regard your back from then on. And finally how would you relearn to trust people, or life itself?

These were just some of the issues Laura had already coped with before we met. In our years of study and work together those issues and others came up many times at deeper and deeper levels. Things like, did she somehow deserve such a blow? Had she strayed too far from home? Had she hurt someone unknowingly who wanted revenge? Was it a karmic debt?

As she worked through these layers she learned how to follow her own process to its deepest available information. Each time she revisited the shooting she dived ever closer to core effects of the trauma. She found important roots of her continuing fear about life on earth. Hadn't the experience taught her that life here isn't safe? That she couldn't expect human help or comfort? She discovered how the event had affected her self-esteem. Just when her woman's body was about to bloom it had been brutally attacked and disfigured. She had been unprotected and humiliated.

That early piercing of innocence and initiation into the reality of the dark of this world permanently imprinted Laura's life. Yet, as dramatic and horrible as those dark aspects of her story are, they are not the most important part. What is profound is how she triumphed over them and claimed her direct experience of Divine intervention.

Piece by piece Laura overcame the negative psychological effects of the trauma. As they resolved she went deeper, into soul work. She claimed the power and guidance of her own soul and her irrevocable connection with God. She realized over time that this event demonstrated to her that "God is always present."

Even though she never understood just *how* it happened she *knew* that benevolent light had saved her life when there was no human help. She knew the strength and life assurance of lightning in her spine. She clearly remembered the hand of the angel over her heart. She realized that her unshakable faith and compassion for others were born in that excruciating experience.

She says, "That event set me firmly on my spiritual path. Who knows where my life would have gone without that 13-year-old opening?"

When Laura and I went over the story once more for this telling we met that inner 13-year-old again, face to face. Even after all the brave healing Laura had done with her there was still a shred of fear, a shard of shame, as she said, "still a broken-open place in the heart."

We prayed together for and with that child: "What grace can we have now to take into that broken-open place of the 13-year old?"

Laura received: "Take in the knowledge that you are deeply loved by God and will always be protected."

Recently Laura consulted an accomplished Ayurvedic healer about other things in her life now. She didn't tell him about the early trauma. After he read her pulses he said:

"You are a rare and gifted healer. All of these painful things that happened early in your life are benefits to your skill and compassion. Even when you were very young people could tell you anything. No one understood how you could take the depth of their pain. You try to protect people from the horrors you've lived through but now you must use your own experiences as teaching stories."

And that is what she does now.

10

More Unexpected Openings

Sanjay and Poonjaji

Sanjay is a fascinating blend of East and West. He was born into a Hindu family in India where he received the religious training of his ancestors and the normal education of an Indian boy. In early adulthood he came to the U.S. to study science in a University where he became enamored of Western technology. Stepping aside from his religious upbringing, he turned to science and rationality, became an American citizen, adopted the American Way and chose goal orientation. After graduating at a young age he got a job as a Professor of Computer Science in an American University.

When I met him in a graduate health care class Sanjay had already discovered a fissure in his life and personality. There was a contradiction of his two sides: the Eastern, sensitive, feeling "wounded healer," as he called himself, and the Western intellectual who lived from his head. At that time he was on a journey to discover his own truth and resolution of these two opposites. He had already quit the Professorship in Computer Science to become a Process Worker and healer.

I liked Sanjay immediately when I first met him in the healthcare class. He was intelligent, well educated and quick-witted. He also had a growing intuitive and caring nature that almost matched his intellect although he seemed somewhat aloof at the same time.

Several years passed before I met him again at a Process Work seminar on the Oregon coast. I saw that he was different from when we first met. He was less intellectual, softer, and more approachable than I remembered.

We met for lunch and I asked him about the changes I noticed in him. He told me about his further studies, now focused on psychology and bodywork, and his practice as a healer. But we drifted quickly into spiritual conversation and he told me the following story about an opening experience that happened to him in India since we had seen each other.

"I went on a five-month spiritual journey to India," he began, "and synchronistic events led me to Lucknow and the spiritual teacher Poonjaji.

I had heard about Poonjaji several times, both in India and the U.S. Gangagi, the American woman guru, now teaching in the United States, had been initiated and enlightened by Poonjaji. My friend Chloe Goodchild, a special person and sacred singer, had been similarly empowered by Poonjaji. She recounted to me how she had been recognized and encouraged by him on her own path. Thus I was intensely interested to hear Sanjay's experience with this teacher.

"Poonjaji's ashram was an amazing place," Sanjay continued, "He was a Master at awakening people into their true nature."

Sanjay explained that Poonjaji literally provoked his students to awaken through a question and answer format. A person would ask him a question and then he would invite the questioner to discover the answer at the center of his or her own Self. Sanjay said he observed this interplay for some time before he wanted to engage with it but finally he was ready:

"When I asked him my question, he invited me to find out who I was, without concepts, and to drop name, forms and all personal history.

"His presence and the question completely stopped my mind. It was as if my ever-present sense of suffering just dropped away, and here I was, simply being present."

As Sanjay told of this riveting moment I immediately had a flashback to my own experience with Sai Baba in India when he had made a similar command.

I felt again the power of confronting the Self head on. The energy increased over the lunch table. I watched Sanjay carefully for any signs, in addition to his language, that would show the effects of Poonjaji's invitation.

A serene transparency came over Sanjay's face. He looked completely at peace and there was a far-off cast in his eyes, as if he were right there again, simply "being present." We sat in stillness for a few minutes. There was electricity around us as the hair on my arms stood up. I could feel that Sanjay's experience was true and that in this moment he was transmitting some of it to me. I was peaceful and vibrant at the same time, throughout my whole body.

"Then Poonjaji and I both just laughed. I could no longer understand what my so-called problem was. In fact all my problems seemed like a bad dream. I was suffused by a blissful feeling of celebration, in just being. And this state lasted for a few weeks. Each time I saw Poonjaji we simply laughed with each other. It was the most clear and blissful time of my life."

Just listening to Sanjay's experience evoked a feeling of liberation in me. The emergencies in the world, the complicated psychological turmoil we had been dealing with in the workshop, our own personal problems—all seemed removed for a time, only superficial. For those minutes of his story we were transported into the realm of timeless *Isness.* We remembered for a few brief moments something of the magnitude of what we are. Similar to the laughter Sanjay and Poonjaji had shared, our life circumstances seemed hilarious just then.

I asked Sanjay how this opening had influenced the rest of his life. He looked disappointed,

"Unfortunately I wasn't able to keep the experience. After I left Poonjaji it dissolved and there were even more complications in my life after that."

Sanjay looked so dejected that I was sorry I had asked the question. The expansive space we felt just moments before had subsided, even though the memory of it was still strong. We changed the subject.

But I kept remembering what Sanjay had recounted that day. I continued to feel the truth of it. So I wrote to him, and asked if he would give me permission to share it in this book.

Not only did Sanjay graciously consent but he sent me a further report of what had happened after the opening.

He explained that his mother had also been in Lucknow with her guru during the time he was with Poonjaji.

"My mother was shocked by my transformation. I had undergone an ego death, and felt free of all identification with being a son, or anyone in particular for that matter."

Sanjay went on to explain that his mother has been very bonded to him since childhood. She was "intuitively nervous" about the changes she saw in her son. When she was ready to leave Lucknow she wanted Sanjay to come with her. Feeling duty-bound, he went back to Delhi with her "instead of nurturing the tender shoot of awakening that had just sprouted."

But as many of us have experienced, going back to familial surroundings was a disaster for Sanjay. It stirred up all the early conditioning he was trying so intently to grow beyond. He wrote that he "lost my sense of awakening."

In a desperate urge to reclaim the experience Sanjay rushed back to Lucknow and Poonjaji. But "there was no going back." Instead of recapturing his enlightenment Sanjay ran right into his unfinished personality issues and entered a "darkening/death phase" which was very traumatic. He couldn't emerge from it there so decided to go back to the West where he could do Process Work.

"I had to once again descend into my own darkness before I could ascend to freedom. Poonjaji had helped me realize a mental union of opposites but that enlightenment hadn't penetrated through my body, and my life yet." Sanjay wrote that when he returned to the west he had to do the "hard work of embodying my enlightenment."

Sanjay's analysis about his expansion into freedom and the subsequent fall into darkness was very insightful, not only about his own process but it also sheds light on the general progression toward enlightenment after an opening.

Just as my opening experience did not permanently clarify my consciousness, nor relieve my ongoing struggles in life, and just as Fritz' opening did not assure the manifestation of his transcendent insights, Sanjay had to systematically unravel his cocoon of conditioning that kept him from fully living his own soul.

When I met him at the seminar it was evident that he had done a lot of that work. This showed in the way he related compassionately to others, by his penetrating insight about people and the world situation and by his clarity and humility about the enlightenment process. He realized, and was living, that process that takes us through many depths before it is stabilized into blissful freedom.

Sanjay is grounding his enlightenment as he pursues his spiritual journey. And he puts it into practice through healing and world service.

For now, Poonjaji's lightning strike still glimmers around Sanjay. You can tell he is a person who has been touched by something deep and true. I believe he will never forget his opening in Lucknow and I feel sure he will recover its full promise in this life.

Cathy's Spontaneous Baptism

Cathy is an accomplished musician and deeply sensitive woman in her forties who wrote to me about the spontaneous baptism that occurred after her session in our class.

We were focusing on soul work that day in a Process Acupressure class. The client is chosen to work in front of the group by the spin of a pen. The pen landed on Cathy and she came forward boldly to participate in deep work, something many don't feel ready to undertake.

Cathy's description of her experience on the table and afterward is so beautifully stated that I quote it here in entirety from the letter she wrote to me afterward:

I was so blessed that day to be chosen by the spinning pen as the one to work on the table with you. So much happened that afternoon, during and after that soul session—I knew I would eventually write to tell you about it.

I seem to be in an initiation process and though it's probably not surprising to you, I am continually in awe of how the universe provides exactly what I need.

During my soul session with you that day I felt so conflicted and almost disappointed that I didn't have a "bigger" experience. This work has rocked my world, and I had expected that a soul session at the culmination of such an amazing weekend would be huge.

My soul message that day was to be "soft enough to dance" and basically to be patient because things would unfold just as they should—and of course they did, though I didn't realize it then. As I sat up from our session and looked you in the eyes there seemed to be a misty veil between us.

I went for a walk that afternoon rather than participate in the next portion of the class. I followed my feet, weeping as I ran and walked to the top of a grassy hill. There was a stream with rocks at the bottom of the hill. I went to the rocks and walked on them up the stream to an old stone bridge. The sun sparkled on the water and through the trees.

I made my way under the bridge and stood barefoot in the water, up to my knees, singing Amazing Grace, and weeping and I felt my body begin to move. As I breathed more deeply, my voice became resonant, vibrating through all of me, like I was a bell.

I've been a musician all my life and I've never experienced such an exquisite embodiment of sound. As I sang, my body became softer and looser.

There was a deeper pool of water, lighted by golden sunlight, right at the edge of the light. Great waves of emotion, unnamable grief and rage began to come through my arms and out the ends of my hands. I moved in ways and breathed in ways I have never done before, and I continued until it was finished moving.

When I felt quiet again I stepped fully into the light, and I knew this was a baptism.

I looked down into the lighted pool around my feet and saw flecks of gold in the sand. As I put my hand down into the water to pick one up I saw my flesh illuminated—like it was glowing from within.

It came to me that I should leave something in this place—something valuable. I took off my grandmother's gold and ruby ring—meant for my daughter someday, and her daughter. It represented a history of pain and addiction that I've spent years reacting to. I offered the ring, with both hands, down into the water, nestling it into the sand among all the other golden flecks.

I left it there, as an offering of gratitude, but also with the knowledge that its absence would remind me of that moment, that new beginning—that turning away from so much "pain and suffering of my past, to align with my soul in that precious moment."

Since that afternoon this initiation into the second half of my life has continued to unfold and I find that I am so grateful.

I looked up baptism in the dictionary after reading Cathy's account. It said, "Baptism is a Christian sacrament of spiritual rebirth by which the recipient is cleansed of original sin through the symbolic application of water, or an ordeal of initiation."[1]

Yes, this felt like a rebirth.

Cathy's experience illustrates how an opening can affect many levels simultaneously, and in a short time. She not only gained a true feeling understanding of the Divinity of her own soul but she was able to shed ancestral bindings that had plagued her all of this life. And all of this had come about naturally, with no analysis, facilitation or even support beyond the initial one-hour soul session.

1. The American Heritage Dictionary. New York, Dell Publishing Co., Inc., 1973.

I saw Cathy again a year after this experience. Her eyes still had the liquid sparkle that showed up that day. Her creativity has flourished and she is training to be a first class health care professional.

Marguerite's Alignment between Heaven and Earth

Marguerite was the demonstration client in an Ancestral Healing class one day. Her intention for the session was "to live in alignment with Light in the midst of my very difficult life circumstances." Her husband had been ill and in constant pain for some time. Although she wanted to spend her time teaching and assisting Process Acupressure classes, a soul message kept coming to her: "You have to stay here with your husband and work it out."

She lay on the table, holding her intention, while she received hands-on acupressure. She grew more and more relaxed, looking peaceful, as the work progressed.

After awhile she said she was feeling a powerful energy through her spine. It seemed to progress through her whole body until all the chakras felt aligned. At that point she started feeling ecstatic. Her face took on a beatific expression. She said she was feeling just how her energy was connecting her into a clear column between Heaven and Earth. Suddenly her consciousness was clear and blissful.

At that moment she said, "So this is what meditation is all about!" Later she explained that she had read many books on meditation and tried and tried but never got to this place.

In ancient Chinese Taoism a human being is seen as the bridge between heaven and earth. Connected with heaven, she receives transcendent guidance that she will implement on earth, for the harmony and well being of all.

In yoga terminology Marguerite's experience could be called a "kundalini awakening." Yoga teaches that a powerful source of energy is locked at the base of the spine. It remains there, untapped, until some force opens it. Then it can shoot up the spine, enlivening the chakras and stimulating consciousness to new levels. Both these teachings give a foundation for our objective in Process and Basic Acupressure to promote full human development, through consciousness in all the chakras. Traditional psychology emphasizes strength in the first three chakras: survival skills, sexual vitality and ego development. In addition to these levels we wish to stimulate further growth through the heart, throat, brow and crown chakras which open a person to compassion, creativity and truth telling, clairvoyance and spiritual realization.

Certainly a full enlivening process was happening in Marguerite with this burst of energy through her central channel. We could feel the energy of it in the room. We were more awake in her presence as we witnessed how she had opened into heaven and demonstrated these ancient teachings in her body and consciousness.

Marguerite was radiant during the remainder of the class. She looked ten years younger. Her natural shyness was replaced by a buoyant charm and she was saying truths straight out that would have shocked her past self. She smiled and joked with her classmates and helped several through their processes. She was an obvious instrument of harmony that day.

When Marguerite left the workshop she vowed to do a daily practice to stay aligned with the experience of being a clear, lighted channel between Heaven and Earth.

After-Reflections About Opening

As we have seen with the experiences reported in this section, an opening can happen when a strong influx of energy blasts through our normal consciousness and reconnects us directly and consciously with Spirit. It may last for only a few seconds, it may last a lifetime. But it makes a gateway into the spiritual channel that may open again and again, each time revealing more of that limitless expanse of Source.

There is a story about a famous spiritual teacher who came to Bapak to check him out. He asked Bapak just what he was teaching. Bapak told the man that he wasn't teaching anything but if he wanted to be opened Bapak would be happy to do that. The man agreed. After his opening that man said he had realized more than he ever had before, even more than he imagined possible.

An opening brings a momentary liberation from suffering, personal or planetary, and a feeling of great spaciousness. Consciousness expands beyond its normal constrictions and comforts. The heart opens into greater sensitivity and caring. As Fritz said about his opening, "You fall in love with everyone and every thing." There is compassion for everything as one feels the suffering in the world more acutely. The coverings over our souls start to fall away.

Even though the opening lightning bolt is a dramatic and unforgettable experience the work of "embodying that enlightenment" will still have to be done, as Sanjay said. The cocoon of conditioning is so dense and so deeply rooted into our bodies, minds and emotions, that even a major opening will not permanently dissolve it. The cracking open is a blessing but it is only a first step in the process of awakening. It must be followed by a sincere dedication to its unfoldment along an uncharted path.

Usually massive life changes are required to make an opening permanent. Edges marking the boundaries of our known reality will have to be crossed. Familiar relationships, even marriages, will sometimes dissolve as an awakening progresses. Often the adjustment to a new level of consciousness can be arduous. Expanded awareness, including extrasensory perceptions, can crowd the mind with unwanted impressions. Many people have reported feeling that they were going crazy, just as Fritz did.

And what about the world's reaction? As we saw in Bapak's transformation, family and friends can't always tolerate the process.

For example, I worked with a psychiatrist client, a beautiful, intelligent and sensitive woman, who told me about an opening she experienced after an intense meditation retreat. She said she was transported to another dimension altogether. For several days she felt, and knew, the oneness of all life and she loved everyone. She could see right through her clients' defenses and pretenses into their basic motivations (a very helpful skill for a psychiatrist) and she felt only compassion for them. She was in bliss for days and hardly felt like sleeping. She tried to tell her colleagues, and especially her roommate, also a psychiatrist, about the wonders of transcendence. For this she ended up in a psychiatric ward, labeled "psychotic break," because her roommate feared she was losing her mind.

I saw this woman a year after the episode. She was very lucid, down-to-earth and pragmatic as any good psychiatrist should be but there was still a spiritual aura around her. She told me that for the psychiatric record, and release from the hospital, she had said all the things she knew would be acceptable to the medical community. But privately she never thought for a moment that she had a psychotic break, nor did she doubt the validity of her transcendent experience. She said it had permanently changed her perspective on life and her work for the better, although she normally didn't talk about it. She pursued that experience of Divinity through a commitment to regular meditation.[2]

So is opening worth seeking then? Is it even worth the risk?

Only the individual soul can know. It depends on one's aim in life, and perhaps soul age or karma. As Bill Dodge told me in those days before my opening in Subud, "If your life is working the way you want it nevermind being opened."

My life wasn't working the way I wanted it then, nor many times since, even after Subud. But through that opening, and the practice of

---

2. Fortunately, a new branch of transpersonal psychology has been developed to address the possible chaotic changes that can happen when a person is abruptly opened into the spiritual channel. Called "spiritual emergence," it studies and defines the difference between psychotic states and higher human development. Transcendent experiences, formerly labeled psychotic, are now examined with more allowance for spiritual awakening. Even in traditional psychology a new diagnostic code for this occurrence, named "religious or spiritual problem," has been added to the DSM-VI, diagnostic manual.

the *latihan*, I have remained connected to the Greater Unity of all life, and been steadily led along my own soul path and into the true work I was to do in this life. Deep inner contentment comes from that.

It has been my experience in my work that some form of opening, gradual or abrupt, must occur in order for a spiritual awakening to begin. Whether an opening is permanent or temporary, it will always leave an indelible marking in our life story. It may become prominent in that story or fall away into the category of "curious happenings." We have the choice of simply remembering that lightning strike as a moment's transcendence or of doing the work to ground it as a permanent promise through "embodying the enlightenment" in ordinary life.

Although the opening is the beginning of the journey, once a person is opened, the possibilities are unimaginable. Each opening reveals more of those transpersonal dimensions known well by saints, mystics and enlightened beings. As the ancient Buddhist sage Joko, wrote:

> There is no end to the opening up that is possible for a human being. Eventually we see that we are the limitless, boundless ground of the universe. Our job for the rest of our life is to open up into that immensity and to express it.

Section V: Life-Changing Lightning Strikes

Unlike an opening or initiation that happens in a spiritual field, a lightning strike can hit in a way that could never have been anticipated. The ones I tell about in this section permanently changed the lives of those who received them. Their consciousness, behavior and outlook on life were irrevocably altered. One was instantly relieved of drug addiction. Two received remarkable healings as a result of the strike. All were fast-forwarded into subsequent spiritual development.

11

The Angel Who Came in the Night

Lisa and I were both opened in Subud on the same day. We hardly knew each other then but over the next months and years we became close friends, as we shared our *latihan* experiences and the woman things of our lives. She was the woman I mentioned in Chapter 5 who saw the car that hit me.

She was an exotic, remarkable person. Her beauty was startling, like Elizabeth Taylor's. Men crowded around her the same way in any social situation. She was extremely talented as an artist with anything she turned her attention to: painting, pottery, fabric, jewelry, home and garden design. A walk through her home was an art gallery experience from the first step into her garden and through to the bathroom.

Lisa's ideas and behavior were entirely unorthodox; she had given up almost all conventions before I met her. Raised as a Catholic, she had violently flung it all aside in late adolescence when she went after alcohol, drugs and sex with unreserved passion.

Lisa didn't reveal these facts of her life to me until we had become very close. By the time we met her passion had turned to a spiritual commitment. She didn't drink, take drugs or engage in sex with anyone except her husband. She still produced art, still wore dramatic clothes (either pure black or brilliant yellows, purples, oranges and reds) and she still smoked tobacco but most of her attention went to practicing the *latihan*, going to see Bapak wherever he was and talking about the miracles in her life.

One night she and I were having dinner together and the subject of drugs came up. I think we were talking about people who still used drugs even though Bapak had told us they were not good for us and that if we expected the *latihan* to work we should give them up. I said that I couldn't understand why anyone would ever take drugs anyway.

"Oh, I understand it very well," Lisa said nonchalantly, "I used to be a drug addict who had no intention of ever giving them up."

I was shocked. I couldn't imagine this holy-seeking woman as a drug addict for a minute.

"You're surprised?" she smiled wryly, "That's good because I never tell anybody about those days. That's one of the reasons I moved here, to get away from all the friends and influences of my drug days."

"My God, Lisa, how did that happen and how did you ever get out of it?"

I wanted to know everything about it.

And so she told me the following remarkable story.

Lisa explained that she had started drinking alcohol at about age 13 to cope with the psychotic and alcoholic chaos of her family. By eighteen she was married to a motorcycle bum, had a baby, was alcoholic and pursuing drugs as well. When her husband left one day after beating her up she threw all his belongings out the second story window of their apartment, smashed his motorcycle and flew to Los Angeles with her baby where she knew he could never find her.

"Why did you go to LA?" I asked.

"There was an art school there I wanted to go to and I knew I could get all the drugs I wanted."

"You expected to go to art school and take drugs at the same time?" I asked incredulously. I knew she was very smart but I couldn't imagine how she could succeed in school while taking drugs.

"Sure," she said, "I could function on drugs and I wanted to study art. You have to understand that at that time I had three principle goals in life—drugs, art and sex, in that order."

I had never heard anything like this before and I listened with rapt attention as she continued.

She enrolled in the art school and immediately took up with the crowd that could get, and used drugs. Within a few months all her connections were in place, she produced art in the day and partied at night with her drug buddies.

"And what about your baby?" I asked, remembering the horror documentaries I'd seen about babies of addicted mothers.

"Oh no sweat," she answered "everybody loved her. We took turns holding and playing with her. If I was too stoned to give her the bottle somebody else would.

"The whole scene was just perfect from my point of view. I was making art, having fun, no parents or husband around giving me orders. I never would have changed a thing if it hadn't been for the visitation." She looked off into the distance for a few moments as if traveling through space.

"The visitation?" I asked.

"Yeah, there was this light being that came."

She stared off into space again and grew quiet, as if deciding whether or not to continue. We both sat there in silence for awhile. A charged feeling filled the space around us. I waited, hoping she would continue, even though I could see that she was sorting it over in her mind.

Finally she sighed and said, "Well, I've only told one person in my life before this but I guess it's time to tell you."

Then she went on.

She said that one night she was at a party with all her drug friends, a party like so many others she had attended. There were drugs, alcohol, rock'n roll and sex in most bedrooms of the house. Lisa was restless as she walked from room to room, hoping to find someone to either talk to or have sex with. She remembered being high and sitting down in a corner where she could get a look at the whole scene. She had just started looking around when…

"This huge light being showed up straight in front of me. It was so bright that its light almost wiped out everything else in the room. Then came the most amazing feeling of love and peace that I have ever experienced. Actually I had never known anything remotely similar to that love. He—I call it he for convenience, I never knew its gender—started communicating with me telepathically. Although there was no sound I could hear his words in my head as clearly as I hear you right now."

Lisa described how the light being had directed her to look even more carefully around the room, inspecting each person carefully. She said this took a number of minutes because as she watched each person she started to see things she had never seen before.

"The light being gave me a deeper sight and hearing. I could see what was really going on in a person's head. I saw envy, jealousy, resentment, and even hatred. I could hear the real thoughts behind the statements. For instance, in back of: 'You look so cute tonight,' I could hear, 'you slut, that's a hooker's outfit,' stuff like that."

Lisa said she saw the real inner person behind the mask. For example, one very elegant woman looked like snakes and worms inside. In that moment I remembered how Bapak had told us once that whereas we all thought X, an international movie star whom I won't name here, was very beautiful, if we could really see inside her we would be repulsed. I imagined that the light being had helped Lisa see like that.

"He did," she said, for that moment reading my mind. "He showed me so many things in that room that I had never seen, and never would have, without his help. For example, he showed me how a person's drug use would progress over time and how he would be in ten years. It was horrifying. He showed me how the "good times" we were having now would crash into illness, death, deformity and loss after loss."

After the light being had given Lisa plenty of time to view the entire scene with new vision he said, "This is Hell you're seeing. Right here. Right now." And she could see with her own eyes then that it was true.

He offered Lisa a choice.

"Now, this is your choice," he told her. "You can continue in Hell as you have been, or you can leave this room and this world right now, stop taking drugs and live the life that is available to you."

She said it was not a choice at all. Her interest in Hell had suddenly vanished in the light of what he had shown her, especially contrasted with the feelings of love and peace she experienced in his presence.

"What do I need to do to live that life?" she asked him.

"Just leave this room with me right now, go home and get rid of all your drugs and you will be guided. I will come to you whenever you ask."

And that's exactly what she did. She stood up and left the room with the light being. No one seemed to notice her exit nor question her later. The light being accompanied her to her home where she gathered up all the drugs in her cupboards throughout the house. Then she flushed them all, to the last pill, down the toilet.

"How much did you have?" I asked, still astonished at what she was telling me.

"Oh lots," she answered, "Probably six or seven bottles worth of various types, legal and illegal."

"Wasn't that really hard, to throw them all away when you were addicted? I've read that addicts are possessed by drugs, that they really need full time help to get off them and still go crazy in the process."

"Yep," she answered, "that's the way it is for most everybody but it wasn't for me."

"And how about when you woke up the next morning without any? How hard was that?"

"Not hard at all. In fact, after the visit by the light being and seeing what he showed me, I had no craving for drugs at all. I've never had another one since."

"Then what happened in your life?" I asked.

"It was permanently changed. Everything changed, absolutely everything. I stopped hanging out with that crowd altogether although I stayed on to finish art school. Then I moved down here, married a good man and started looking for the right religion or spiritual practice. Very soon I met you and you introduced me to Subud. You know the rest."

"And what about the light being? Did he come again?"

Lisa grew quiet then and looked pensive. I waited.

After quite a long pause she said, "Yes, for some time it was just as he promised. Whenever I needed him I asked and he showed up. He gave me very clear guidance for quite awhile and there was always that infinitely comforting love in his presence." She paused and looked sad. "He always answered my call. He always guided and strengthened me. That is until I told someone about him. Then he never came again."

"What do you think happened?" I asked, feeling her sadness at his loss all around us.

"I know exactly what happened. He told me never to tell anyone about him and I didn't for a long time." She looked down at her hands. "I never intended to tell but one time my sister-in-law, whom I loved very much, was having a terribly hard time in her life. She was so depressed and had lost faith in God. I told her about the light being because I thought it would help her. But he never came again after that and I'm sure that's why. That's also why I hesitated about telling you but since he doesn't come anymore I thought I might as well."

"Thank you very much for telling me," I said, with a catch in my throat.

The two of us sat in silence for some time, both following a private train of thought. I was in a state of awe about the light being. Was it an angel? And what had brought him to Lisa when she hadn't even asked for help and certainly had no thought of changing her lifestyle? It felt like a miracle to me that she had quit drugs because of the many stories I'd heard about how difficult it was to give them up. And I pondered why he didn't want her to tell anyone. It seemed to me that the story would help people; that's why I have asked her permission to tell it now.

I assumed that Lisa was again feeling the loss of that amazing being. Perhaps she was re-evaluating whether she should have told her sister-in-law or me about him, and whether it had actually helped her sister-in-law after all.

It didn't seem appropriate to question her further then though. I remember that we sat there in a kind of time suspension, almost as if we were held in a bubble of wonderment. Nor did we ever discuss the light being again.

I have always felt very grateful to Lisa for telling me this story. It helped me many times. And I was grateful to the light being for surely saving her from a life of self-destruction. The Lisa I knew devoted the rest of her life to the *latihan*, her daughter, grandchild and helping others.

12

Loss and Gain

John, our dear friend and colleague of twenty years, walked to the door on his crutches to meet Laura and me. One pant leg dangled limply where his calf and foot had been only a week ago. I didn't expect to see him upright so soon after amputation.

"Shall I hug you, John?" I asked awkwardly. I didn't know if he wanted to be touched and didn't quite see how to navigate arms around the crutches.

He looked me straight in the eyes and said, "Sure," as he deftly took both crutches into one hand, leaned against the wall and reached the other arm out to me.

In that hug we exchanged a hundred things of our history together—intense study and practice of Process Work, in big groups and small, shouting, wrestling, crying, resting in silence, sharing notes, giving each other feedback to perfect our skills, supporting each other in the hard times, celebrating the triumphs. The late afternoon when John, his wife Flo and I stood on a riverbank and cried out our dreams over the river. The ten years when he and I met weekly with another psychologist to practice and supervise cases. The laughter at birthday and New Year celebrations. The sorrow over a colleague's premature death. All those years of love, work and play we had already shared.

Now an entirely different reality had shattered his world. The abrupt shock of a deadly cancer diagnosis only two weeks before. The agony of making a decision to sacrifice his foot and half his leg to save his life. The swift overnight dash to the hospital and surgery. The stark reality of waking out of anesthesia, missing part of himself. The searing nerve pain and even worse emotional pain. All of that also radiated between our bodies within a minute or two.

Say something? What could possibly be said about this?

I think maybe I said, "John, John, John, I love you so," but I'm not really sure.

John released his hold and I stood back. We looked into each other's eyes again. His eyes sparkled with the inner light of his spirit. For a few seconds everything else fell away. Only love and the touch of soul to soul remained.

Four of us—John, his wife, Flo, Laura and I—stood there, clustered together for a few moments in their entry hall, savoring our love, and our lives, with profound respect.

"Let's go outside," John said, as he took up both crutches again. He led the way as we followed carefully. An athlete, long distance runner, explorer of treacherous terrains, in robust fitness only a month ago—all that flashed across my mind as I watched how he gracefully maneuvered with the crutches past couches and chairs and through the door onto the porch. He eased himself onto a chaise lounge and positioned his legs, first the whole one, and then the half.

We sat around him. Afternoon light slanted through the trees. The slight brush of a breeze sounded in our silence.

"I haven't been outside much," John said, looking around at the softness of nature. A tiny smile crinkled the edge of his mouth.

I stared at his face, amazed at its clarity. It was washed right down to the light of his soul.

"You look so beautiful," I said, as I looked directly into his eyes again, "like your true self, shining right here."

"Well yes, that's the thing. I'm right here now but the work now is to stay here, fully present, fully embracing life instead of the false never-quite-enoughness I've pursued most of my life. You know," he looked at me piercingly, "I've always been a little depressed, always after the achievements I couldn't quite reach, always longing for what wasn't here."

This," he gestured toward the lax pant of his lost leg, "cut me down to the realization that I had everything right before me all the time."

We sat there on the porch for awhile in silence. Then we moved, moment by moment, in the process way we had practiced so long, straight into the truth John was living.

"I want to live! My foot, my life, were caught in a trap and they were coming to get me. I had to sacrifice that foot to save my life. That's it. Now I'm afraid that if I don't get it, that if I slink back into the depression, the cancer will come up someplace else."

I put my hand on the still-there part of his leg and pressed it firmly. I would have felt too shy to do that in the past because John has always been a ready helper of others who found it difficult to receive.

"You've already got It, John. It's right here now," I said. "This is It."

He took hold of my hand on his leg and held it tightly. He looked around at each of us, wide open, receiving our love.

"Yes," he said "that's the thing, will I be able to stay with It, to cut away those old patterns that I have nursed as my identity for so long?"

Through all the horror, the fear, the still-present medication, John was more clear, more powerful than I had ever seen him. Although I have known him as a brilliant therapist—helper of hundreds in trouble, sensitive husband, superlative teacher and loyal-to-the-battle friend, I saw more of who he is that afternoon than ever before. He shone from inside with soul light that came straight out through his eyes. He spoke the truth of his insights and fears with unwavering honesty.

I thought I knew him quite well. Now I realized that all I had seen before was only the smallest part of him. Here is a great soul, I thought, the stuff of a bodhisatva.

Please God, I prayed, let him seize that and live It. Help him leave all the rest behind with the foot he sacrificed.

Aftermath

The next year was an agonizing adjustment at all levels, especially the physical, for John. Pain went on and on in the leg, physical and phantom—that mysterious effect of a missing limb that still sends its signals of distress into consciousness. Each time Laura told me about his and Flo's grueling struggle of sleepless nights, trips to the hospital, repeated adjustments of the prosthesis, I winced. Could this athlete, this warrior, come out of the tunnel of such a nightmare? Would it never end?

Then one day I received a brochure in the mail with a post-it note which read:

"Aminah, Here's a taste of what I'm up to. Wish me luck!

Love always, John"

I quickly scanned the tasteful brochure with a picture of John. It began:

"We are not who we think we are...We are the silent, free-flowing spring from which body, mind and the world itself pour."

I haven't said that John is also a writer and poet. His brochure displayed those talents eloquently.

"We are not any image," it read, "Our essential nature defies description, yet it can be experienced directly. We know it exists because we can feel it calling. It has been calling for all time. The call's source seems mysterious, yet we know beyond thought that it is our supreme task to find it, because we sense it is the wellspring of our life."

I quickly read through the whole brochure, more delighted with each sentence. Then I called Laura.

"What's happening with John?

"Oh it's fantastic," she said. He's doing this beautiful event with people, anyone who wants to come, to elicit the essential truth of their own being. I just attended the first one and it was a winner. He told the truth so beautifully about his near-death experience, his struggle and how he emerged into a new reality. It was so honest, so direct, beautiful. And then he worked, one-to-one with several people. He was masterful. Each person came to a much deeper place of knowing self and the truth beyond their problem. Oh I wish you could have been there. And he looked so happy, just wonderful!"

"I'm going to come to one! I can't miss this," I was deeply relieved and so happy myself that John had not only come through the tunnel, apparently he had come into the full light.

Within a few weeks I did get to John's program. I re-read the brochure before I got there. It reminded me that:

> We name it—the source of our calling—god, truth, the self, essence, or adamantly refuse to name it at all, knowing that no name describes it. We hear the call, feel its resonance, catch a glimpse of it luminosity, but it seems to vanish in the noise of the world, and of our minds.
>
> It is time to give up the quest. Our essential self is already here.

And this is exactly what I experienced with John and others who responded directly to him in the group that met. With each person he elicited that essential self that was already there, in that moment, in such a compassionate, respectful way. I watched with intense interest and admiration as he led person after person through the rapids of their problem or tangle, to that place of holiness within.

Between sessions of working with an individual he talked easily and clearly about some of the things he had discovered. For example, dual awareness. He said it was possible to be completely here in this reality while at the same time fully present in the reality of I AM THAT, in both worlds at once. John made this point exquisitely by describing it as Not transcendence and Not immersion in the mind's creations. Observing the mind, using it as an instrument—it's a very fine tool, he said—but not being trapped by it. I was so impressed by this knowing because John's mind is incredibly sharp and subtle. He has a mind and an ego, which would be very easy to identify with completely.

I noticed during the talk that he adjusted the partial leg several times, now perfectly prosthetized and shoed beneath his pant leg. I thought it must be hurting or stressing him in some way. When I asked him afterward if he still had pain he replied easily, "Sure, sometimes...there's still phantom pain."

But there wasn't a trace of the old veil of depression I had seen so many times in the past around John's beautiful face. His smile, his sparkling eyes were right here, right now.

As he worked with each person the room became lighter and more joyful. What a pleasure it was to sit there with that group, to hear straight truth, delight in, and love for, each person's realization of freedom. It was one of the best Sunday afternoons I have ever spent.

I experienced John as a clear instrument of awakened intelligence. I saw him elicit the I Am That in people and then support that moment of truth, soul-to-soul in the relationship.

Toward the end of the afternoon he said:

> When you meet life where it is, it bursts open to reveal its flowering. Then your life becomes a prayer, and every moment a blessing.

I sat quietly with that statement for some while.

I thought about all that John had lost in his battle with the monsters of cancer and amputation and what he had gained. And what a blessing his life looked like now, as he blessed others.

John and Flo, Laura and I, sat over dinner after the program. The old buddies together again, after all that struggle. Laughter. Reminiscing. And especially loving one another, appreciating one another, like the soul friends that we are.

John looked so happy,

"This is what I love to do!" he exclaimed as we talked about the program. His face was glowing, eyes crinkled in frequent smiles. What a joy to see him and Flo like this. It was a pleasure to be with them and to rejoice in John's self-realization. The Dalai Lama has written that the purpose of life is happiness. This is that kind of happiness, I thought, as I appreciated John.

13

Scorpion Medicine

Lightning can strike in a bizarre and foreboding way.

A whack on the door at 3 am awakened us. A loud voice, toned with doom, called:

"Fritz and Aminah! Please come immediately! Donna has been stung by a scorpion."

A wave of fear and dread flooded through me as we jumped out of bed, threw on our clothes and hurried up the rocky hill to Donna and Bill's room.

My thoughts raced over the possibilities.

Donna carried a core fear from an abusive childhood that I knew well, having worked with her for years. It was a fear so pervasive that it stopped her cold whenever she wanted to move forward. Any unknown territory—geographical, social, intellectual or emotional—would provoke it. She had to prepare herself beforehand with extended research, a clear structure and a strong drive. Over time she had constructed, piece by piece, a huge courage to combat the fear that always percolated just below the surface.

Nevertheless, she and Bill had made the decision to attend our wilderness ranch retreat even though they fully understood how isolated we would be, and about rough accommodations, snakes, scorpions and the demand of intense personal work we did there.

Just before the trip Donna had written in her journal:

I am on an edge and a threshold. It permeates every aspect of my life. As I watch it unfold it is wonderful, awesome, intoxicating, scary, chaotic and confusing.

Since their arrival two days earlier Donna had asked many questions about scorpions. She watched out for them everywhere she went, swept all corners of her room, always checked under her bed covers and sitting cushions. She said she had sensed the aura of scorpions everywhere from the first moment they arrived by taxi to the ranch. She told Bill at the time that she could feel them around her.

As she repeatedly brought up her concern about them I worried that her fear alone might call a scorpion.

"Look Donna," I said to her, "this week could present a big opportunity for you to transform your core fear." At the time she looked at me with a mixture of trust and fear.

We already knew that the particular scorpions at the ranch weren't fatal to an adult. But a student who had been stung before was ill in bed for three days with fever, extended numbness in various parts of her body, distorted eyesight and lots of fear.

I prayed, "Please God, help us through this night!"

When we arrived in their room Donna was in bed. Bill lay beside her on raised elbow, holding an ice pack on her arm. Wayne, the student and acupuncturist who had called us, lived in the next room. He had immediately answered their call for help and now knelt at the end of the bed, holding Donna's feet.

"Oh thank God you're here," Donna said in a weak and shaky voice. Then, with more strength, she blurted out her experience.

"It woke me from a sound sleep. I knew I'd been stung by a scorpion. I was instantly sick. I threw up. My gut was red hot with fear. I stumbled to the bathroom and immediately evacuated an unbelievable amount of stuff into the toilet." She looked up at me in awe. Her eyes were wide with an inner fire.

"Aminah, that was my fear, I know it! My whole system got flushed out in one huge rush. I'm empty." Her voice had an insistent tone in it and she continued to look at me in wonder, holding that realization in suspension for a few moments.

Then her eyes glazed, and her voice became weaker.

"But I'm still a little scared now. What's going to happen? I feel really strange."

I didn't know what would happen. All I knew from the manager of the ranch was that panic and hyperventilation were dangerous. When the poison hit her throat, which it would do as it spread throughout her body, it could close off her breath if it combined with panic. I said to myself, "don't allow panic, no matter what!"

"You will not die!" I said, as I looked her in the eyes and firmly put my hand on her arm to send the message into her core.

"OK. I trust you. But don't leave me."

"We aren't going anyplace until you're through this," Fritz assured her. I wondered just what that would mean.

She was quiet, more relaxed, for a time. Then she said,

"I'm starting to go away now, far away."

I pressed her arm more firmly. "That's fine. You'll Be OK. Just stay with what's happening and keep reporting to me. We're all right here and we will be here."

Her eyes closed and a shudder quaked her body. I wondered if she would go unconscious and if so what to do next. Beads of sweat popped out on her face. She started to moan.

"Donna, tell me what's happening."

"I'm so cold. I've never been this cold. And it's getting very dark."

We piled an electric blanket over the mound that already covered her and turned it on high.

"We're right here, Donna. Just keep breathing, stay with it and keep telling me."

In the bed next to her Bill started to sob quietly. He held the ice pack on her arm with one hand and wiped at his tears with the other. I sympathized with him. They had been married only three years and I knew that he loved her deeply. Probably he feared she was dying. But I had to keep all my focus on Donna just then.

Donna started gasping. Then she threw her head backwards, as if in spasm. A wave of fear about the throat closing up struck me but I knew I couldn't afford that for more than a few seconds. I tightened my grip on her arm.

"Donna, tell me what's happening now. Stay with us. You're OK. You're very strong. You can get through this and you'll be stronger than ever."

Suddenly she took in a sharp inhalation and her whole body went completely still. She said,

"Oh! Oh, thank God, Jesus is here!"

"Good. Wonderful! Thank Jesus for coming and ask for his help."

"He says He will be with me. He says He will never leave me."

A long pause.

"Now He says that we're going to a very dark place for awhile but He will be with me."

"OK. Take Jesus' hand and know that He, and we, will be right here."

Donna relaxed more deeply. I could feel her body softening under my hand. Then she said, in a barely audible, dreamlike voice. "OK Jesus. I will go with you anyplace. I surrender to you completely."

Then she was quiet.

The whole room became quiet. It was quiet for an uncomfortably long time. I could see her fairly regular breathing and feel her blood pulse under my hand but I was getting nervous. I suddenly remembered what I had read about Sai Baba being stung by a scorpion when he was a young boy. He almost died, went into coma and became delirious. A medicine man type was called in who resorted to severe measures; he buried Sai Baba in the sand up to his head, cut into his scalp and poured burning acid into the wound. When Sai Baba eventually came out of this extreme state he was very different. In fact, his world mission began shortly after that when he left home and told his parents that he no longer belonged to them, his students were calling him.

I hoped Donna's experience was nothing like that!

"What's happening?" Fritz asked, mirroring my anxiety. I shook my head, then repeated to Donna,

"Can you tell us what's going on where you are, Donna?"

Her only response was a kind of groan. She moved her head slightly to one side and weakly pulled at the blankets.

"Are you still cold?"

She nodded slightly. Fritz found one more blanket and tucked it around her. Wayne worked more vigorously on her feet.

There seemed to be little else we could do during that long period except remain intensely present with her. Occasionally one of us would ask,

"Donna, are you OK?" Are you here?" and touch her firmly. Although she would always give some minimal response, like a groan or slight nod, we had no idea what was happening to her inside during that time. Her body movements and periodic groans indicated that a lot was going on though. Later she showed me this part of the journey from her journal:

> *Jesus appears. He says,*
>
> *"I am here to take you on a journey needed for your soul's progression. Stand strong with me, trust me. Do not be afraid. I will lead the way."*
>
> *I am afraid, for my body. It feels as if it has been packed in ice. My lips are numb and tingling. My head is the same way. And yet I know that I must go. I leave my body in capable, loving hands of the four. They take care of it while I go with Jesus.*

If we had known then that Donna felt she was actually dying we probably would have intervened with dramatic measures. Such as, first CPR, then probably called an ambulance which would have taken her off to a hospital 45 minutes away, sirens blaring all the way. Then she would have been rushed into the startling procedures of Emergency Room medicine. Fortunately Donna was saved from that. Instead, as we found out later, she was entering a remarkable inner journey as we waited quietly.

Her journal recorded it:

> *I ask him: "Jesus, are you taking me home? If you are I want you to know that I am 100 percent willing and ready."*
>
> *Peace, freedom and joy fill me up. I want to stay with Jesus. I hope he is taking me because life has been so hard for me sometimes.*
>
> *But Jesus says, "No, you have to go back. Your work is not done. I need you on Earth.*
>
> *He explains: "We are going into darkness and we will be there for awhile. We will enter through your brain."*
>
> *My brain is tingling. The brain cells are opened, awaiting surgery by the Master Surgeon.*
>
> *Ah, the black hole, I know it only too well. Scraping the sides, holding on for dear life. I spent many years clinging to life by a thread in this hole.*
>
> *"Let go and come with me."*
>
> *Jesus leads me deeper into the hole. The way is a long arduous descent into the dark, the passage narrow. It is completely dark, more cold and lifeless the deeper we go. Every step is an exercise in trust.*
>
> *Now we come upon a very big old tree. At the bottom of it is the root of my ancestral line. I have asked for healing of my ancestry before.*

The path becomes more narrow, darker and colder with each step. It is void of all life, save ours. I think, I must adjust to the darkness. It's so cold, lifeless, an unimaginable void.

I see that there are many ancient roots here. Much bigger than me. Other humans have roots here. We continue to the core of my ancestral root.

The first we knew anything of her experience at that time was when she abruptly started sobbing heavily. Her breathing came in short gasps with the sobs. I worried again about choking.

"Breathe, Donna!" I commanded.

She gasped in one breath and then words started pouring out of her mouth in rapid fire.

"Oh my God. Oh my God, it's so dark here. Black. A pit. Oh, the horrors. This place is terrible, terrible. Beings are in agony here. They're writhing around in such pain, such torture. Oh, I've never seen anything as horrible as this, never been in a place like this."

I recalled how many traumas Donna had already been through in her life, some of the worst I had heard. This must be really bad, I thought.

"Tell me, Donna. Keep talking!"

She writhed, as if in pain, gasping, but no words came out.

Her journal record told it this way:

Now I see a sea of souls, lost and suffering. The agony is beyond the worst that exists on earth. Too much for me, or anyone, to grasp. I feel Jesus' hand turn me to leave.

I resist. How can I walk away from these souls? Leave them to endure such suffering?

She cried out aloud to us just then: "These beings are trapped here for eternity. They can't get out!"

She was sobbing more heavily now, out of control. So was Bill. I looked at him in alarm, wondering what was happening to him now.

Over a year later he told me that he was crying because as he touched her he felt and saw the same things she did.

"Breathe, Donna! What's happening? Talk to me!"

"Oh Aminah, I've got to help them! There are so many of them and they're in hideous pain."

I could hear the desperation in her voice and feel her body weakening under my hand, as if she were in the grip of some invisible force.

"No Donna!" I raised my voice and put all the authority I could call up into it. "You can't help them! It's too much for you. No ordinary human being can help them. Only God can help them. Leave them and come back from there!"

Her body startled a bit from the force of my voice but she pleaded,

"Isn't there anything I can do? How can I just go away and leave them in this terrible place?"

"You can pray for them. And tell them to cry out to God themselves. God will not deny anyone who earnestly calls out to Him."

"OK," she said in a subdued voice. Her sobs started to taper off.

"Oh thank you, Jesus. He says I have seen the worst now. And during all of it I have experienced that He will always be with me."

Her eyes still closed, Donna relaxed into a deeper state. Her breathing slowed and she was quiet for some time. I could literally hear the rest of us breathing easier too. Jesus had said the worst was over. We relaxed a bit.

After awhile, in a new voice, completely devoid of emotion, Donna went on,

"Now He wants to tell me about my son's problems and about my work in the world."

So began an extraordinary time in those early dawn hours.

Donna entered a full blown transcendental state, beyond the hell she had apparently been visiting. All tension seemed to leave her body. Her voice was quiet and serene, even soothing. She reported later that

Jesus was talking to her the whole time, objectively, with steady authority.

Bill lay next to Donna, still holding the ice pack on her arm, not crying now but intensely present. Wayne continued to rub Donna's feet but his face had transformed. The expression of anxiety and helplessness I had seen there when we first entered the room had changed to wide-eyed awe. He was listening intently. Fritz was also listening with full attention. I thought I saw reverence on his face.

He and I sat close to the bed, our hands on Donna's body. I breathed very deeply for the first time and opened up to the charged field that was building by the minute.

There was grace in the room. All of us remained still, in stunned respect, as it expanded. It went on for what seemed like a long time. It might have been minutes, or an hour; it was a timeless place.

Although we didn't know just what was going on inside Donna then, she told us about it the next day.

She said that Jesus took her into a "golden room" where there were Masters, Divine Mothers, and what were called Mentors. In addition to Jesus she saw Sai Baba, Mother Mary, Mother Theresa, Martin Luther King, John F. Kennedy, John Lennon and Mahatma Ghandi. Several of these holy beings spoke to her or embraced her. As a group they offered her "strength, integrity, uprightness, righteousness, courage and ferocity." She felt tremendously strengthened and inspired.

Then Jesus taught her. He told her not to engage in "meaningless trivia," actions and projects that had no real purpose, but to hold every moment as precious because each was "plump with possibility of healing."

He told her about the grand scale of our time. September 11 is only the beginning, he said. "It will get much worse...This is an age-old battle between good and evil, light and dark." But he assured her that the end result would be "unity" and to hold that truth in front of her. He said that although He could not promise her safety in the body that if she would "stand upright and walk in the light you have nothing to fear. Your soul will be safe."

Although we knew none of these messages at the time the vibration in the room was so uplifting, so expansive, that we weren't worried anymore. Rather we were inspired and rejuvenated. Simply being in that field was nourishing. The lack of sleep and our former fear were washed out of us. In fact, we felt blessed, a feeling that remained with all of us for several days.

The peacefulness of that period was broken only once when Donna began to sob again and twist around in the bed.

"What's happening now," I asked her.

Oh," she moaned, "I'm in pain, chaos and suffering about my son. I need to know my son will be OK. What can I do to help him?"

"Ask Jesus," I advised.

Donna was quiet for some time. After awhile she relaxed again and her face became very serene. This is what she reported in her journal:

> *Jesus answers, "You have just done something big to help him by severing the root of your ancestry. He still has to do his own work for his male ancestry. You cannot do that for him."*
>
> *I persist, "But I need to know he is going to be safe."*
>
> *Jesus says, "Put him in My hands. Let him into Me. I will always hold him in a sacred and safe space."*
>
> *Then Jesus took me to Mother Mary. She filled me with the strength and compassion to be present while my son does his own work, even when he suffers. She infused me with some of her own strength that she had when her son suffered.*

Even so, Donna said she was still overwrought.

Mary took her back to Jesus, who "opened his arms to me and then his heart. I climbed into his heart." Then she felt like she was "in the heart of Jesus, in the holy flame." She was at last "in peace and power."

After some time Donna announced that she was being given messages from Jesus for all of us. She spoke them out clearly to each one of us and they felt charged with blessing. The last one was addressed to herself:

"Donna, you are no stranger to war. You are a true and accomplished warrior, which is why I chose you for the work I have for you."

I could vouch for that. I had witnessed Donna's long hard work in therapy to overcome massive early trauma, her considerable skills, well earned over a long period of practicing and teaching, used with difficult cases, and parenting a boy alone before Bill came along. Yes, she was a warrior. Otherwise, I reflected, she wouldn't have the strength to go all the way through this present ordeal.

I felt a profound sense of strength and affirmation from these messages. All of us were filled with gratitude. We realized we were gifted with one of the most remarkable journeys we have ever witnessed.

Only hours before we had come to this room heavy with fear and dread. Then we had watched a potentially extreme trauma transformed into healing and enlightenment. We had seen a primal fear pattern released after a lifetime struggle. We had even heard of the severance from ancestral bindings that had freed not only Donna, but her son as well.

Therapy of many forms in the past had weakened Donna's fear and helped her cope with ancestral burdens. But this lightning stroke went beyond them all, even beneath all personal history conditioning, to free her completely. Personally, I had no doubt whatsoever that Donna's core fear was banished and that her life would be forever different.

And the witnesses—Bill, Fritz, Wayne and I—had received with her, in our own bodies, a remarkable flow of Grace that had awakened and healed us as well. Now we were light with wonder just as sunrise was beginning to burst into the transformed room.

The feeling of blessing persisted with all of us for the remainder of the retreat. When Donna shared some of her experience with the entire group, she shone with the light and authority of a true spiritual warrior while she told it. She imparted some of that strength to everyone in the telling.

Aftermath

After they returned home many dramatic changes happened to Donna and Bill.

Lightning experiences like this abruptly elevate consciousness to a higher level, beyond the life as it has been lived before. How idyllic and comfortable it would be if that new state of consciousness simply endured.

It rarely happens that way. Powerful energy that evokes higher states also inevitably flushes up spaces in the body and consciousness that are not yet able to tolerate its frequency. Such as negative emotions, thoughts, past illnesses and karmas. Just as openings are followed by purification, a transcendental experience usually requires many adjustments, in the body, mind emotions and lifestyle, before a full embodiment of its gifts are realized. A new life must be constructed around the new consciousness.

For about a month after the retreat, Donna and Bill continued to feel the great protection, grace and guidance they had experienced during scorpion medicine. They were "high all the time."

But in the year that followed their blessed awareness crashed. It seemed like all peace and order in their lives unraveled around them. Bill had an accident at work that resulted in extended pain, many doctors and four surgeries. Later there were demanding legal procedures with a resistant worker-compensation bureaucracy. Their son went through many personal and work setbacks that threw him into a deep and extended depression.

Donna called me several times during this stress-packed year. She was upset and confused, at her wit's end, with the continuous flood of trying episodes. Miraculously she was never afraid.

"What is wrong, Aminah?" she wanted to know. "Jesus said I was to go on with my new work, that it was important. But I can't do anything now except hang on to my sanity with all these stresses."

"I realize how severely trying all this is, Donna. But remember that He also told you that you're a warrior and that He would always be with you. Hold to Him. Keep praying for His guidance.

"But we do!" she protested. "We pray every day to be shown the right path. Does all this upset in our lives mean that my journey with Him was just wishful fantasy?"

"No Donna! We were there. We know the experience was true. You're being tested." I said this with trepidation, not so sure inside. "Keep appealing to the Divine. This can't go on forever."

"Then when will it all end?" she wanted to know.

Certainly I had no idea.

"Although your nerves are worn very thin, you haven't once collapsed in fear," I pointed out. "Remember that miraculous fear transformation." I hoped recalling that fact would restore some of her faith in what she had experienced. It did seem to comfort her momentarily.

She and Bill continued to pray. They held on.

Then, after about 15 months, all the tangles came to resolution. Bill recovered and the legal case was satisfactorily completed. Their son suddenly found the right work and expressed a personal pride he hadn't felt for many years. It was like a miracle. Of course Donna and Bill were immensely relieved.

Since then Donna has taken up her true work with gusto. She is now a true warrior, fearless, brilliant and joyful. The once fearful and angry girl has turned into a mature, spiritual woman. She has become one of the very best therapists for survivors of sexual abuse I know. She has published about her work and is preparing to train others in it.

Bill is at last finding and perfecting his true work as an artist. The hard physical labor he had done for thirty years is in the past. Their son is blossoming into the fine young man his childhood talents promised.

After severe trials, Donna, Bill and her son are now living the guidance Jesus gave, in confidence and deep inner satisfaction. Blessings continue to shower upon them and they are a happy, grateful family.

The other three of that night, Fritz, Wayne and I, feel that we were gifted with a remarkable teaching—a journey through terror, awakening and healing, clear through to transformation. And all within a few hours.

Section VI: Teachers Who Light the Path

About Teachers

The path of spiritual awakening is often obscure, fraught with obstacles and exhilarating at the same time. Our present world is formulated from energies and examples of the lower three chakras—money, sex and power. We are dominated by material and submerged in its hypnotic spell. One who goes against these currents will meet constant resistance. He or she needs help and guidance along the way.

A spiritual teacher is especially indispensable after an opening to tutor the embodiment process. Although every soul must find its own way eventually, a teacher can greatly assist the process. The great sage and saint Yogananda admonished his disciples to stay close to spiritual people who lived from higher values and purposes in life than those of the ordinary world. Bapak urged us to realize that we were higher beings than material and to learn how to direct material to accomplish our true human aims.

But in this material world, how shall we hold steady on a path of truth, right motivation and right action?

Eastern wisdom claims that a spiritual journey is not remotely possible without a guru who has already achieved a higher state of consciousness and the selflessness required to truthfully tutor his/her disciples. It is hard for Americans to accept such a tenet. We believe we can do anything at all by ourselves if we set our minds to it. The thing is, enlightenment defies mindset. In the West we hold to a similar tradition when we accept that only the priest, the pope or the rabbi can correctly lead us to salvation.

Surely we need teachers who have seen beyond the illusions of the world and stabilized their consciousness in the great flow of the Creative. We need teachers who are instruments of higher energy that they can transmit directly to students who will be uplifted and enlightened by it. We need teachers who are wise, compassionate and dedicated to service of a higher evolution.

The world has not been deprived of such true teachers.[1] All traditions, East and West, have records of their teachings and actions. All major religions are fundamentally based on those teachings. As Bapak said, "God has already given all the teaching man needs to become human."

Great spiritual teachers have left footprints from their searches for the rest of us to follow. Trails of their awakening processes that inspire and guide us, for a certain distance. Whatever their backgrounds, skills, or spiritual practices, all true teachers have eventually awakened to the Holy Spirit within themselves. Every one I have studied taught that the trail begins and ends within one's own being. I call it soul but whatever it is called, everyone can know it.

Not all the great teachers and prophets were male. Although their records have been mostly lost or ignored, many great female teachers

1. American prosperity created a breeding ground for many *untrue* teachers, in all traditions, in the last decades. Many books and articles have been written about the misuse and abuse of these teachers, who have used their heightened psychic or magical powers to extort money, power and privilege from gullible seekers. I have also known such "teachers," and am not blind to their abuses but I leave their exposure to others.

also taught through the centuries. Scholars in Western and Eastern traditions are now digging up the stories. There are also female saints now in the world delivering their God-force to starving seekers. It is not by accident that three of the teachers described in this section are women.

Our problem here and now, after Jesus, Buddha, Yogananda, Krishna, Lao Tzu and hundreds of others have already gone on to another dimension, is: how do we live those teachings?

In Hinduism it is written that when the world is endangered by false teachings, wrong actions and loss of righteousness, the Divine will send an incarnation of Itself, an Avatar, to set things right.

Surely our world is endangered now. And God is generous. At present there are many enlightened teachers alive on the planet, working literally around the clock to help us climb out of the pit we have created.

But how do we discern the true teachers from "false prophets"?

Amaji, whom I write about in Chapter 14, says that a true spiritual master is beyond the mind and ego. She says the experts of the world, seeking to lessen their inner pain, dwell in their minds "within the small world created by their egos. As long as they themselves are in the grip of their minds, how can they help others to get beyond it?" she asks.

Jesus gave very succinct advice about true teachers: He said, "By their fruits you shall know them."

That advice has helped me greatly in my own search for truth. I apply it everywhere, not only in the spiritual realm. For example with ordinary teachers of bodywork, psychology, physics, music, shamanism, or medicine, I ask, is this teacher truly knowledgeable in his field? Is her knowledge matched by skill? Is the knowledge grounded in practice? Does she "walk her talk"?

I have been privileged to study with many fine teachers, both professional and spiritual, and I am grateful to them all. I focus on spiritual teachers I have met in this book because I think our need for them is neglected. With Bapak, they have shone light on the path and renewed my resolve to seek enlightenment when it weakened.

Even though Bapak's perspective was radical about spiritual teachers, since he continually repeated that we would each receive our own inner truth through the *latihan,* I have always regarded him as my spiritual teacher, once awakened from my adolescent arrogance. I saw his consciousness and his wisdom as far far beyond what I could yet know. I wanted to stay close to that source of truth while my own inner source was gradually being excavated. And as I held close to his source my own spiritual channel and soul consciousness eventually awakened.

I have also sought to draw close to spiritual truth in other remarkable teachers, some of whom are described in the following section. Those I write about here have steadily enhanced my awakening process. They all contributed immensely to my journey toward wholeness, and the development of my work.

14

Evelyn: Lightning Herself

Evelyn was walking lightning, all ninety-three pounds and five feet of her.

When she opened her front door a burst of light seemed to shoot out from her bright eyes, frame her body and light up the entry.

"Hello girls!" she'd call out cheerfully, and it felt like you had come home, to a sane and wonderful place.

During the ten years we worked together her lightning spread out through and around me until it seemed to illuminate this whole lifetime, and beyond. We traveled back and forth in time, through this life and others, healing one event after another, correcting mistakes, erasing memories, until I felt Evelyn knew me inside out. Long before life coaching hit the mainstream Evelyn was a life-death-eternity coach supreme.

Even now, ten years after she has gone on to her next dimension, I can still hear her distinct voice, feel the energy she transmitted through my body and reach out to her Spirit for counsel. In fact, Evelyn's spiritual force was so great that my Process Partner Laura and I often said she was the only human being we knew that we were really really afraid of because if we stepped off the righteous path she whacked us.

Evelyn treated and taught Laura and me once a month for those precious ten years. We drove for an hour one-way to receive her teachings. Each of those days was a ritual of celebration.

We would arrive at her modest home in San Mateo full of happy anticipation. If we were even a few minutes early, we sat in the car to wait for the appointed hour. Evelyn didn't like anyone to arrive before the exact time and if we were late she scolded us. Just at the appointed minute her front door would swing open and there she stood, a light beam of cheerfulness and grace. As I write this I can still see, and feel, that vivid impression of her.

She was so beautiful to me. Her wrinkled-all-over face radiated an inner light. It was made up just so, complete with eye shadow, mascara and bright lipstick to match her colorful outfit. Her thin wispy hair, perfectly coifed, was colored strawberry blond. It looked like a glowing halo. Her shapely little body looked like twenty-something and she was always dressed impeccably in a smart dress or suit. If fact, if we arrived in the casual clothes we wore in Santa Cruz she would look us up and down for a moment, eyebrows raised, and make some simple remark like,

"My, that dress looks a bit baggy on you, don't you think?"

When we got back to the car Laura said,

"Wow! I won't wear that again!"

Once inside the house she went straight to work. No small talk. No visiting. Onto the massage table you went without a word. Then Evelyn started sweeping the field around your body, with the vigor of spring cleaning. By this time she rarely touched the body anymore—she held her hands about three inches off of it. But just as soon as she stood at the head and held her hands over it a bolt of strong energy would surge through your whole body. That energy started exposing, clarifying and correcting many layers within me—thoughts, feelings, symptoms, behaviors. As these layers were revealed Evelyn gave explanations or corrections.

For example, many times, as she worked at my crown chakra, the energy center at the top of the head, she said,

> "Here you are again, all fogged up with your clients' problems. Oh you girls, (by then I was fifty and Laura thirty but we were always "my girls" to Evelyn) you must stop taking all

this on as if *you* could fix it. Remember, 'the Father within, He doeth the work.'"

Then, as she held her hands above my head she would brush over the crown center forcefully and send a blast of energy through it. After a few minutes she would say,

"Yes, there's that beautiful golden light streaming in again. Now try to keep it that way!"

I was introduced to Evelyn by a clairvoyant classmate, Chako, when we were in graduate school in transpersonal psychology.

"Aminah, I've met this unusual woman who does curious treatments. I don't really know if she's crazy" (as graduate psychology students we were thinking a lot about crazy) "or a true master, but I'd like to ask her if she would see you also."

I thought it could be an interesting experience.

"OK," said Chako. "I'll ask her. She won't see just anyone. She checks you out on the inner planes first."

That intrigued me and I wondered if I'd "pass." Apparently so, because Chako announced that she had an appointment for me with Evelyn the next week.

I drove to an older industrial complex outside San Mateo and eventually located an unimpressive office that looked something like a 1930s doctor's space. There was no receptionist. Evelyn herself came to the door. I was amazed to see a diminutive "little old lady" of indeterminate age. She wore a white jacket over a colorful but conservative dress. I had expected someone more exotic from Chako's description.

"Come in," Evelyn said rather formally and gestured toward the interior. No big smile. No handshake. Certainly no hug—greetings I was used to in Santa Cruz. Boy, I thought, this lady means business.

She ushered me into one of two very small "treatment" rooms and told me to lie on my back on the massage table. Then she put her hands lightly on my body. At this time I had worked on bodies myself with acupressure for about ten years. My experience was that you needed to put fairly firm pressure on explicit acupoints for some minutes before you, or the client, could feel energy moving. But now I was experiencing something quite startling. Energy was streaming through my whole body even though Evelyn's touch was very light, and she wasn't even on specific points! I realized that this woman knew something about energy that I didn't and I was eager to learn.

But when I started to query her about what she was doing and what system it represented she discouraged any talking.

"Just relax and accept the treatment," she said, rather sharply. So I shut up, feeling that I had been properly put in my place. In fact it was probably two years of regular sessions with her before Evelyn explained something of what she was doing and how it had come about.

I left that first session feeling rejuvenated and light in my body and spirit but rather unsatisfied in my mind. Evelyn hadn't explained what she was doing, what her aim was, nor told me any of the esoteric secrets Chako implied that she knew. It would take some time before I realized that Evelyn was doing soul work in the flow of the Tao, beyond theory or technique. Her aim was nothing less than soul liberation as she attended the body, mind and emotions simultaneously. But at the time I thought I hadn't learned anything.

Nevertheless I made another appointment.

And so began the ten years of regular treatments and teachings from Evelyn. I came to treasure these times far beyond my initial curiosity and expectations.

After I had visited her a few times and come to value her powers, I asked if Laura could come also. Evelyn said she would see her once and then decide. When they met though there was an immediate positive resonance between them and Laura was "in."

In the first years we continued to work in her little industrial office. Then one day she announced that she was retiring from practice. In my mind I thought, "it's way past time, Evelyn must be over eighty."

Yet my heart sank. By then she had become one of my most important life and spiritual counselors. I relied on her wisdom continuously in my personal life and in my practice. I often consulted her about difficult clients. In fact, I didn't know any psychotherapist supervisor who could replace her. She had opened up and revealed herself as an endless repository of fine medicine. I developed a tremendous respect for this little wizard who was able to tune my body, emotions and spirit within an hour while she simultaneously spouted gems of wisdom offhandedly. What I said was,

"Oh Evelyn, I totally understand and support you wanting to retire after all your years of service. (I knew she had treated people for fifty years but it was touchy to say anything about years!) But I will really really miss you. Could I call you now and then for a consult?" I asked.

"Well, I've decided to keep a few of my favorites," she answered, with a conspiratory wink. "You and Laura can come to my home from now on."

I was overjoyed and very grateful. From that day on, until the illness that caused her death, Laura and I had the great privilege of seeing her every month.

We brought general and specific questions, about our study and practices or personal problems, to her each visit. Sometimes she answered these exactly and wisely. Sometimes she talked about entirely different issues that we weren't even thinking of at the time.

While she was working Evelyn received continuous higher guidance, from the "Masters" as she called them. She was told how to apply the energy with each client, and often received explicit instructions for them.

These Masters had been introduced to her in childhood by her father who was an unlikely combination of sea captain and metaphysician. Later she followed up his instructions by studying many metaphysical teachings. But she was not a follower of any particular system or religion. She referred equally to Jesus, Buddha, Mohammad and saints from many traditions. In fact, when the subject of religion came up—which was best, or what spiritual tradition had the truth—her instant response was, "There is only God and none else! Man has created the 'else' and spends his time worshipping and fearing the 'else."

Evelyn was a fountain of these metaphysical sayings. We marveled at how she could possibly remember all the hundreds of pronouncements she called up instantly for any condition or problem. When we first heard them they sounded archaic and we didn't always get the point. But she delivered them with such authority, they were so appropriate to the situation at hand, and they produced such powerful effects that we came to respect them over time. They rang in our minds after a session. Even now they continue to jump back into awareness.

If we were tired she told us to say: "I am one with Universal Life Energy. I see it; I feel it; I know it. I feel it flowing through me now."

When there was conflict, threat or pain in our lives she said to repeat: "I have put off darkness and clothed myself in light and acquired bodies free from pain and affliction."

If an explicit trauma arose from the past, as they were always doing in graduate school, there was no analysis or processing. Evelyn had a powerful intervention. She would invoke her metaphysical warrior voice, practiced over so many years, and declare:

"We do not deny that this has happened. What we do deny is that this is happening now. By the power invested in me I erase the cause, the core, the record and the memory!" And afterward, our attachment to that trauma would magically fade away. Then it simply became just another learning on our soul path.

Evelyn never explained, and we never asked, who or what had awarded her with "the power invested in me," but we accepted its validity. Its potent effects were proof enough.

If we felt weighed down with our clients' problems, or worried about the world situation, she reminded us that: "We work for the world, but it is not a burden on our shoulders! When something begins to weigh you down say: 'I cast this burden upon the Christ Spirit and I go free.'"

For example, one day she touched my heart and then paused reflectively.

"Your heart was deeply wounded in the relationship with x," she pronounced. "Now open it to the love of God and forgive. Just let it go, say: 'I cast this upon the Christ Light and I go free!'"

Another time she was holding my knees when she abruptly announced,

"These old old fears in here. Give them over! 'Let nothing affright thee; let nothing disturb thee; all things pass but God.'"

Afterward I felt much lighter and more courageous as if she had simply lifted an old burden away with a magic wand.

She usually found "too much congestion" in my head, which of course was exactly correct since at that time I was studying many things at once and worrying about various clients and situations. She would hold her hands over my head for some time. Remarkably it felt as if she were vacuuming it out; I could definitely feel a clearing there.

During one of those times I told her this. She said, "Yes, They were clearing out both the medicine you've been taking and also the effects of it. They want you to be free of both pain and medicine."

Then she commanded in her power voice: "Let the fire of creation come in and cremate the old ideas!"

After the session I could think more freely.

The instructions she gave us from the "Masters" were always helpful, and are still a valuable part of our work. She didn't hold the Masters possessively to herself either; she told us we could also call upon them directly when we needed assistance.

Yet with all her metaphysical power and authority Evelyn also expressed an ordinary humanness by sharing truthfully from her own life experience. This beautiful quality took her off any pedestal of "guru" and placed her right in the lap of this present life-struggle reality. We could believe Evelyn because she had been there.

For example, she reminded us to "clear out" all the useless debris—of problems, symptoms, worries—accumulated throughout the day, within ourselves or from our clients. She instructed us to always "sweep the field" of clients before working on them directly.

She told us that every evening she took a walk to let go of whatever had stuck to her from clients that day.

"Then I stand in the shower and see anything that remains pouring off my body with the water and going right down the drain!"

Often I spoke to Evelyn about my children's' problems. She would listen attentively and then make some amazing statement that showed a deep understanding such as, "Oh, Rosalind doesn't realize her real talent yet. This is why she is so confused and distressed. We'll send light into that." Then she would pause for a few moments and concentrate deeply.

"There, that's better," she announced confidently.

When I expressed worry over my daughter Paulina's illness Evelyn paused in the session to send light and healing. Then she spoke directly to my daughter, as if she were right there in the room, "Paulina, put all worries aside and know that you are well in God." In the next visits Evelyn asked after my daughter's health. When there was still a problem she prayed accordingly.

I told her I was concerned about my son Philip's difficult decision about which residency to choose after medical school. That choice would easily affect the rest of his life.

"Oh, we will speak for his Right Place," Evelyn said, and then did so in her Priestess Authority voice. My son chose a residency that served him well. I felt that Evelyn's prayer contributed in his favor.

Once my daughter Rosalind was visiting from out of town during a time when she had returned to school but was undecided about her major. She has a remarkable mezzo-soprano voice and has loved singing since childhood. She had been advised that a career in music wasn't practical. I asked Evelyn if I could give Rosalind my session that month. She needed wise counsel just then. Evelyn wasn't enthusiastic about it but agreed "as a special favor."

So Rosalind joined Laura and me that month. As we drove to the appointment Laura and I begged Rosalind to sing just a measure or two for Evelyn. We felt that if she heard that voice she would know exactly how to advise.

I introduced Rosalind to Evelyn and then said quickly, before Evelyn could object, "Please, Roz, sing just a bit for Evelyn so she can hear what is part of your career choice decision."

Evelyn looked chagrined; she wanted to get to work.

But then my daughter sang.

I saw Evelyn's face change entirely. Her eyes widened and she said, "Not much gives me chills but I've got them now right down to my ankles!" Then she spoke very directly to my daughter, "That voice is a gift from God! Why aren't you out there using it?" She paused and bore those sparking eyes straight into Rosalind, "Now, let's get to work!"

After that validation it was easier for Rosalind to declare her major, go on to finish advanced degrees in music and become a professional singer and teacher. Laura and I felt that Evelyn had supplied the nudge that launched that direction.

In these ways Evelyn touched my entire family and many of my clients over the years.

After a time of receiving Evelyn's remarkable "treatments" which impacted our lives and work in so many positive ways, I was empirically satisfied that she certainly wasn't crazy. Rather, she was a gift from God. Not only did I come to deeply respect her work and her character but I felt that many clients and students could benefit from her lifetime of wisdom also. I was developing my work, Process Acupressure, at that time and beginning to explain it to a small group. So I asked her one day if I could organize a group of us for her to teach.

"Absolutely not!" she replied emphatically. "It's not my job to teach in groups. I only work with individuals who then serve others. I work for the world inside my own home."

I was surprised and disappointed. She contained so much wisdom; I didn't want it to be lost. It was only much later that I understood her response more fully. She had been working for the world since childhood, first with her mother and father who had a difficult relationship, later with her own children and husband and finally with hundreds of patients in pain and all kinds of distress.

But that phase was over now. In these later years she saw a few healer-clients who passed her teachings on to others. And she worked for the whole world inside her little temple-house. She told us she could no longer even go out into large crowds unless she put "127 shields around myself."

I found out, after one New Year's Eve, what she meant by "working for the world inside my own house." While the world was partying and igniting firecrackers, Evelyn was watching it all on TV and praying for various trouble spots over her world globe. She also watched the news on TV every night and prayed specifically over each malfunction and destruction she saw there. Then she "saw" each situation corrected.

She also worked for the "other world." She told us that during one long period she was guided to shepherd souls who had just died toward the light and into the next world.

One day Evelyn volunteered the story of how her present work had evolved. She was trained in the 1930s as a physical therapist. She went to work in a doctor's office where people with all kinds of severe ailments were seen. Within a year or so she was taking x-rays, operating all the exercise machines, conducting many of the exams and working 8-10—hour days doing hard physical therapy, "cracking bones and pulling muscles," as she put it.

Then, after several years of doing conventional physical therapy she had her hands on a patient one day when a "bolt like lightning came through my body and into the patient. I was shocked. I didn't know what to do. The patient jumped and said, 'what was that?' and I said I don't know."

Later, in her meditation, Evelyn was told that she would be entering a new phase of her work. She would be given the energy that she had experienced with her patient and instructed how to use it. When I first met her she had been working with this energy for many years and applying it to everything from physical symptoms to spiritual distress. It felt like no energy I had ever experienced though I have been treated by many fine therapists.

As we brought every kind of problem or inquiry to Evelyn, for ourselves or our clients, we learned that no subject, from the most base to the most exalted, was beyond her consideration. Money, illness, breakdowns, sex, birth control, relationships, infidelity, job loss, or healing, prayer, meditation, abundance, angels, death, past lives, work between the worlds—all of these subjects came into her treatment room. She must have heard thousands of secrets in her life.

One day Laura confided one of her deepest secrets—the fear of going crazy. Laura was clairvoyant since childhood, has a very sharp and penetrating mind and is deeply sensitive emotionally—a combination that in her young years made her seem markedly different. In graduate school we were doing so much study and inner work, some of it focused on "crazy," that Laura's early fear had re-surfaced. She asked Evelyn if she had ever been afraid of losing her mind.

"Oh for God's sake, honey, of course I have, many times, everyone has. But it might comfort you to know that you have no mind to lose. There is *only* the One Mind. And that is the mind of God."

When I complained to Evelyn about not being able to surrender my ego at school where there were so many subtle competitions over student performance-in papers, exams and speeches, unexpectedly she replied, "There is a place for your ego. But you just can't let it run the show!"

Another time I was perplexed about how to balance surrender and discipline. I asked Evelyn, wasn't discipline required to manage many responsibilities? Her response was direct and instructive: "Discipline and disciple come from the same root. To be a true disciple of God, of the Truth, you need discipline. This planet is about discipline and the sooner we get on with it the better."

She let that sink in and then, in a more gentle voice, explained,

"Responsibility means respond to God. You know that 'the Father within He doeth the work,' so just let go and let God!"

Then she added a "practical" tip:

"Anyway, when you have too many things to do ask Holy Spirit to expand time."

Evelyn would tolerate no self pity, complaining, blaming or whining, yet she was one of the most compassionate and objective persons I've ever met. She listened to some condition or problem very closely. Then she responded with fresh wisdom that applied directly to that problem and that person, without judgment or conventional doctrine.

Her advice was entirely down-to-earth even though it originated from a "Higher Source." For example, she taught us about abundance. As working students we were often struggling with money and we took our worries to Evelyn. She listened attentively and then told us about the law of abundance:

"You girls need to learn to trust the Source of all Supply. Say: 'I am not subject to material law, I am subject to Grace!' Then call upon that infinite Source," she instructed us. "When you need or want something, speak the Word. Think it, see it, speak it! Then simply know, and see, that you already have it!"

She told us that during her early years as a householder she had verified the law of abundance in her life many times. It was a concept she had already learned from metaphysics as a child—namely that the Universe is infinitely abundant and will always supply us according to our need and intent.

She recounted how so often when the bills were due she didn't have enough money in the bank to cover them.

"But every time a bill came in I would say in my mind, 'Paid in Full" and then I let God be my banker," she explained. "Then when I wrote the checks I would say 'I am writing this check out of the Bank of the Infinite.'"

When we looked somewhat unconvinced—our bills were due right now—she reported,

"And I always paid my bills, never bounced a check!"

Even though we believed in Evelyn's mastery we were still not sure this would work in our own lives. We had many unexpected bills, emergencies and special wants. Each crisis gave us an opportunity to practice her instruction and then she would coach us further.

The most notable opportunity came in the spring of 1984 when we were offered the chance to visit Egypt. Patricia Sun announced that she would take a group of healers there to see many temples and the Great Pyramid. We respected Patricia's spiritual teachings and certainly wanted to experience Egypt. But of course we didn't have the money. And the trip was in three months. At first we simply gave in to "no money." But then we decided it was the perfect time to put Evelyn's teaching to the full test.

The night is indelibly stamped in my memory. Laura and I met to INVOKE SUPPLY. We sat together and visualized ourselves in Egypt. We "saw" the Great Pyramid, felt ourselves walking up to it, anticipated meditating in the King's Chamber and being so happy with our adventure. Then we put our two foreheads together, at the brow chakra, and concentrated with everything we had to MAKE IT SO. Then we *spoke the word*, as Evelyn had taught us. The next day we sent in a registration, even though we had no idea where we would get the money.

Of course we went on the trip, and it was an event of a lifetime. I can't even remember where all the money came from but it did come, magically just in time. That manifestation has been a marker for us ever since.

When we got home Evelyn was one of the first people we told of our extra-normal experiences. And she celebrated them with us like a doting Grandmother. Even now we think of telling her about some special development in our lives.

Often she repeated: "Let nothing afright thee; let nothing disturb thee; all things pass but God."

Evelyn lived this last teaching throughout all the hardships of her life.

Until she was past forty there were many struggles and sufferings. She was the sole provider for her two small daughters and an alcoholic husband who couldn't work during the Great Depression. Even though she had a job her salary was small for a family. She told us about the times she didn't have bus fare to go to work and had to walk both ways. Even this difficulty, she said, couldn't really dampen her spirits because "I just walked along, admiring the flowers and giving praise to the Father for my gifts. I said, 'Glory be to God in the Everywhere!'"

She said she had loved God from earliest childhood. And she depended on God throughout her life, first and last.

"God was my Mother and God was my Father and I never had another," she often repeated, especially when we tried to rationalize our ideas or behaviors according to our childhood parenting. Of course we were doing this all the time in graduate school. But Evelyn had little respect for psychology.

It was a humorous paradox. We were studying to become transpersonal psychologists with very fine teachers who were instructing us how to work through personal history, principally with Freudian-based theory and methods that targeted early childhood conditioning. At the same time Evelyn, a little-old-lady physical therapist/metaphysician was coaching us with guidance from her Masters' timeless counsel that went beyond personal history. She wouldn't listen to our childhood woes, nor pamper our personalities. She just brushed off our theory and intellectual analyses with a fling of her hand over the body.

"Parenting and ancestry don't matter that much! You were born free, in grace!"

She continued to tell us about the challenges in her life in an objective, even off-handed manner. She said, "None of the hardships in my life, and there have been many, including a difficult mother whom I nursed for the last years of her life, a divorce from an alcoholic husband, raising two children by myself, and six surgeries—none of them could take me away from God."

One surgery she described was gruesome. She woke up one morning "bleeding from both ends," as she put it. In the hospital she was rushed to surgery. It was touch and go afterward. Her life was barely saved from a perforated ulcer.

"I had tubes coming from everywhere, was strapped down to keep me from moving, the pain was indescribable and I began to black out. But even in that blackest moment I cried out 'nothing can take the light of God from me!"

She added reflectively, "Actually, with all the crises and surgeries I've had in my life I don't know why I'm still here. It's certainly longer than I ever expected. I've been given life extensions already."

Believe me, we were very grateful for those extensions because by this time she had become an anchor of Grace in our lives. We prayed for as many extensions as possible and told her so.

"Thank you," she said without too much enthusiasm. Then she added thoughtfully, "Yes, I think I've come this time to finish up with those I was teaching in the past. All of my children I love. But I'll be glad to go on to the next level. So when my time comes just pray for a speedy crossing."

I said, "Evelyn, if you go on before me I don't know what I will do without you."

She responded sharply, "Of course you'll know what to do! Remember! God was your Mother and God was your Father and you never had another. You'll go straight to God." Then she added matter-of-factly, "And I'll still be around for awhile to help you if you need me."

Laura and I tucked that statement away for future reference! We felt sure we would need her and those words seemed to be giving permission to call upon her. Which we have done a number of times. And she has answered us.

Evelyn's methods were often as unconventional as a Zen Master's. A mighty strength of Spirit would surge out from her slight body in sharp words, a look from her eyes or even a light slap to the body.

For example, one day Laura was feeling burdened with several problems in her life. When she lay on the table she let out a few big sighs.

Evelyn said sharply, "Stop that!" and hit Laura on the belly gently. Laura was so startled, and scared, that her body jerked on the table. She said, "Oh, excuse me," and didn't sigh again.

It was experiences like this that caused us to say Evelyn was the only person we feared. Which on the surface of things seemed absolutely ludicrous, considering the size and lack of worldly power of this woman.

When we wanted a picture of her we were afraid to ask. All of our favorite teachers were pictured on our altars and we felt Evelyn belonged there too. We knew we couldn't have her in physical form forever and we wanted some way to remember her exactly. But she had told us in no uncertain terms that she didn't want pictures of her "at this age floating around." Age was a taboo subject in any form.

Nevertheless we talked about how we might persuade her to allow us, two of her favorite students, to take her picture. And which one of us would have the guts to ask. Several times we brought the camera, intending to bring up the subject, but then lost our courage and left it in the car.

Finally one day I resolutely put the camera in my purse. Almost before she had time to greet us I blurted out,

"Evelyn, would you *please* let us take a picture of you, just one, as a keepsake?"

She was taken aback, faltered for just a moment and then, to our amazement and delight, said, "Oh, all right. But get it over with."

We snapped three pictures very fast, one of her and Laura, one of her and me and one by herself. That picture graces my altar now, along with my family and other great teachers.

Just after that the inevitable came. For over a year we had been remarking to each other that Evelyn looked frail, that her so erect posture was beginning to slump. Even though the strength of her Spirit never wavered we had watched her body growing fainter as the years went by.

One of the last times we saw her she told us about her evening walk the day before. She said she felt so expanded, and so full of gratitude for her life and the work she was given to do.

"And imagine," she said as she stared into the distance, "just imagine all the wondrous adventures and dimensions we will travel *after* this life."

Laura and I looked at each other with realization, and dread.

When Evelyn's daughter called one morning to cancel our appointments because her mother was sick, we slumped, sick at heart. We prayed for another extension, "*if* it was God's will." We clearly remembered Evelyn's instruction that we were not to hold onto her when her time came.

As the weeks went by her daughter reported by phone that Evelyn was growing weaker each day. She didn't want to see us, or anyone, her daughter said, but she had a dream about us. In the dream we had come to see her and stayed too long. She told her daughter, "I was so tired when they finally left."

Then we knew it was time to let go and "pray for a speedy crossing."

I was teaching in Baltimore when Laura called early one morning to report that Evelyn was gone.

I sat in meditation for some time that morning, thanking and blessing Evelyn. I realized the profound event of her passing, how it would change our lives and what an empty space it would leave. The stark severance, even though we knew she was dying, was a jolt, hard to take. I recalled then all the times I wasn't fully present with her, thinking of the next thing, as I almost always do, not soaking deep down into the moment. I realized my habit of thinking: I'll do, finish, take care of, that...later.

I heard Evelyn's voice, loud and clear: "THERE IS NO LATER! This is it. This moment will never happen again. Do and be all that you can, all that is spiritually true and righteous for you, IN THIS MOMENT."

Hearing her was comforting, even in a reprimand. Still at that moment I had to admit that I had expected her to stay around here awhile longer. How well would we cope without Evelyn to help us? I realized how deeply I had come to love and trust her wisdom.

I reflected on all that her life and teachings had brought me.

Evelyn lived, and served others, aligned with the single light source she knew as God.

She lived her service, not from theory and doctrine, but through a long, complicated life of the householder. She learned from a difficult marriage, childbearing and child raising. As a professional therapist for over fifty years she treated and counseled people in pain and chaos, of body, mind and Soul. She had navigated through most of the life-altering events of the twentieth century and adjusted to them, for herself and others. More than adjust, she even corrected whatever she could. She had learned, first-hand, from it all. She was full of reliable wisdom and steady as a rock in its delivery.

Evelyn had demonstrated to us the true blessing of an Elder. She showed how one who embodies Light can spread it out to everyone she touches simply by being in It. Light came out of her as palpable energy through her hands. It came out of her mouth in short, cryptic messages of wisdom. It permeated her modest little home so that it felt like a temple. She had been steady lightning to us, through all the twists and turns of graduate school, clients' problems, family upsets, illnesses, and relationship tangles.

She had helped thousands of seekers and wanderers stay on the righteous path of soul growth. She was a Pure Gift to us all, and still would be.

Then I remembered the declaration she had blasted at me several years before. Her death made it more clear.

> Come boldly to the throne of Grace
> and resume and assume your inheritance incorruptible
> and go out boldly entrenched in Holy Purpose
> to dissolve the great illusion of the many.

Even though my heart was very sad to part with her physically, our dear precious teacher, spiritual mother and deepest friend, I rejoiced in her Spirit, standing at the throne of Grace, flying free.

15

Mother Meera

Fritz and I heard of Mother Meera two times in one week while we were teaching in Europe. In England our good friend Murray, a long time spiritual seeker, told us that a bright light had hit him in the head while he walked behind several strangers. He turned to follow them. They were talking of their pilgrimage to a holy woman, Mother Meera, in Germany. He said that he immediately got in his van and drove there to find her. He had Darshan with her and said that he had felt transformed for weeks. He looked that way as he spoke about her too.

Just a few days later another colleague in Switzerland, Marcella, raved to us about her trip to Mother Meera and how deeply it had impacted her. She asked,

"Would you like to go with me next time?"

We decided to travel with her by train to Germany. On the way Marcella explained more about how Darshan with Mother Meera worked. She said we would be allowed to visit her only three nights in a row. Because there were so many people who wished to see her, spacing had to be arranged this way.

"Besides, three experiences will be all you can handle at one time," she said.

We reached the tiny hamlet of Thalheim in the afternoon where we found rooms in a home and prepared for Darshan that night.

There was no temple, no ashram, and no sign of anything unusual in Thalheim. It looked like any other German village. The Lutheran church was unremarkable, and locked. Marcella told us that Mother Meera had asked people who came to her to do it very quietly so as not to disturb the villagers. The fact that she was a young beautiful Indian woman who wore a sari while she tended her garden and attracted hundreds of people to her door hadn't disrupted village life thus far, although Marcella didn't know how long that would last.

Marcella explained that Mother Meera's extraordinary spiritual abilities had been discovered by her uncle in India when the girl was just eleven years old. The uncle, Mr. Reddy, was a longtime devotee of Aurobindo, a great Indian teacher and saint. He recognized the girl's astonishing spiritual capacity and became her father protector, guide and closest devotee. He brought her to Aurobindo's ashram in Pondicherry where a group of devotees began to form around her. She gave Darshan to them through silence and touch. The experience was said to be an initiation into the Divine Light beyond all religions. Mr. Reddy claimed that she was an incarnation of the Divine Mother herself.

All of this sounded very intriguing and we were eager to see and experience this holy woman for ourselves. Being an empiricist, and having directly experienced living spirit within my own body through the *latihan*, I don't accept the truth of reports alone.

We asked Marcella why Mother Meera lived in Germany and not India. Certainly the northern climate, with winter snow and dark skies, must have been a big adjustment to her after the tropical weather of her home.

"She has said that Germany is where she is needed most," replied Marcella. "Mr. Reddy brought her here in answer to an invitation from a German devotee. They stayed on and people began to hear about her throughout Europe. Although there is no publicity about her, word-of-mouth reports traveled swiftly. Now people come here from everywhere, even the U.S. You'll see quite a mixture of cultures and languages there tonight."

We arrived at the "meeting place," a public parking lot at the edge of town about 6:30 pm. Already a number of people were gathered there, all standing in silence. Around 7 pm we walked in a group through the village to Mother Meera's home, still in silence. Her home looked like the other rectangular blockhouses on the street, and was unremarkable.

An attendant motioned for us to file into the foyer and beyond into the meeting room. Inside, the house had been transformed into an Indian temple. Marble floors shined from polishing. Sumptuous Indian silk drapes and hangings glimmered against the snow-white walls. There were several very large pictures of Mother Meera. A gigantic and exquisite crystal chandelier, fit for a palace, hung from the center of the ceiling.

There was no talking at all as people moved respectfully into the inner temple. Each found a chair among the tiered semi-circle of seats around the center front of the room. Fritz and I were directed to sit in the front row because it was our first Darshan. From that position we could see the whole room and we were close to the elegant throne-type chair at front center, obviously meant for Mother Meera. It was empty. Beside it sat another chair, much less decorated than the throne but still more distinct than the grouped chairs.

After all the waiting people had filed in we sat quietly for perhaps another twenty minutes. Most people seemed to be meditating. A few were restless, looking around. The vibration in the room was electric and the silence soothing. At first it felt wonderful to simply sit in that field but after awhile I began to wonder if Mother Meera wasn't coming that night.

Then there was a gentle rustling sound and I looked back at the entrance to see the attendant coming toward the throne. Behind him walked Mother Meera. I craned my head around to get a closer look at her. She was arresting. She wore a regal sari of red silk, which framed her entire body like a heavenly cloud. Her face was extremely beautiful in a classic Indian way, black hair pulled straight back from her face, heavy, well-arched eyebrows, porcelain skin. Of course no makeup, she needed nothing to enhance her natural beauty. Her eyes were averted.

There was only the sound of the silk sari swishing as she followed the attendant.

As the attendant sat in the side chair, Mother Meera settled herself on the throne, as graceful as a snowflake falling. Her eyes were still averted. There was no chanting, no incense, no talking. Mother Meera never spoke a word the whole evening. We learned that she taught only through her hands and eyes.

The attendant rose from the side chair and knelt before Mother Meera on a cushion in front of her. I noticed that when he left the side chair another person came forward to sit in it. The attendant's head was positioned just in front of Mother Meera's lap. I watched as she laid both her delicate, unadorned hands on either side of his head. Then she leaned closer to him and stared into his eyes as he watched back. They remained in this still pose for perhaps thirty seconds.

It is reported that Mother Meera has the ability to go straight through a person's eyes into their spine where she "unties knots of karma," to free that person from parts of the soul's history. I had never heard or read of such a phenomenon before. It sounded outlandish to me, perhaps someone's fantasy, but I wanted to be open to experience what happened here for myself.

So I watched as the attendant rose from the kneeling position and motioned for the person sitting in the side chair to approach. That person similarly knelt before Mother Meera and again she held the head and looked into the eyes, perhaps a bit longer. And so it went, person after person, until all 160 people in the room had been touched. There seemed to be an intuitive flow to the procession, no two people approached the chair at once and the rhythm was steady.

During all this time there was almost no sound in the room except for an occasional cough or shift in a chair. We sat in stillness. It felt like a vast soothing balm. I remember that early in the evening my soul voice said to me "now you can go Home for a little while." That's exactly how it felt, heavenly, free, the soul spreading out.

I remembered a quote from Mother Meera in a book Marcella had shown us. She said: "Our consciousness is quite free from the body…It will work in and beyond time, and beyond space…The soul is free from limits."[1]

It was such a relief to sit there in silence, relaxing into the feeling of being in the right place. My body felt mildly electrified as if it would never sleep again, the energy was intense.

Both Fritz and Marcella went up to her before me. I waited a long time that first night before approaching the side chair. Of course I wanted to experience Mother Meera but I was also nervous. What might she find in my eyes, my spine? Would she see my faults, weaknesses? Would she judge me unworthy?

Finally I heard "now" inside so I moved to the side chair. Once there I felt even more heat in my body. My heart beat faster. It was the sensation of fear in the body without an actual emotion of fear.

As I knelt before Mother Meera and put my head at her lap it felt as if I were being cradled by the primordial mother. I felt a surge of love for her and the work she was doing for the world, far from her homeland and family. I thanked her inwardly. The energy that had been circulating throughout my body began to gather in on the upper part and the head. I had the distinct sensation of both crowns in my hair being intensely stimulated, first one, then the other, then back to the first.

Mother Meera held my head between her hands. An indigo light came into my left brain, which tingled in response. When she looked into my eyes it felt as if she were probing me. I tried to open up inwardly so she could see or do whatever her task was. I couldn't quite see her eyes well enough. They were beautiful but like two infinite dark pools, which I couldn't penetrate. I wanted to stay there as long as possible but presently her eyes closed distinctly, like a shutter closing, and the connection was broken. She removed her hands and I stood up to return to my chair.

---

1. Goodman, Martin. *The Mystery of Mother Meera.* Harper, San Francisco. 1998.

I felt somewhat dizzy as I sat down. It was impossible to process or make sense of what had happened. I was able to meditate for a short time and became even more aware of tingling in my head, which felt as if my hair were standing straight up. But mostly I sat in a daze for the remainder of the evening, eventually feeling that I might doze and wanting so much not to.

The following day Marcella, Fritz and I visited a tiny medieval chapel on the top of a hill in the area. Built in the 12th century in honor of Saint Blaisal, it has been a pilgrimage site for centuries. Many healings had been claimed there.

We walked the 12 Stations of the Cross from the bottom of the hill to the top where the chapel was humbly nestled in the forest. There was nothing remarkable about it except its age.

There was no one inside. The only light came from the faint glow through one stained glass window and many lighted offering candles. They burned around the base of a simple and very old statue of Mother Mary in the corner of the chapel. She stood in perfect peace there, her eyes looking down with compassion upon all who would stop before her. A number of individual tiles, giving thanks to Her for various miracles, marked their pilgrimages. There was a feeling of great peace and comfort in the chapel. The Great War hadn't touched this place. Isolated as it was at the top of the hill, bombs, guns, troops and the inevitable terror of people under seige, hadn't affected it.

Marcella and I stopped at the candles. We found some unlighted ones and each lit one, I for the healing of my daughter who had been ill.

Spontaneously I went into a *latihan* state and started singing "Oh, mother mother, mother of all things…" over and over. Marcella joined in. As we sang the feeling of the Divine Mother opened all around us. She said to me, "I am here with you now as I was in Egypt. I have always been with you".

I continued to sing quietly in that *latihan* state, opening to the joy and love from Divine Mother. But when a man entered the chapel I stopped, too shy to go on.

He said in German, "I would love it if you would continue to sing." Having just received the Mother's encouragement I continued for just a bit, pushing through the shyness. The man stood quietly with us and a feeling of heaven and love for everything flowed over me.

I remembered another quote from Mother Meera in the book Marcella had shown us.

She said, "You will know that you have received the light because you will experience love of all humanity and an infinite concern for all life."

Fritz, Marcella and I stood together then and sang Amen as a sustained chant. This spirit-filling experience was a perfect integrating interlude before our second Darshan that night. I wondered if Mother Meera had directed us there.

In the second night's Darshan I again experienced a strong infusion of energy as we entered the temple. But this time it felt like thousands of tiny acupuncture needles being inserted all over my body. Not an unpleasant feeling, just awakening. I looked forward to the next contact with Mother Meera with less anxiety and more exhilaration.

Soon after we sat down in Mother Meera's chamber my attention was drawn to a reflection of the giant chandelier in the polished marble floor. There in the shiny surface of the stone hundreds of tiny lights sparkled as they reflected the crystal drops of the lamp hanging above. Each light had distinct facets, which twinkled effervescently. All the lights together shimmered in a continuously changing pattern, like an undulating nest of diamonds. This array of brilliance leapt out of the floor right up into the foreground of my consciousness. It hovered there, calling me to a deeper meaning. My mind drifted into a kind of hypnotic reverie as the patterns shifted.

Then I heard Mother Meera speaking inside my head. She said, "This is what I see. I see the light that is here all the time, yet hidden from people. It is perfectly visible and yet they do not notice it. And this is what I'm looking for when I look into your eyes—that brilliant light of the Divine self." This teaching struck me profoundly then and has remained with me ever after—an image of the chandelier reflection that was so pure, so luminous, so obvious, and yet unnoticed.

This evening I was moved to go to Mother Meera earlier than the first time. When she held my head I saw yellow and red lights shoot into the right side of my brain. Again I experienced frustration at not being able to see her eyes adequately. I wondered if she had found the light within me and what might have obstructed it.

When I returned to my chair I could feel big energy shifts within my whole body as if currents were being subtly re-routed. There was tingling along my spine. I tried to follow these changes with my mind, hoping to identify them according to what I knew of meridian flow and chakra energy. But the experience was so expansive and disorienting that I realized my analytical mind was far behind what was happening. Instead I relaxed and settled into a state of wonderment, just observing without interpreting.

I became more aware of other people in the room. I noticed that some had expressions of great pain on their faces, and some held their bodies in postures that indicated discomfort. Several cried softly. I remembered something Mother Meera had said in the book about the effects of the light on people's bodies:

> "Wherever it (the light) enters, it produces a burning sensation and that part of the body feels numbness. If the body is not strong physically, severe pain is felt for ten to fifteen minutes, as severe as a scorpion sting. Those who are unwilling or unreceptive feel the pain especially. The pain may last for ten or fifteen minutes but will vanish completely after two hours. When the body is fully charged with light, even though the pain is severe it should not reject the light. On the contrary,

> aspiration for it must grow, despite its effects. Afterward a supreme Joy and Peace will be felt and all obstacles to the furthest spiritual progress will be removed."[2]

I observed more carefully as Mother Meera touched people. Her expression never changed. It was one of calm, but focused, intention on each face. And each time there was the abrupt disconnection as her eyes closed with finality. I wondered at her inner strength to be able to deeply contact so many people and then leave them. Did any of their pain linger in her body or consciousness? She showed no signs of fatigue, no wrinkles of concern.

Toward the end of the evening, as before, I became restless and tired. I was beginning to understand what Marcella had said about three times being all one could handle.

On the third day we went to the chapel again where we sat and prayed for an hour. The stillness and peace there pervaded our consciousness. The usual sufferings and struggles of the world were far away, they didn't penetrate the forest or those sacred chambers where people came to pray and give thanks.

In the solace of that holy place I suddenly became aware of how ashamed I have been about my spiritual yearnings for most of my life. How I have tried to hide what I actually crave the most-God consciousness—because there was so little space for it in a culture that values money, power and competence above other things. This was a sad realization and I made a commitment to turn that shame into appreciation for the spiritual longing that had led me to places like this, no matter how the world reacted to me. Then I prayed for guidance to serve Spirit, to understand more and be shown the right ways to do it.

---

2. Ibid., p. 120.

At our last Darshan Mother Meera seemed to press our heads harder between her palms, and perhaps a bit longer. When she looked into my eyes I heard her talking to me again,

"You know what you're doing," she said, as if in direct answer to my prayer in the chapel. "Just trust yourself and go on. Don't hold back. Keep going, as I do."

After I returned to my chair I meditated to align the chakras and integrate what she had told me. Then teaching happened. I felt Mother Meera directing me to a great expansive dimension far beyond this earthly reality. She showed me the shape of it and how it expanded out into eternity. I heard her saying:

"You can visit this dimension often. Become more familiar with it so that you can bring that energy and information into this one. This is part of your work."

The message seemed quite clear, and normal, at the time. Later, away from her presence and the temple, it was difficult to translate into ordinary life.

I felt recognition and encouragement from Mother Meera. Some tender place deep within me that had been unsure—too shy, not quite ready to go forth—was being healed.

Each of us felt peaceful after being with Mother Meera. Fritz said that his mind was less busy. When we taught the next time I noticed that the first thing he wrote on the board was: "Quiet the mind."

After Mother Meera I felt more objective and less attached to the strife of the world. In the book she had said "You will be able to work and save the world and at the same time feel a complete and peaceful detachment from the world."[3]

I certainly didn't feel "complete and peaceful detachment" but I did feel less attached to my world concern because she had reminded me that there is always infinite help. Mother Meera had shown me that the

---

3. Ibid., p. 20

light and guidance of the Divine Mother are here with us all the time. And that our own light is always present whether we can see it or not.

16

Amaji: The Hugging Saint

Amma, or Amaji, for Divine Mother, is known throughout the world by her followers as "the hugging saint." She literally embraces, close up to her body, thousands of people a day, for many days each year. At last count, in 2002, twenty-one million people in the world had been hugged by her. Countless numbers of those people are suffering from physical, mental, emotional or spiritual illness. Many of them have testified that they were completely healed by her touch. She has said of her hug, "It is not a mere hug, but one that awakens spiritual principles."

Fritz and I were blessed by Amaji's embrace three different times. Each hug delivered healing and enduring inspiration.

We had heard about Amaji for several years from a close friend who had been seeing her. She urged us to attend Amaji's Darshan. Finally we planned to travel to San Jose where Amaji was holding her yearly meeting.

Just on that day I became ill, a debilitating flu was coming on. I told Fritz to go ahead without me. At the last minute we decided I should go but we would leave before the nightlong hugging session was over.

When we arrived at the auditorium a ceremony was already in progress. There was chanting, food being served and a long line of at least one hundred people waiting to approach Amaji. We took a place at the end of the line but I didn't see how I would ever wait it out. By this time I was feverish and feeling very weak. Still we stood for some time before I told Fritz that I'd have to return to the car. He wouldn't let me go alone so we started to leave the building. Our friend spotted us and came rushing over with a big smile on her face.

"You're not leaving yet, are you? Amaji is just getting started!" she exclaimed.

Fritz explained that I really wasn't well and we needed to drive home.

"Oh please, wait just a moment! I'll be right back," and she hurried off into the crowd.

We stood waiting although I was feeling worse by the minute and really wanted to go. Within minutes our friend returned.

"Follow me," she said, "Amaji always takes sick people first," and she started right for the front of the line.

What could we do? I really didn't want to stay in my condition and I also felt bad about going to the front of the line but our friend grabbed Fritz' hand who grabbed mine and we were being pulled right through the crowd.

Within seconds we were third in line and Amaji was right in front of us on a raised platform. The first thing I saw was her wide smile and sparkling eyes, in an ageless face. She was beaming love straight out to the next man in line. He stepped up onto the platform to face her and then knelt down in front of her lap.

She reached out and gathered that man into her bosom and then held him there for a few moments, wrapped in the embrace of a comforting mother. My heart melted. This was no perfunctory hug like those from new age dignitaries. It was the real thing, full of true caring and penetrating healing. My mother's heart felt the quality of it and my ill self soaked in its healing.

Then she released the man and he bowed in appreciation before he moved on to make way for the next person. Amaji reached to an attendant beside her for a handkerchief, wiped her brow and then looked directly into the face of the next person, with that same broad loving smile.

I looked at her plump body, nestled into a throne-like chair and draped in an elegant sari that was soaked in sweat already. I wondered how it would be possible for her to hug all these hundreds of people before she was finished for this one evening. Suddenly I felt very worried about transmitting whatever I had to her. I had felt so rotten, trying to figure out how to go home, that this thought hadn't occurred to me before. I wanted to tell the attendant, or her, that I was sick and she shouldn't hug me.

But in those few seconds it was already my turn. She motioned for me to step up on the platform. As I did she reached out for me and pulled me down on her lap.

All thought, worry, and reservation dissolved instantly. I was simply engulfed in the great abiding nourishment and compassion of the Divine Mother. That quality—so rich, so penetrating, so healing—is beyond words and comparison to anything. How could anyone voluntarily leave it?

My body filled with warmth beyond fever. It tingled all over. She put her head down next to mine, just like a mother does to her infant, and then squeezed me tighter. It was a timeless moment. I soaked in that comfort through every fiber of my being. Then she gave me a gentle lifting touch that signaled it was time for me to rise. As I did she motioned to an attendant to give me something. I held out my hand and the attendant dropped a small color-wrapped object into it. I clutched it tightly and stepped on.

As I started to descend the platform an attendant motioned for me to sit down, right there on the platform. I noticed that several others were also sitting there already. I obeyed, with confusion and gratitude.

From that height I could see Fritz quite clearly as he approached Amaji. She beamed at him as if he were her only son and pulled him down into her lap. Then she put her head right down next to his and started saying, or chanting, straight into his ear over and over

"Um mum mum mum mum, um mum mum mum"

I could see that Fritz let go into the chant and her embrace. He looked like an innocent child in that moment, surrendering himself completely to the Mother's comfort. Later he said that her embrace was deeply nourishing and the chanting so sweet in his ear, like a mother's milk.

Fritz was also motioned to sit on the platform so he sat down next to me. We were aware of what a blessing it was to stay that close to Amaji's presence. At first I worried that I wouldn't be able to go home to bed quickly as I'd planned. But shortly I noticed that I was actually feeling a lot better already, it seemed I would be able to stay, for awhile.

So we sat there, as person after person received this extraordinary and intimate contact from Amaji. Some arrived eager and smiling in front of her. Others came sobbing: I couldn't tell if it was from suffering or deliverance, maybe both. Men, women, children, old and young, of all colors and shapes. They were incredibly varied but Amaji remained just the same, hour after hour. She never rose from the chair, never sagged for one minute and her expression of joy never lessened. The only sign of strain to her body was the perspiration she wiped from her brow frequently and the increasing wetness of her sari. Eventually it seemed as drenched as if she had been standing in heavy rain.

I continued to feel better and better as we sat there in her presence watching one person after another receive healing and compassion. We stayed on for a long time but eventually our bodies were too tired to remain until the end, which we learned later was at 2 am. We drove home by midnight.

The next morning I had no sign of flu and felt better than well.

I placed the small colored object Amaji had given on my altar where it reminded me of the extraordinary gift of her Divine Mother love. It stayed there for a year or so, blessing my treatment room, before the candy inside finally crumbled.

Amaji has been traveling around the world, far from her native India, for the last 20 years, performing this ceremony of love for thousands of people wherever she went. She said:

> "It is for the benefit of all the crying souls out there that Amaji is traveling. Those who live in other countries are also Amaji's children. It is to soothe their pain, to alleviate their sorrow, and to show them the eternal light that Amaji is going abroad.... Mother's sole mission is to love and serve."[1]

When we first saw Amaji we knew almost nothing about her. Our experiences then were uninfluenced by information, belief or persuasion. Because of what we had seen and felt though, we decided to see her again when she came to San Jose.

In the meantime I wanted to read something about her. By a fortunate synchronicity a good friend, a book reviewer, sent me a review copy of Judith Cornell's biography.* I learned that before Amaji could become a world spiritual teacher her path was as difficult and painful as any saint or prophet.

She was born to a poor Indian family in the country. Her skin was much darker than other family members, an embarrassment to them and a demerit for her. As a baby she was neglected and later shunned as a growing child. Her prospects of becoming a world spiritual leader would have seemed preposterous.

She was often abused by her mother and brothers. At one time she was even sent off as a maid to another family where she was treated like a slave. Yet even though Amaji was abused she didn't ever become an abuser, as is common among those who have been mistreated. Once she healed one of the very brothers who had severely abused her.

It is probably reasonable to say that she received no love from human beings. She was not cared for by family, teachers or priests. Still

---

1. Cornell, J. Amma: Portrait of a Living Sage. An imprint of Harper Collins Publishers, 2001.

she was a devout little girl. She often prayed so fervently that she sometimes floated off into an ecstatic trance-state. Her friends were little animals which she healed. She held devotions in nature, offering prayers for anyone who was hurt or neglected.

Perhaps it was the deprivation of human love that led her to seek, and finally receive, Divine love. Certainly she learned how important love is, for children and all people. She teaches now that love is her only religion. She says, "although people may come from different religious faiths and have different cultures and ways of thinking, the language of the heart is always the same—love." Ibid., p. 235.

Amaji had only a fourth-grade education; she was needed as a household servant and besides, girls weren't commonly schooled in rural India at that time. She didn't receive teachings from books or priests either. Yet her present understanding, intellectual and otherwise, confounds and impresses pundits, educators and doctors all over the world when she talks to them about religion, education, healing and world problems. They are astonished by her wisdom and clarity.

For example she explained western suffering in the following terms:

> "There is a need for both physical and mental healing in Western countries. But the more important of the two is mental healing.
> It is their minds that are causing people their greatest problems.
> Though there is greater freedom in the West, people also have twice the amount of a different type of suffering...
> What people really need is love and mental healing...
> In the west much money is being spent on therapy and drugs to help solve marriage problems, heal depression and other mental illnesses. People turn to experts to lessen their inner pain, but all the experts in the world—the doctors, scientists, and psychologists—are people who dwell in their own minds, within the small world created by their egos...As long as they themselves are in the grip of their mind and ego, how can

> they help others to get beyond the mind and ego? Only a true Master can heal the mind."* Ibid., p. 104.

Amaji's prayers and austerities eventually resulted in her complete immersion in the Divine Mother. Apparently her solitary search led her all the way through the veils of illusion until she pierced straight to the Source of all love and truth. Relying on That only, she found enlightenment and freedom in the One.

Amaji's transformation was complete. Soon others began to see the difference in her and they flocked to her feet to receive blessings, even while her family continued to shun her. She embraced all alike—the poor, wealthy, ill and brilliant—and all received upliftment of spirit. Finally her family realized her holiness and former tormentors became her servants. She took up her world mission, which she has described:

> "Amma's world mission is to awaken her children to their divinity by reestablishing true spirituality based on the legacy of India's great sages. There is a Krishna, Devi, Rama, Buddha or Christ hidden within each one of you. The great masters are able to see that hidden Divine Light, which is waiting to break through the walls of the ego...In reestablishing true spirituality, Amma continually reminds her children that they are divine and immortal souls, no matter what religion they follow or what country they come from." Ibid, p. 237.

Like many great spiritual teachers of our time Amaji is committed to selfless world service. She fits her own definition of a true spiritual master who is beyond the mind and the ego.

To facilitate good in the world she travels wherever she is called, leaving her ashram for long periods at a time. She works tirelessly among people of all cultures and religions but especially among the poor. Perhaps her exposure to thousands of suffering people around the world led her to make the following interesting comment about another great spiritual teacher. She said,

> "The greatest sacrifice Christ performed was to live in the midst of ordinary people with bestial tendencies. And living with them, finally transforming them into God. That is the biggest sacrifice that Christ did." Ibid, p. 200

Among Amaji's great accomplishments are the schools she has established throughout India. Although they are based on spiritual principles they also provide the highest level training, for both sexes and any religion. They teach basic practical skills in reading and writing as well as advanced computing, management and engineering. Students learn about human character and exactly what the mind is. They are also given the opportunity to develop their innate creativity so that they can experience life as a joyful celebration and be well prepared to take on the challenges of the world.

Although students are taught traditional moral and spiritual values, they also learn how to access their own inner knowledge. They are taught to meditate. And how to put their training into practice by giving part of their time to selfless service. Her schools are based on spiritual principles because Amaji wants to re-establish the true spirituality of ancient teachings. She says,

> "The sages recorded in the Upanishads taught people the spiritual science of how to turn within oneself to find the Truth-the Soul." Ibid, p. 127.

Amaji proved the truths of these ancient scriptures—that real knowledge comes from within—through her own enlightenment experience. Therefore she embodies the teaching she gives to her children.

In both her schools and other world work Amaji has renewed an ancient concept of true spiritual equality by providing opportunities to girls and women. She has empowered women to take up their rightful place in the spiritual community.

To research her biography Cornell traveled around with Amaji for several years in order to write a definitive, first-hand account. She became convinced that Amaji was healing on a massive scale,

> "...far beyond that of any saint or healer I had ever known or read about. The immensity of Amaji's global reach made it quite clear to me that she is playing a key role in healing our hearts and fragmented minds so as to help humanity take the next step in the evolution of consciousness." Ibid, p. 235.

Cornell is a young woman but during her travels with Amaji she grew exhausted and even ill trying to keep up with Amaji's schedule. She asked Dr. Raglan, a medical doctor who had examined Amaji on several occasions, about her phenomenal endurance. His reply was informative:

> "What she does physically, a normal healthy person could do for maybe one or two days, and then they would need a lot of rejuvenation. They could not repeat every day, morning and evening what she has done for the past twenty years.
>
> When I examined her she said, "You won't find anything." Her body seems to have adapted itself to her requirements. The problems that I would expect to find are just not there. Her body doesn't follow the normal physiological rules, that is sure." Ibid, p. 104

A year after our first meeting with Amaji we were in the line again but not at the front this time. We waited our bona fide turn with hundreds of others and were happy for the opportunity to soak in the chants that surrounded her from many voices and the sacred space created by Amaji's presence.

Finally we were at the front. Amaji motioned for us to come up together. As we reached her she extended her arms around both of us simultaneously and then pulled us down to her lap. It was absolutely delicious to be squeezed tightly together at her bosom. She nestled us there for a few moments and then beamed her radiant smile at us as if to say, "Now. Be good and true for each other. You are blessed."

We savored the blessing as we left. It felt like a spiritual marriage ceremony. In fact, we learned later that this double embrace was meant to seal partners in a spiritual union.

One evening recently I had dinner with Sanjay, whose story I told in Chapter 10, and his wife Kelcie. Our conversation drifted quickly to spiritual interests and they told me the story of their first visit to Amaji in India.

At the time they were traveling together as two spiritual seekers, not mates. They weren't married and in fact had no idea of marrying. As they approached Amaji she motioned for both of them to come up together. Kelcie said that just as they stood in front of Amaji, "There was a single explosion of light over our heads."

Sanjay nodded as Kelcie related the rest of their story. She said Sanjay had turned to her after their encounter with Amaji and said vehemently, "Now don't think that means we'll get married!"

And even though they both tried to avoid it for some time, they eventually surrendered to the inevitable and were married. I enjoyed our evening together. They seemed to match spiritually even with entirely different backgrounds; Sanjay is Indian, Kelcie, American. Although Kelcie was raised Christian, and Sanjay Hindu, both had left the religions of their families to seek spiritual truth in other realms. Like Fritz and me they are eclectic explorers, having visited with several teachers in addition to Amaji. Sanjay is now a follower of Zen Buddhism but both remain devoted to Amaji.

Our third visit to Amaji happened at a center in London. Our dear healer friends, the "Heavenly Twins," invited us to go with them when we were their guests at Yewden Lodge where we stay each year when we teach in England. The twins are aptly named. They are gorgeous women, identical twins, with long curly blond hair, luminous blue eyes, model bodies and compassionate hearts they use so effectively in hands-on healing work. Every year when we visit them we are exposed to yet another new healer, healing tool or spiritual teacher. This time we had all been excited for several months that Amaji's stop in London would coincide with ours.

For the first time we were able to see Amaji in the daytime since Darshan starts early in the morning in London. As we approached the building we could hear the chants and smell the incense. There was a jubilant feeling in the air as we joined people of all ages and backgrounds in the hall. So many colorful clothes, from saris to punk. Everyone was smiling.

Another colleague, Carol, joined us at the door. Carol is a psychologist and ex-nun who left the habit but not her spiritual devotion. She is a longtime student of spiritual traditions but this was her first exposure to Amaji. She and I have worked together as teachers and co-therapists for many years so we know each other's personal histories well. We were both daughters of wounded mothers who were unable to give what we felt we really needed. But both of us had made peace with that early condition.

It was restful and fulfilling to sit on the carpet for a long time, waiting to get in line. We watched person after person go up to Amaji; we saw how they were as they approached and how they looked after her embrace. For example one man was obviously resisting the whole experience, perhaps his wife had begged him to come. He looked scornfully around him, one eyebrow raised, obviously critical of the exotic scene. He made snide remarks to the person beside him. I watched him for some while with a psychologist's curiosity, wondering why he had come and if Amaji's love could penetrate his defenses. When he arrived at the platform before Amaji his body was visibly hanging back from her.

Then he was before her. She reached out and pulled him down into her lap, engulfing him in that wave of unconditional Mother love. The man's body started shaking, it looked uncontrollable. Then he sobbed like a small wounded child. She held him there for longer than usual, cradling his shaking body in her arms and chanting something in his ear as he sobbed. Finally he rose, still sobbing, and stumbled down from the platform. I got a good look at his face as he passed down the aisle, assisted by an attendant. It looked quite different from the one I had seen approach Amaji. It looked like the tears were wiping it clean; it was lighter and clearer. His cold hard expression had softened into one of open awe.

We sat for two hours at least before it was our time to get in the line. Fortunately we were asked to remain silent. It was peaceful and renewing. Fritz and I had been working hard, interacting with many people. It was so restful and interesting to sit there is the meditation-field of Amaji's presence, hear the chants and objectively watch Amaji's effect on people. Several times my eyes met Carol's and I could see that she was deeply touched by what she saw and felt.

When it was finally our turn to approach Amaji I was disappointed to be ending our time there. This time it felt I could absorb her hug and her love, even deeper than before. I surrendered myself into it, with intense gratitude. Those few seconds again brought a timeless sense of the Infinite and the endless love of Source. I felt renewed at all levels. I thanked Amaji and God for such enormous blessings.

Carol was just behind me. I stood by and watched as Amaji embraced her and then as she descended the platform. She looked stunned; her face was luminous. There were tears in her eyes. We stood looking at each other for a few moments, acknowledging and affirming what we had received. Then we hugged and I said in her ear: "We've been waiting our whole lives for that, haven't we?" As have many of the world's children I suspect.

At the Global Peace Initiative of Women Religious and Spiritual Leaders in Geneva in 2002 Amaji said that the salvation of this world lies in our ability to recognize and honor the great mothering and creative power within the Divine feminine aspect of our natures. She said this too-long suppressed treasure lies not only within women but also in men and that when we give it equality with the masculine aspect, our world can heal and rebuild.[2]

Amaji speaks to many professionals and world leaders about world problems but she doesn't merely talk about them. She demonstrates through example. With the help of her devotees, she has created practical and creative solutions in the fields of family life, education, the sciences, medicine, psychology, religion or the sacred arts, all within the context of affecting the whole person—body, mind and spirit. And they are offered to all people, regardless of sex, culture or religion. Her influence extends around the world with a thousand arms of compassion. For, like a true bodhisatva, she gives all that she has received from the Divine for the benefit of all sentient beings.

I am deeply grateful to Amaji for touching me, at all levels. Her touch endures.

Afterword

As I was writing this chapter an old friend and spiritual sister called me from New Mexico where she is living near one of Amaji's ashrams. She told me Amaji is still hugging between three and four thousand people a day, in addition to all the other world service she administers. World corporate leaders are now coming to her to study her systems of education, assistance to the poor and health care because she is accomplishing a revolution of care in India beyond anything yet known in the business world.

I thought how ironic and beautiful it is that the money powers of the world are finally paying attention to the quiet revolutions of social change being carried out by the poor and non-violent seva workers in India. And they are led by two single individuals born into neither wealth nor power, Amaji and Sai Baba.

---

2. Sri Mata Amritanandamayi Devi, The Awakening of Universal Motherhood. Kerela, India, 2002.

17

Teacher of Teachers—Sai Baba

Sathya Sai Baba has millions of followers throughout the world who are contributing to a quiet revolution of human consciousness through *seva,* selfless service. They come from all religions, all faiths and no religions. They are old and young, rich and poor, the powerful and helpless. Many heads of state seek his counsel. Yet no advertising of any kind, no radio or television announcements, have drawn them to him. His non-violent revolution has spread entirely by word-of-mouth. People must travel from around the world to India to see him because after he traveled to Africa, just once in the 1940s, he said he would not leave India again until its social and economic problems are resolved.

But let me back up to the first time I ever experienced him. That was an event that left an indelible imprint within me which continues to instruct me to this day. It happened in a dream—at least that's what I have to say logically—that was more real than life.

One evening friends and I had been discussing whether the miraculous reports we had read about Sai Baba could be real. The healings, uncanny readings of visitors' entire personal history without prior knowledge, manifestations of holy ash, jewels, statues, on and on.

"I've read that if you call out to him he will appear," my friend said.

"OK, I'm going to ask directly," I vowed emphatically.

So when I went to bed that night I asked: "Please God, show me who this man is. Show me if he is actually real."

Shortly after I had turned out the light and tucked in for the night I heard a tap tap tap on my window. I lived at that time in one room in the country on the bottom floor of my landlady's home. Sometimes Laura would tap on the window as she came to visit. But it was after midnight and she never came that late. I listened, startled, and called out,

"Who's there?"

Another tap tap.

"Who's there?" I cried, louder, with more urgency.

Suddenly all the lights in my room came on at once, lighting every single corner. I knew I hadn't tripped a light switch and I knew that all the lights in my room wouldn't create this noon-sun brilliance. I jumped out of bed, really alarmed by then. Perhaps there was a fire in the house, or a massive short in the electrical system.

Then the lights started flashing off, and on again.

"What's happening?" I practically shrieked, both frightened and intensely alert.

I grabbed up the bedspread, wrapped it around me and ran up the indoor-stairs toward my landlady's rooms. I cried out, "Mama, mama, mama!" like a little child. That frantic feeling of running for mother in a crisis enveloped me. At the same time I knew I wasn't calling for either my own mother or my landlady.

Then abruptly I was back in my bed. The room was dark and completely quiet. Not even a flicker of a light, no tapping. My heart was beating wildly. How did I get there? I knew something incredible had happened. How could I suddenly be back in bed when I had been on the stairway? I was completely confused and disoriented but totally alert.

What happened? I kept asking myself. How could the lights flash on and off? Who or what was tapping? I lay there for a long time, wide-awake, puzzling over these extraordinary events. They seemed so real, not like a dream at all, and yet how else could they be explained? Could they have been an answer from Sai Baba? I wondered.

Even the attempt to write about Sai Baba seems impossible. There are hundreds, probably thousands, of books about him by now. Millions of devotees from all over the world stream to his ashram in the Indian desert just to catch a glimpse of him. How can I possibly describe this transhuman being who has been giving spiritual teachings now for sixty-seven years, who has performed more recorded miracles than any other person in history, changed the quality of Indian education through the many schools and universities he has established, created a program throughout India of free service for food, water, and medical attention to the poor and disadvantaged, built three of the most advanced hospitals in the world which give free care to all who can't afford medical help and who says that he has committed three incarnations to bring this world back to righteousness? In fact he has literally said that his mission "will not be stopped and it will not be slowed down."

Impossible to capture Sai Baba in words. "You cannot understand me," he has said to both theologians and scientists.

Yet the awakening journey I'm describing in this book wouldn't be complete without the experiences I've had with him because he is clearly the most astounding streak of lightning I have ever known, or read about.

I saw Sai Baba at close range for the first time in India in 1989.

A busload of one hundred of us from the First International Holistic Medical Conference in Bangalore was headed for Sai Baba's ashram in the desert. We shook and heaved over the primitive road, wiping sweat from our faces every few minutes as the temperature soared in the hot desert. Will we ever get there? Will we be able to see Sai Baba once we do?

For some of us this was a miraculous opportunity we had awaited for a long time. As we bumped along that rutted country road I reflected back over the miraculous series of synchronicities that had brought me to this unlikely place.

Shortly after the astounding dream experience with him I attended a prenatal psychology class with Dr. Graham Farrant from Australia, one of the world's authorities on prenatal therapy. I learned a lot and the class was great but the most arresting part of it happened at lunches and dinners when Graham would regale us with stories about his high-charged experiences with Sai Baba. The miracles he claimed, the excitement he radiated, and the *vibhuti* (holy ash) he passed around—all these kept us on a constant high of Graham's wave. On the last evening he showed a video of Sai Baba for those who were interested. That was the last straw. I decided it was essential for me to check out Sai Baba for myself.

Fritz was at that class too. Besides agreeing that Graham was a "flaming Sai Baba devotee," he also wanted to see Sai Baba for himself. Even though it was completely impossible at the time, we agreed to go to India to see Sai Baba whenever it was possible. We shook hands on it.

Exactly two weeks later Fritz was teaching Zero Balancing at Esalen and I was assisting him. A colleague from Baltimore, Jerry Toporovsky, came up to me and asked if I would consider presenting at a world holistic medical conference in India the following year.

I wrinkled my nose, thinking about it. Conferences are a lot of stress and I didn't know if I could possibly afford to go to India, even though I had always wanted to go there. Then Jerry said, "And by the way the conference presenters who are interested are invited to Sai Baba's ashram to see him after the conference."

"Yes!" I said immediately without any further thought about preparing a presentation. I wanted to see Sai Baba!

It turned out that Jerry had also asked Fritz to present at the conference that same day and of course, Fritz had also said yes!

So now here we were eighteen months later, in a bus lumbering along a pitted road in India. I was going over this amazing series of events in my mind and reliving the conference we had just attended. It was an inspiring event that began with a panel of India's most esteemed spiritual leaders, including the Dalai Lama. Then alternative medical practitioners from around the world reported on their promising research.

I was aroused from this reverie when a feeling of stirring excitement washed over me like a gentle electrical charge. We're getting close to Sai Baba, I thought.

Within a few miles the bus entered the village of Puttaparthi surrounding the ashram. It looked similar in many ways to other rural Indian villages we had seen. Animals and humans walking in the middle of the road, children playing in the potholes nearby, women carrying bundles on their heads. But there was another quality as well, like a vibrant stillness in the atmosphere and happiness in faces.

A prominent sign, "Prasanthi Nilayam," (The Eternal Abode of Peace) marked the entrance to the ashram. The bus lurched to a stop near a large temple and we started filing out, almost blinded by the brilliant sun as we looked around a magical world. It was a bit like Disneyland, with its giant brightly colored statues, shiny cleanliness and electrified atmosphere, except that all the statues here were of Gods and Goddesses.

Already hundreds of people were crowded together in the temple, sitting on the marble floor. We squeezed into the entrance and stood, crunched together, in the back rows since there were no places left to sit.

As representatives of the Medical conference we hoped for a private interview with Sai Baba, a time to meet up close with him. But there was no assurance of such a privilege. Even though Dr. Matthai, the Director of our Conference, had been encouraged by officials about our chances for a meeting, it was explained that Sai Baba never made advance plans but only responded to the moment.

A complete hush came over the crowd.

Sai Baba walked slowly into the temple. Rather he seemed to float like a soft brilliant orange cloud. He was a tiny figure, only about five feet tall, but his presence filled the entire temple. He walked ever so slowly along aisles between the seated devotees. His hands lifted in simple graceful gestures now and then. Occasionally he stopped in front of someone. He twirled his right hand in a small circle and then, out of thin air, the holy healing ash, Vibhuti, poured out of his hand into that of the recipient. There were sharp inhalations all around as people watched this miracle in amazement. I was transfixed. I had read about this phenomenon many times but seeing it was stunning.

I was still struggling to integrate this experience when I felt a rustle and urgent whispering near me.

"Come, come quickly," our group was urged, "Baba will see you!"

I almost stumbled as I hurried behind the others to an enclosed room inside the temple, Sai Baba's inner sanctum. We crowded into the room, some of us slightly informed about what an extraordinary privilege this was, others simply curious, entirely ignorant of Sai Baba.

He was much more visible here. The wrinkleless chocolate-brown face, the huge black halo of thick hair, the delicate graceful hands and the simple ankle-length orange robe. I remember thinking that he looked about forty years old although I knew he was already over sixty.

He stopped among the crowd, raised his hand in blessing and started to speak to us. He spoke about healing, about the responsibilities of it and its Divine origins. I was intensely interested. I wanted to take notes but at the same time didn't want to take my attention for a split second from his voice, his face, his gestures.

For almost forty-five minutes Sai Baba talked lovingly to us like a father to his children. A rich uplifting discourse about the necessity, the benefits and risks of healing which included comments about contemporary medicine, how it served and where it erred, as well as where it should, and would, go in the future. I realized that this was an understanding and vision far beyond what I had ever heard or read before. I thought, how grateful I am to be here.

As he concluded the talk Sai Baba walked straight up to Dr. Matthai and spoke to him individually. He seemed to be asking the doctor something. Then he lifted his right hand and spun it around. Special vibhuti for this doctor, I thought. Suddenly gasps came from the people near them and in that moment I saw a sparkling object fall from Sai Baba's hand into the doctor's. I watched Dr. Matthai look at the object in his palm and then slip it onto his ring finger. A ring! I strained to see it closer but there were at least thirty people in front of me. Later, when Fritz and I were alone with Dr. Matthai, he showed us the ring and even let us touch it—a ten-carat emerald in a beautiful gold setting. We asked him what Baba had said to him. He said that Baba had blessed the conference and also the holistic health center Dr. Matthai hoped to build near Bangalore.

But everything was happening so fast, so magically at the time that I hardly had a chance to cognize that miracle when Sai Baba started walking among us, distributing little packets of vibhuti at every turn. I prayed silently, "Please let me have some of that special healing vibhuti for my children and clients!" Within minutes he had dropped a packet of it into my hands. I held it close and thought, Oh Thank you! This alone was blessing enough to travel all the way to India.

Then Sai Baba was walking back in my direction! I watched him intently, amazed at this gigantic presence in such a tiny body, the lightness of his face, the humor sparkling in his eyes. He stopped very close to me. I quickly asked him silently if I could touch his foot, a rare privilege I had seen others do. I thought I heard him say yes so I reached down and touched one sandled foot ever so lightly.

Immediately a bolt of electricity surged through my body. I almost fell over with the shock of it and had to catch myself quickly with one hand on the floor. I feared I would faint. I struggled to get inner control of the dizziness, the disorientation. I knew I had received a huge blessing but it was far beyond my mind's grasp. What I do remember thinking is that this one dose of the Divine was enough to last for the rest of my life. At the time I just stood there in a daze, filled with wonder and gratitude. The intensity of my earlier attention widened and softened.

Yet it wasn't over. I was still stunned when he came back in my direction. A woman next to me handed him an envelope. At first he took the envelope and held it in his hand for a moment, as if reflecting on its contents. Then he handed the envelope back to her and said, "You keep it. I want only your love." And he turned to walk away.

> Suddenly a wave of love surged through me with such power—from my toes up through my legs, torso, and throat—that it burst straight out my mouth as,
>
> "I love you, Baba!"

There was absolutely no thought of stopping it. No wondering how it would sound to others. No reservation about the force of it. No second thought whatever.

Sai Baba wheeled around, like a bolt, and faced me. He looked me straight in the eyes, grabbed my right hand and replied with force,

"I love you!"

As I write this I can still feel the imprint of his hand in mine and the life-changing power of that tidal wave of love. Fritz said later that as he watched Sai Baba touch me he could see a profound healing of the death of my father envelope me. It was only later, after I had read many books about Sai Baba and talked with devotees, that I realized what rare blessings we had received that day.

After that I didn't register details. The remainder of the day is a blur to me. I was floating in some other dimension, quite unable to process what was happening in my usual way.

During the next three weeks, Fritz and I traveled around India as tourists.

The floating sensation continued. The field of India's 3000-year old attunement with the sacred engulfed us. I let my body relax deeply into the rhythm of the car as we rolled through extraordinary landscapes.

Temples, shrines and holy statues, decorated with colorful flowers, marked almost every turn in the road. Sadhus, holy men with scant or no clothing, walked barefoot beside the truck-loaded streets, as did mothers carrying babies, children selling chiclets and farmers herding their goats. People, trucks and ox-carts made way for cows, sacred in that culture.

My mind let go and released its planning and problem solving. I was suspended for a time, free from the burdens of the world, as I knew them. Each moment was a precious gem of indescribable richness. I had never been so contented since the month in Indonesia with Bapak, so able to simply be where I was. And beneath this luxury of perception I could actually feel Sai Baba's blessing working within me. A sense of peace, healing and other-worldliness persisted until we left India.

I now know that Sai Baba's love and touch, transmitted in that one afternoon, has continued to work deep within me all these years. Sometimes I recognize the traces of that power in an unexpected healing of my own memories or in a healing with someone else.

When we first returned from India I could feel his healing vibration in my right hand when I did hands-on work with people. Sometimes they could feel it too. One woman announced, "There's a little brown man standing here by the table. He's wearing an orange robe and he has a huge black halo. Who is he?"

Gradually I became less and less conscious of that sensation in the right hand until finally it almost faded away, although the actual event of Baba's touch never left my mind. Several years later that vibration was brought to my attention again. In one of our workshops an older lady was suffering from severe back pain. She was a good woman who had devoted most of her life to taking care of other people, first as a mother, later as a healer. I felt a lot of concern for her and wanted somehow to stop her pain. Although she had already received our styles of bodywork she was still suffering.

I put my right hand on her back as we talked about other things. I prayed for Baba's help,

"Please Baba, heal this woman's back pain."

Baba's answer was swift and a bit sharp.

"I have already given you all the healing you will ever need in that right hand. Now use it!"

I felt reprimanded but also empowered. As I meditated on his command I realized that yes, the vibration was still there, but it had to be activated by my conscious request and attunement to that God-frequency.

Of course the first reality that confronted me when we returned home was spiritual allegiance. For thirty years I had been a faithful student of Bapak even though I had read about many spiritual traditions and met some of their important teachers. I recognized his mission and had pledged myself to be true to it. The *latihan* is the spine of my spiritual life and my work. I was both confused and feeling a bit guilty. What did it mean to be so deeply drawn to this Indian teacher, Sai Baba?

Bapak had died in 1986. I mourned the loss of his physical presence yet I also accepted that he was available to us, across the worlds, when we truly needed him, just as he had promised. So I decided to go straight to him for a consultation. In the *latihan* I asked Bapak,

"Am I being disloyal to you and Subud by this attraction to Sai Baba?"

Then in the most amazing impression I actually saw and heard Bapak throw his head back in that beautiful way as he laughed. He answered me, "Haven't you realized yet that we are all Brothers in this together, serving the One Source?"

That was the end of my confusion and guilt about Sai Baba. I continued doing the *latihan* and also returned to Sai Baba many times.

When we got back from India I read many books about Sai Baba; I couldn't get enough of the miraculous stories of his youth as a wonder child, of the advent of his teaching when he was only fourteen years old, of the hundreds of healings he had performed, and of his extensive service at all levels of society.

Several authors reported that Sai Baba had made a curious declaration.

"I am your mother," he said on many occasions. Of course I remembered my own dream of crying out, "Mama, mama, mama!" and then I understood the mother I was calling for.

One of the books I read, *Sai Baba: The Ultimate Experience*, by Phyllis Krystal, impressed me with its open honesty, and objective reporting of miraculous events. For example she reported that when she was flying to India one year her plane was hijacked by terrorists. Naturally she was terrified, as were all the other passengers, as the captors marched through the aisles carrying machine guns and ordering the passengers to sit still and be quiet.

She thought it was the end for her. She remembered that Sai Baba had told devotees to call out for him in emergencies. It was all she could think to do. So she held the prayer beads Sai Baba had manifested for her and cried out silently for his help. Shortly thereafter radio negotiations were successful. The plane landed and the hostages were released.

When Phyllis arrived at the ashram she had an interview with Sai Baba. Before she could finish thanking him for saving her life he said, "Yes, yes I know. I heard your voice calling, "Baba! Baba! Baba!" He mimicked her voice perfectly.

Not long after we returned from India we contacted Phyllis. We were interested in the unique meditative techniques she was teaching all over the world and we invited her to teach a class in Santa Cruz.

Phyllis told us on the phone that she would wear one of the strings of prayer beads Sai Baba had manifested so we could recognize her at the airport. But she stood out from the crowd like a light, a handsome woman in her seventies, smartly dressed with a beautiful smile. She came right up to us, extended her hand and said, "You must be Fritz and Aminah!"

We were amazed at her vitality, lightheartedness and sensitivity from that moment on. Her class was electric. We learned very helpful techniques for dealing with everyday problems at a transcendent level. She taught us how to anchor awareness in higher consciousness which she called HiC. I realized this was the same thing I was calling soul consciousness in my work.

But it was Phyllis herself who made the time special. Each morning she would show up like a sunbeam, smiling and attentive to each person's need. Her vitality and lightness of spirit would continue throughout the day. She had more vigor than any of us although she was the oldest. She said that teaching was no effort at all because she, Phyllis, really didn't do it, Spirit did the teaching. "Whenever I hear a teacher complain of being tired after a day of teaching I know that he or she is trying to do it," she said.

Phyllis told us that all through her youth and far into adulthood she had been intensely shy. Even the thought of speaking in front of people had terrified her until Sai Baba instructed her to start teaching her work. At the time she was astounded and argued with him. "Baba, how can I teach when I can't even speak in a social setting?" He told her it was time for her to overcome that shyness and he would help her.

During the class Phyllis told us many marvelous stories of Baba's miracles, his advice, his incredible ability to know the whole history of anyone he was addressing. For example, she said that he had described events in her life that only she knew. All these stories echoed many I had read from other authors. They fueled my wish to return to India for more first hand experience.

So we went again to see Sai Baba in 1994. When we arrived in Bangalore we were told that Baba was giving daily Darshan at Whitefield, his ashram near Bangalore.

The minute we entered the temple I could feel the vibrant field of Sai Baba's love, that same pervasive flood I had experienced in 1989. It was off-season and there were fewer people in the temple although it was still almost full. But this time we could just sit in that love, meditating, for several hours daily. I soon learned that I could sit quietly in a state of *latihan* receiving and feel the downpour of grace. Those hours were like going straight to heaven and being bathed in a shower of love so powerful that it erased almost everything else.

Consciousness would open wide and high out of the crown chakra. I was in another realm, timeless, spaceless, infinitely peaceful and happy. I was content to simply bask in It.

This state probably would have been termed cosmic consciousness by Richard M. Bucke, the early twentieth-century author of the extraordinary book by that name.[1]

Occasionally something I wanted to know would pop into my mind. Then I would ask a question and the answer would come in a hologrammic way—in sight, hearing and feeling.

One time I became aware that my body was screaming with cramps from sitting so long. The parts that weren't screaming were entirely numb. But it didn't matter at all because this transcendent consciousness was worth any amount of physical pain.

When the temple was closing for the day some of us would linger as long as we could in that vast peaceful field. I would have to forcefully remind myself that it was time to go after most of the ladies had already left. One such a day, as I gazed carefully around the whole temple to indelibly imprint that scene for life, I spotted Fritz across the way on the mens' side. He was also lingering and his face looked just

---

1. Bucke, Richard Maurice, M.D. *Cosmic Consciousness*. New York, E.P. Dutton and Company, 1969.

like I felt, peaceful and far removed from ordinary reality. I felt so much love for him, a true spiritual mate.

I brought questions, projects and problems to these meditations. It's not that I thought about them while sitting there. Rather I posed them to Baba's field and then simply waited, in a quiet state of *latihan* receiving. During the course of days answers for a number of these things had just come in lightning flashes. In the seconds of their arrival understanding was complete, hologrammic, and it pervaded all parts of me. As they accumulated over the days I grew more and more grateful and engrossed in the process. I began to inhabit another realm altogether, one that became much more real than the reality I had been living in. I wanted to be silent most of the time so as not to leave that dimension for a moment.

It was a wonderful time, peaceful, illuminated, electric. It didn't matter that Baba didn't once walk close to me or that we didn't receive an interview in the inner temple as before. His grace and love were so pervasive that we felt full to overflowing. Gratitude engulfed me.

One day I realized that soon we would be leaving the ashram and my questions couldn't be put into that field anymore. A bit alarmed I asked, "Baba, how can I sustain this connection, this grace, when we go away?"

An astounding response happened immediately. Just in front of my brow chakra, about 2" from the forehead, a tiny hologram appeared. It was animated and talking, very similar to the hologram of Princess Lela in Star Wars. Except that it was Sai Baba! I could hear his voice quite clearly.

"What do you want to know?" he asked, "I'm right here."

My eyes were wide open. I could see the people, the temple all around and the trees outside it, as usual. And at the same time this tiny hologram was as real as the lady next to me. I blinked my eyes but still it persisted. My psychologist mind asked, "are you hallucinating now?"

The soul answered, "You're an empiricist. Try it out. Ask something."

So I asked one of the Big Questions: "Why are we here?"

The answer came swift and clear. It was shown to me in a hologrammic instant, flooding my body, feelings and higher-than-mind understanding.

"Principally to evolve your souls. Earth is a great training ground."

I was amazed, could this be real? I asked another Big Question: "Then why am I here"?

And again the answer came immediately in the same way:

"This world is in severe crisis/opportunity. You have skills, only some of which you have yet brought forth. You agreed to apply them here at this time to serve the Divine plan and evolve your own soul."

I let that soak in for awhile, as it would continue to do in the following years.

Then I tried another: "Why is there so much anti-life behavior on this planet?"

"Karmic patterns, separating you from the One. A struggle to wrest power from It started in ancient times, within individuals and groups. Now these karmas have accumulated on earth, to a level of explosion, like a great volcano. They are arising to the surface in full force. Hence your mounting conflicts, wars, and abuses of all forms of life. These patterns reside within individuals. You have forgotten that all life is connected in One creative current. At this moment you stand at a brink of either extinction or an evolutionary leap. Humankind can seize this opportunity to choose the One over those ancient karmas and let go of the past, or you can repeat them over and over for another thousand years."

This answer stimulated an intense sense of urgency within me. I felt little and overwhelmed with its implications. I appealed for help:

"Baba, couldn't you heal this world, as you have healed so many individuals?"

"Yes, I could, but if I healed the whole world in an instant those patterns would quickly recur because they are threaded through the very fiber of individual human beings. Past mistakes must be realized within each individual and set right by individual choice. But don't worry," he added as if speaking to a helpless child, "I have come to restore this world to righteousness. Listen to me. I will guide you."

After the stunning impact of these messages I continued to ask smaller questions. For example, I was planning an inner child healing class and book at the time so I asked Baba for guidance about them. He told me that the most important part of the healing was to guide the inner child to the Divine Parents, especially the Divine Mother. He said,

"Guide the inner child into a Divine healing space. Set her in the lap or heart of a spiritual person. Wait until you feel the influx of spiritual energy and healing. Let the child soak in this energy. Then leave her there in that healing chamber, for as long as it takes, until the work is done. Tell her not to think or worry about the ways or time but to simply know that it will be done."

This question and answer process engrossed me for the remainder of that morning. By the end of Darshan all the questions I had at that time were answered.

Still I worried if it would continue.

"How will I have access to this information when we leave?"

"Don't you understand? I am here with you always, no matter where you are."

"Baba, do you mean I can have you here, in my brow chakra, in this hologram, anytime, anyplace?"

"Exactly. It's only a matter of your concentration."

Since that time I have had an inner contact with Sai Baba. That is, whenever I remember to give it attention.

After we left India I consulted the hologram many times and almost always, according to my concentration, it yielded immediate counsel. But through the months, as the thicket of daily life entangled me, with its problems, projects and demands, the pervading reality of his voice began to fade and I forgot to ask Baba directly. After awhile the ten thousand things of ordinary reality crowded out the vast space of the ashram. It seemed far away, like a fantasy, in another world even. Finally I couldn't confidently remember its validity. Sometimes I longed for that illumination, that peace, that love, if even for a few minutes.

Fritz also felt that longing so we decided to return to India in 1995. We planned the trip with two dear friends and soul sisters, Deirdre, a Buddhist bodhisatva and Paula, a yogini bodhisatva. We had agreed to meet them at the ashram in Puttaparti. The arrangement was that Fritz and I would arrive first and secure accommodations for all four of us. Fritz and I already had a reservation at the ashram. It was only for three days, yet we felt confident that we could arrange something for all of us once we got there.

But it was the year of Sai Baba's 70th birthday. We hadn't exactly understood what Baba's birthday meant to his devotees. People from all over the world were streaming to the ashram for the gigantic celebration. It was estimated that there would be three million at least.

As soon as Fritz and I arrived at the ashram we went straight to the accommodations office to reserve additional days for ourselves and another room for our friends.

"Absolutely no rooms available," said the person in charge. "Baba's birthday."

Immediately we went across the street to the only "hotel," in the village at that time, Sai Towers, to secure rooms for ourselves and our friends. We were a bit relieved to visit the hotel since the ashram room we had seen was almost uninhabitable by our accustomed standards.

We asked the hotel clerk if we could reserve rooms.

"Oh no," he said brusquely. "It's Baba's birthday time. We have no rooms. We are booked solid for the remainder of the month."

My heart sank. We were to be in India for two weeks and wanted to spend all that time at the ashram; three days weren't enough. And what could we do for our friends? They were depending on us. Perhaps our ashram room could be extended. I asked for Baba's help,

"Please Baba, help us find a room. We want to stay the whole time near you."

More people arrived at the ashram each day. The village itself seemed to bulge with the sheer force of numbers. I couldn't imagine how all these people would even be fed so far out in the desert.

On the third day, when our ashram reservation was up, we packed our bags, and went straight back again to the accommodations office to appeal once more for an extension of our stay.

"Oh no," said the officer in charge. "It's Baba's birthday time. The people who are moving into your room are already here."

We went to Darshan for the last time. As I sat in the temple I could hardly surrender because it was so sad to be leaving and also I felt let down by Baba—it seemed that he hadn't answered my call for help.

Just near the end of Darshan I heard Baba say clearly,

"Go back to Sai Towers and ask for a room."

"But Baba, we have already been there and they have no rooms," I argued.

He repeated, "Go to the hotel and ask for a room. Go right now!"

Oh boy, I thought. Fritz will think I'm crazy. What if this is just my wishful fantasy? Nevertheless I hurried up to him and tugged at his arm.

"We must go immediately to Sai Towers and ask for a room."

He looked at me curiously, as if I had lost my mind. "They told us they didn't have any."

"I know, but Baba just told me to go over there right away. Please. Humor me. Let's just go!"

So across the street we went as I almost ran on ahead, suddenly possessed with urgency.

I approached the desk clerk shyly. "Do you possibly have a room now?"

He looked up at me with annoyance as if to say, oh, you again. But then he turned to the registration book and started tracing through the columns. His finger stopped halfway down the page.

"I do have one room, just vacated this morning, that will be available tomorrow. But you would have to pay for it right now to secure it."

I wanted to jump up and down. There was a room! Baba had helped us after all! I felt such joy I couldn't respond to the clerk.

"We'll take it," Fritz said, and pulled out his wallet.

That gave us a day to return to Bangalore and our fancy hotel there, to clean up with luxurious hot showers and buy what we would need for the next days in Puttaparti. Then we could come right back and move in. Perfect. Except of course what we would do with Deirdre and Paula.

We arrived back to Sai Towers the next day, refreshed from our overnight stay in an elegant, air-conditioned hotel. The room at Sai Towers was up three flights of narrow stairs and it faced the street, which was getting noisier by the hour as more people continued to arrive. It was a small room with two cots pushed together to form one double bed. It was lackluster and frugal. But it had a bathroom of its own with a toilet, and a faucet with a bucket for bathing. One thin dingy towel hung on the towel rack. A sharp contrast to the luxury hotel we had come from in Bangalore but I was so happy to have it. I could hardly imagine then that before we left that little room it would become a temple.

I worried aloud to Fritz about what to do with Deirdre and Paula.

"They will just have to stay with us in the room," Fritz said, in his eminently practical way. I looked at him in amazement. Where? I thought. There's hardly enough room to turn around in there. And Fritz is a particularly private person. Three women in the same bedroom and bathroom seemed unlike anything he would choose. But in Baba's field worry and obsessions melt away. So we went to Darshan and I surrendered it.

Still, on the day Deirdre and Paula arrived I was nervous. Where could we put them, how to explain? Buses were arriving one after another in the village. People poured through the streets in crowds. We hadn't made an advance plan for where or how to meet them and now, amid these droves, it seemed impossible to even spot them.

We were just coming back to Sai Towers after Darshan when a taxi stopped in front of it. And out popped Deirdre and Paula as if by appointment. We dashed up to them in relief, and hugged all around. I took a deep breath, now for the moment of truth.

We grabbed up their bags and led them into Sai Towers. I went straight to the desk while Fritz swiftly explained the predicament to Deirdre and Paula.

"Have you another room?" I pleaded with the clerk, "Our friends here have just arrived, a long trip from Europe. They're tired," I tried to appeal to his sympathy, "they really need a place to stay."

"No rooms," he said impatiently, "Baba's birthday."

We stood at the desk, looking at the clerk. I hoped that Fritz' technique of just waiting there in front of him would yield some solution. But the clerk turned his attention to other guests as if we had become invisible.

Fritz spoke up. "Then do you have two extra mattresses we can put in our room for our friends?"

The clerk looked at us in a perplexed way. Three women and a man in one room? In India women and men are separated, in the ashram, often in the home and at work, and certainly in the bedroom. I could see his mind wrinkling. Nevertheless he shrugged and said, "I'll bring two mattresses to your room."

When we unrolled the two mattresses there was no floor space left in the room. This meant that in the daytime we rolled them up against the walls and at night we had to tiptoe in a squiggly pattern to get to the bathroom. It also meant that we all needed to go to bed and to sleep at the same time. Then, when we awoke to the alarm at four-thirty am to go to Darshan, there was a hilarious scramble of bumping bodies in the dark.

But the love and abundance of Darshan swiftly cancelled all concerns about our lodging. We were in heaven inside the temple despite the heat and squashing crowds. It was quiet—no talking in Darshan—and clean marble floors gleamed from twice-a-day scrubbing on hands and knees. But mostly the temple was filled with the electric charge of Baba's grace. In that field meditation was automatic, sudden insight common. Everything that happened—swallows flying just beneath the ceiling, a sudden cool breeze on the back of the neck, a penetrating glance of the lady sitting nearby, the baby peacefully sleeping in her mother's arms—everything, every moment, seemed to announce meaningful, synchronous progressions.

Baba himself was more luminous than ever, ceaselessly distributing gifts and sweets to everyone. In the first Darshan attended by Deirdre and Paula he came gliding through the women's side of the temple, handing out silk saris with his own hands to every woman. It took several boys, running after him with their arms loaded, to keep the supply flowing. That sari graces my altar now, a constant reminder of Baba's love and generosity.

In comparison, the village outside the ashram was like a little Hell. As soon as we stepped through the gate into the village the ordinary world impinged on our consciousness. Car horns and blasting music. Rickshaws, buses and trucks vying for the same narrow road space. A continuous din of hawkers calling out to sell everything from prayer beads to Sai Baba alarm clocks.

It was a big shock to the senses after the serenity of the temple. At the same time there was something so real, so down-to-ordinary-earth about it, that in a certain sense it was a relief. Also amusing and exciting. Everyone was gearing up for Baba's birthday celebration. Beneath the commercialism there was also a kind of worldly piety and generosity, as if Baba were watching all transactions.

"Oh, you buy Baba's prayer beads for friends in US? OK, half price."

So the four of us went twice each day to Darshan, back and forth from our room to the temple. Through the village crowds each time. Such a curious mixture of the sacred and profane and yet a rich feast for the senses.

Each of us was working hard internally. We spoke little; the intensity of boiling inner processes triggered by Darshan demanded most of our attention. Eyes deepened, and penetrated whenever you glanced at them. Now and then you saw a tear wiped away. We felt each other's presence and kindness without sharing our processes.

One day at Darshan Deirdre and I were sitting next to each other on the front row, a coveted position where Baba would pass very close if he walked down that aisle. I was praying that he would. We were deeply inward when Baba started to come our way. My heart jumped. I hadn't been this close to him since the time in the inner temple in 1989.

I had been harboring a deep desire for him to look at me again as he had then, so I called out silently, "Please, Baba, look into my eyes."

He floated near us and then passed by without even glancing at us. My heart sank, disappointed. Then about ten feet beyond us, just as we were watching the back of his orange robe, he stopped abruptly. He turned around and looked straight at Deirdre. He focused on her intently for what seemed like an eternity though surely it was only a few seconds. He recognizes her, I thought, how wonderful. Then he looked at me. His bottomless dark eyes penetrated straight through me into infinity.

I was filled again with that huge love and overwhelming gratitude. "Thank you, thank you, Baba," I said inside.

He passed on.

Deirdre and I sat in silence, too overwhelmed with the magnitude of this blessing, to even move, much less speak. We were transported to an unfathomable realm by his gaze.

Within four hours I was as sick as I have ever been. Intense body pain, diarrhea, vomiting all hit me within an hour. At first I was thinking, how inconvenient, I might not be able to go to Darshan, let's see, what medicines do I have that will keep me up? Which acupressure points shall I hold to stay functional?

But within hours going anywhere was out of the question. I was flat out on our one bed and could barely move. Fever rose until it felt like I would burn up on the spot. Fritz and Deirdre immediately went into their healer selves. They applied needles and salves and gave me the medicines we had for such emergencies in India.

Nothing seemed to touch the symptoms. Hour after hour I kept vomiting until finally I simply slumped on the floor by the toilet, waiting for the next surge, until there was absolutely nothing left to vomit. If only I can get back to the bed and go to sleep I'll be all right in the morning, I hoped. Then through the fog of fever and weakness I saw Fritz' face, creased with worry, a feeling he rarely allows to show. It must be pretty bad, I thought.

That was the last rational thought I had. What I remember next is rolling from side to side with body pain in the bed and spinning through a dark tunnel. Images and experiences I had never known, at least in this life, flashed through and by me at lightning speed. Strange words, like Dakau, came out of my mouth. It was impossible to grab or cognize any of it, even if I had been trying. No way to get my bearings. I surrendered deeper and kept spinning further, further through the tunnel, propelled past places, faces, and images that were only vaguely formed before they dissolved, to be replaced by others in a continuous supersonic stream. I learned later that this went on for many hours. At the time it felt like hurtling through all eternity.

I was vaguely aware of Deirdre kneeling beside the bed throughout the night, one hand on my body and the other holding tiny bottles. Periodically she would hold a dropper to my mouth and squeeze a few drops into it. Whatever she was doing felt like life-sustaining soul work and deeply comforting. In the darkness the plain room had become a temple and Deirdre the Priestess. It felt as if she were keeping me connected to this world with her hand and those drops.

It was a tenuous connection. The realities around me in the room and outside in the street had vanished; I was suspended in another dimension. There was a feeble thought that I might die. It didn't matter.

Sometime the next day, still in the spinning tunnel, I began to see a bright light ahead and far off. At the same time I had the sensation that I was reaching the Beginnings. Of what? There was no thought. Simply the intimation of First Things.

The spinning opened up away from me. The light got much bigger and brighter, like a huge sun straight ahead. Then the spinning suddenly disappeared and I came to a stop.

Sai Baba stood there in front of me, his body filling a luminous sun in the space behind him. He was smiling and radiant. His voice boomed forth like a gong, "Now!" he commanded, "remember what you are!"

A lightning flash of multi-layered consciousness struck every particle of my being. In one moment many memories, prayers, promises, mistakes, triumphs, yearnings, losses coalesced in a gigantic Nowness. It was a clear direct hit in that instant. Afterwards it took years to process and integrate. I rarely told it to anyone either because I was aware that it would sound preposterous. And now, when I try to translate lightning into words, it dilutes, loses charge and doesn't deliver the whole-being dose that pervaded me then.

It was something like this: a fogged realization of what I am and where I come from, a knowing that Baba and I, as well as all life and I, are One, feelings of The Beginnings and infinite continuities, the infinite pervasiveness of Love, the knowing that I had traveled through countless lives which were now dreams in a spinning infinity, not recaptured in detail but it didn't matter.

I knew that some kind of miraculous clearing process had happened. That I had been amazingly blessed.

That moment lasted for perhaps a minute in 1995; its teachings have been spreading out through my life and consciousness, like a great gentle wave, ever since. It continues to inform me. Even now it returns periodically to yield some further meaning, as if I couldn't get parts of it until I reached a certain age.

Abruptly I was back in this world, weak but miraculously almost well. The fever was gone, my stomach calm.

I looked at Deirdre in amazement and gratitude, seeing her far beyond any construct I had of her before, as a precious Divine angel.

"Oh Deirdre, you're exquisite, a soul's angel. Isn't it a miracle? I'm here again. I'm alive! I think I'm well."

In fact I felt more alive and well in some ways than I had ever been.

"Thank you, thank you, dearest Deirdre, for staying with me through all of that. You saved me. It felt like an ancient healing temple in here. Whatever you were doing kept the process moving. It felt like I could have got stalled in any part of it but each time you gave me the drops we would go on. What were those drops anyway?"

"Soul essences," she answered matter-of-factly.

When I stood up from the bed though, my body didn't operate as well as I felt. It was quite weak, like a rubbery doll actually. I couldn't make it hop to and get it all together to go to Darshan. I told the others to go on; I didn't need tending anymore. It was our last day in Puttaparti and I felt sad to miss Baba but I rested quietly, still immersed in the extraordinary experience with him.

After awhile I could hear the crowd emerging from the temple and knew that everyone would be back soon. I got up and walked carefully down the stairs to greet them. Just as I stepped out of the hotel onto the sidewalk I heard excited voices and saw people gathering in a crowd. I looked up to see what was going on. Baba's car coming down the street. Blessing!

I got one last look at him, close up, as the car passed by.

We have traveled several more times to India to see Sai Baba. Many miraculous things have continued to happen to us and others who have traveled with us. For example, in 2000 we took a group of international healers to the ashram. Our individual and collective experiences there, and the grace that happened afterward, would consume a whole book.

But for now I'll report the mantra Baba gave me at the end of that trip. He said to tell students to say it at the end of Chakra Tai Chi, a Tai Chi movement I developed to clarify and facilitate our work in Process and Basic Acupressure. It brings more consciousness and alignment to all the chakras.

At first Baba's statement seemed too long for a mantra but after we had practiced it for awhile we began to experience its liberating effects every time we said it. It seems relevant in our world now for everyone:

I shed the suffering and struggles of the past
to align with my Soul
in this Present Moment.

As we were leaving Baba gave me one last strong message:

"Spread the news that there is a new world in the making. Everything has to change!"

Section VII: Calling Lightning

Once we have been struck by lightning and enlightened for a short time, what then? How can we continue to remember the Source that is calling us? To stay with It along our soul path? It is so easy to slip back into the unconscious grave of the cocoon of conditioning. The ten thousand things of the world beckon to us at every turn. They want to keep us wrapped up in what is familiar, already known. How can we keep ourselves awake to our Divine birthright? Shall we call lightning, as the Peruvian shamans do when they deliberately trek high into the Andes, hoping to catch a strike that will further enlighten them? Or can we just wait for another strike? How can we cultivate the soul consciousness that has been ignited during our awakening experience?

During my own journey my guidance has come through the *latihan* and spiritual teachers; they were indispensable to keep me on track. My journey was inextricably blended with my work as a transpersonal psychologist and bodyworker who was focused on soul empowerment. Therefore, as I awakened and learned more, I was able to apply what I found helpful with my clients. Along the way I received various principles that helped me in the full development of Process Acupressure as a body/mind/emotions/soul modality of liberation.

For example I received guidance about the relationship of personal history, the body and spiritual freedom. It was explained to me that it was important to release anything in the physical body that carries the history of this life so that the soul body could fully occupy the physical. I was told to help clear personal history so that the purpose and destiny of this life could be fulfilled.

Yet personal history was not to be judged or demeaned, because wherever it got stuck only showed an important lesson or task to be done which needed attention and respect. I was to ask what the meaning or lesson was in any particular experience or trauma. I should find out if the lesson was complete or what was yet needed to finish it. This guidance helped me and my clients to drop a victim position in life. Now we work from a soul perspective which greets past trauma and new challenges with an attitude of curiosity and the intention to get the teaching and apply it in life.

I was told to keep asking the light of the soul body to occupy cells of the physical so that processing of personal history could be assisted and met by inner soul work. I was to ask the soul to light up those places in the body that needed attention, clearing, or nourishment. This guidance showed me the way to bring the soul specifically and forcefully into the work.

This receiving was very valuable in helping me to bridge the gaps between psychology, bodywork and spirituality. In my own study they had been presented as separate domains altogether. Through the *latihan* I realized the unity of all within my own body. Thus I had been able to bring psychology and bodywork together. But for a long time I still kept the *latihan* separate from either of them—in my mind that is.

Guidance like this came to me continually as I developed my work. It became more focused and natural after Bapak provided the direction to pursue psychology of the soul.

I found that the more clarification I sought and the more I applied what I received in life, the stronger guidance and right action moved through me. In fact this principle was explained early by Bapak and has been demonstrated over and over again through our lives. The energy of the *latihan,* or any true spiritual practice, is very strong. When we keep that energy flowing through us by expressing it in life, it brings more and more strength, clarity and power. On the other hand, if a person doesn't use the blessings given, the energy tends to bunch up within them, and can make a person not only dysfunctional but often a bit crazy.

As I continued to study and practice, I found various people, places and events that also helped me remember my soul and its purpose. Special events or meetings can call lightning to us. They lift us to another level and open doors of perception that we hadn't known before. They heal and empower parts of ourselves we haven't been able to reach in other ways.

In the following section I tell about some of the avenues I found that can attract lightning. I describe a few of the remarkable power places, soul friends and events that coaxed me over my edges toward greater soul consciousness.

18

Power Places

There are special places in the world that can energize, heal or empower anyone who is open to the energy. I say open to the energy because I can remember so vividly when I stood in the Great Pyramid of Cheops being jet-rocketed into a state of higher consciousness. Yet I saw tourists walking around me, looking at the walls and touching them, who seemed entirely unaffected by that energy.

The special places where this energy is experienced are called "Power Places" by authentic shamans and have been identified for centuries. Think of Lourdes, the Great Pyramid of Cheops, Delphi, and other places you have known that had a special effect. Formidable experiences have been reported in these places. They vary from miraculous healings to spiritual awakenings and clarified consciousness.

It isn't known exactly what causes some locations to be more powerful than others. Contemporary technology hasn't yet clearly defined or measured their fields although Dr.Valerie Hunt, in her biophysics studies at UCLA charted the territory. Yet sensitive humans can easily feel the energetic effects of them in their bodies and consciousness, just as a practiced bodyworker can feel the flows of energy and tension in the body with her hands.

Many people believe that the ancients built their places of worship on energy vortices in the earth. They claim that these places are very powerful spots where *ley lines* of the earth intersect. And some say they can see, hear, feel and douse these intersections of energy.

We do know that many of these places hold a vibratory field created from continuous prayer and worship for centuries, as in Assisi, Italy,

Koyasan, Japan and Machu Picchu in Peru. Others, like the Grand Canyon, and some deserts, have no such human imprint. They are beyond and outside human design, yet they also exert a powerful influence upon us. Some deserts have that effect. I agree with Balzac, who once wrote, "The cities are man without God, the desert is God without man."

Many truth seekers in our time have consciously sought out these sites to enliven and empower their awakening process. Books have been written about their journeys.

Fritz and I have visited a number of power places. We've had so many amazing experiences in different spots of the world that it would take another whole book to describe them and our experiences there. With each stop at a cathedral, temple, shrine, ashram or meditation cave, our spiritual journeys were fortified.

In the next chapters I want to tell about some of those experiences that have significantly affected our relationship and our work. About the effects they had then, and later, in our lives.

Power Places of India

India is known by many as the mother lode of spiritual inspiration. It is pervaded by God-consciousness. No matter what the teaching—Hinduism, Buddhism, Christianity, Islam, Jainism, Bahai, Sikhism, Judaism—or sects of these, people in every class and all walks of life are reverent toward the Great Source, by all Its names. They honor It in their daily lives, not only at the temple, church or mosque, but in the mornings and evenings, over meals, before starting projects and while dying.

Everyone remembers the large exodus of young spiritual seekers to India in the 1960s and 1970s. Ram Das was one of those. He met his guru there, as did many others who were looking for spiritual nourishment and clear guidance for higher consciousness. I had wanted to visit India since I was drawn to Gandhi at age eighteen. He was the first teacher I encountered who taught the underlying unity of all religions,

Eastern and Western, and who welcomed followers of every one. But I had to wait until 1989, when I was invited to the holistic medical conference in Bangalore I mentioned in Chapter 17.

India was all I had imagined and more. I had never been any place where God-consciousness was so palpable. After the ashram that year we traveled around the country for another three weeks to visit one holy spot after another. We wanted to feel for ourselves some of the essential spiritual quality of India.

In Delhi we found a meditation center that had been established by Muktananda, Fritz' teacher. We found the humble shrine in a dilapidated section near the center of town. It took about ten minutes to see everything within it. As we started to leave, the keeper of the shrine, a soft-spoken Indian lady said,

"Would you like to see the cave?"

Fritz replied that we would. I asked him quietly if he knew what that was. He said he didn't. We followed the lady down narrow and fairly steep stairs into a basement-like room that was quite dark with only one dim light in the corner. Next to it hung a simple curtain.

"It's there," the lady gestured to the curtain. "Stay as long as you like." Then she went back up the stairs.

I looked at Fritz questioningly. He walked over to the curtain, pulled it back and exposed a big black hole in the wall behind it. The cave. It didn't look inviting but we went inside anyway.

We stood quietly, unable to distinguish anything in the dark except one flickering candle. Eventually we could make out a tattered picture of Muktananda. Gradually I began to feel tingling all over my body. It intensified until it almost felt like stinging bees. I took it as long as I could and then slipped through the curtain to the external room and sat down to meditate.

Fritz stayed longer in the cave as I waited in meditation outside.

"Did you feel that?" he asked, wide-eyed, as he joined me. "That was like high voltage electricity. I felt like I was with Muktananda again."

That charge was a testament to the longevity of spiritual presence in a place long after the teacher has departed. We were to meet this phenomenon many times in subsequent shrines and burial sites we visited.

Outside Delhi we went to Mahatma (meaning "Great Soul") Gandhi's tomb where his ashes are buried beneath a large marble square. People are allowed to walk up to it freely and a number of people were there, standing or sitting quietly. An eternal flame burns in the middle of the square.

As we walked up to the tomb a wave of emotion flowed over me in almost an overwhelming surge. There is no word for that emotion. It had appreciation-wonder-grief-awe-love all wrapped up together. I had to kneel at the tomb because I couldn't stop the tears that streamed down my face.

I remembered Gandhi's mighty leadership of all people—Hindus, Moslems, Christians, and untouchables—in the nonviolence method that eventually freed India from British rule. During all that great struggle he followed prayer and inner guidance at every step to lead his people in a seemingly impossible resistance that finally brought independence. I saw images of his tiny frame, clothed scantily in the Indian dhoti he wore (barely more than a large white sack around his waist), bent over his walking stick, smiling as he walked along. How he offered tea to the antagonistic Englishman, who came to demand that he stop the resistance. Before their meeting Gandhi offered the man a cup of tea, "because," he said cordially, "I know an Englishman needs his afternoon tea." I clearly remembered the day he was shot by a single Hindu who had walked straight up to him, seemingly in devotion. It was reported that as he fell he called out, "Ram (God)!"

Somehow what Gandhi represented for the world was imprinted there in the vibration surrounding his tomb. All I could do to pay homage to this great man, saint really, was to kneel there quietly, give thanks for him, and cry.

I felt a gentle tug at the shawl I was wearing. I looked up to see a young boy, looking at me with…what? Appreciation, comfort, understanding, questioning. His dark eyes looked deeply into mine. We exchanged a soul moment of great tenderness. He said, "You love Gandhiji."

"Yes," I answered, "very much. I appreciate so deeply what he did for this world."

He touched my hand ever so gently and nodded his understanding. He sat there beside me for a few minutes, both of us in silent gratefulness to Gandhi. Then he slipped away.

I thought how this great man, Gandhi, had been able to bring people of all faiths, nationalities, classes and ages together, just as that young Indian boy and I were united in spirit. And how his spirit lives on in the heart of India.

Just being at his tomb imparted some of that spirit to me.

We traveled to Varanasi (Benaras), known as the holiest city in India, and also the oldest city in the world, populated by hundreds of spiritual teachers, aspirants and enunciates. The city sits on the shores of the holy Ganges River, said to be the greatest source in the country of blessings and healings.

There on the banks of the river, surrounded by children and old people holding prayer beads out for sale, we watched dead bodies being burned on their funeral pyres. Members of the family of the dead person stayed, praying, chanting and stoking the fire, until the last bone had crumbled.

One morning just before sunrise we entered the river in a small canoe rowed by our guide. Candles, cupped by banana leaves, are floated out on the water at that time of night, creating a magical array of winking lights. Many canoes are floating among the lights, carrying devotees and tourists like us into sunrise prayers on the holiest of sites. Everyone is silent, or saying prayers and chanting almost inaudibly. It was an amazing and incongruous situation. On the other hand I knew the facts that the Ganges is one of the most polluted rivers in the world, one where people wash, defecate and even float their dead.

As we rowed along in the boat I looked out to one side to actually see a wrapped dead body floating near by. I didn't touch the water even though I heard and read many stories of people being healed from bathing in it and drinking it! This was an unsolvable mystery to me. But it didn't keep me from appreciating the awesome feeling of pure reverence for Something greater than themselves that radiated from so many praying people in those boats as the sun rose over the Ganges.

In contrast to Benaras we visited the ancient temple city of Khajuraho, once the proud expression of the Rajput dynasty that ruled in central India from the tenth to the twelfth centuries. At that time the finest artisans had constructed eighty-five temples, all celebrating the divine power that can sanctify sexual union. Now the city is deserted but remains as a holy and artistic sanctuary where twenty of the original temples still show the amazing creativity and reverence the people had for that holiest of acts that can happen between men and women in Divine union.

The temples and grounds are well tended now so that visitors may study this unusual form of worship. We walked among the temples, marveling at the intricate poses of lovemaking carved on the walls outside and within them. And we smiled at how our Puritan ancestors might have viewed these works of art.

Each day of that trip was like a meditation for us. Already full with Sai Baba's blessings, we were able to digest them more deeply as we went from one experience to another—great ornate temples tended by many lavishly-dressed priests, humble folk, shrines dedicated to the Great Mother by the side of the road, mosques thundering with the call to prayers—one dose of spiritual nourishment after another.

When we returned home I missed that richness of spirit that India embodies. And each time we traveled there again I had an instant lightening of spirit as soon as we entered the airport. If it were possible I would go back to India every year for that lightening even though Sai Baba has said that once you truly *get it* there's no need to ever return.

19

Assisi, Saints Alive

Saint Francis

Fritz and I had wanted to see Assisi, Italy ever since our dear friend Susan Lodi told us about the peaceful, spirit-filling time she spent there as an art student, and because its cathedrals house some of the finest medieval paintings in the world. We traveled there to experience the place for ourselves.

Assisi crowns the top of a small mountain that arises from the Umbrian valley of Soleto. As the taxi wound along the ascending slopes the driver proudly pointed out the church of San Damiano which Saint Francis had rebuilt as his first service to Christ and the giant Basilica of Saint Francis, visible throughout the valley below. It was erected in the Saint's memory and his tomb lies within it. We knew Assisi was the home of Saint Francis and Saint Clare but little else about the 12th century saints except the few references to them from history courses long forgotten, and the many well-known images and statues of Saint Francis with a flock of birds.

The "town," more like a cloistered village than anything resembling a twenty-first century town, looked like it has been molded with the mountain. Cobbled-stone streets wound between medieval rock buildings stacked one upon another.

The night we arrived we settled into a quaint hotel near the Basilica and read the guidebooks we had brought along to gain a glimpse of the area's history, art and the two famous saints.

We learned that Francis, born in Assisi in 1182, was the pampered son of a wealthy merchant. He had been called early to the renunciate's life when Christ, speaking to him through a simple crucifix, had commanded him to "restore my house, which is falling in ruins." At first Francis took the command literally and began to rebuild the humble church that housed the crucifix. Certainly the little church was falling down in ruins and sorely needed repair. But through the years it became clear to Francis that Christ had meant the body of the Catholic Church, which at that time had been riddled with corruption and indulgences.

Others, inspired by the gospel teachings of poverty and chastity, followed Francis. They eventually became the Franciscans who took vows of poverty, chastity and service to the poor. They brought a new spirit and example of reform into the church overall.

We also read that Saint Clare, born to a wealthy family in Assisi in 1193, had similarly been called by God as a young girl. She heard Francis preach and knew she had discovered her guide. She secretly left her home and appealed to him to accept her as a renunciate. Francis encouraged her to join a convent, which she did. Essentially he became her spiritual mentor from that time forward and she followed him exactly. He eventually charged her to establish an order of nuns, who became the Poor Ladies. Claire was to be their Mother Superior, even though she was much younger than most of them. Francis told her to write a Rule of Order for them which mirrored that of the Franciscans.

Both saints lived the vow of poverty and charity to the poor faithfully all their lives and both were canonized shortly after their deaths.

The next morning we quickly bypassed all the interesting shops along the narrow street to walk straight to the imposing, art-wealthy Basilica dedicated to Saint Francis. Its exterior walls tower out of the mountain like a great ship. We walked up to it slowly to admire the many turrets and ramparts, already feeling like medieval pilgrims. We entered the building respectfully, with a line of tourists. The interior walls are covered, ceiling to floor, with world famous frescos or paintings; the windows are sparkled with jewel-toned stain glass figures of

Jesus, the Saints and famous Pontiffs. The ceiling was frescoed by Giotto, some of his most famous productions.

In these days hundreds of tourists file through the various chapels and chambers, trying to be quiet as ordered by entry signs. They don't really succeed; a booming Priest's voice keeps repeating in a megaphone, "Silencio! Silencio." Everyone is looking up, at the art. Perhaps many don't see the narrow, cellar-like stairway going down into Saint Francis' tomb. Anyway, only a small wooden sign identifies it. We noticed it and agreed to come back after our art tour of the upper chamber.

By the time we descended the narrow stairs to the tomb we were ready for rest and quiet. We entered a simple but elegant dome-shaped room, shaped from quarried stone with a large crypt in the center. It was stark, after the Basilican splendor, but appealing. There was an austere feeling, more appropriate to the Saint himself, I thought. It was quiet and cool and dimly lit. There were several benches, similar to church pews, and we gratefully stopped there for awhile. It was restful to feel the finality of earthly life there with Saint Francis' body preserved in the center for all these centuries.

The simplicity of the place invited contemplation of the Saint and his legacy to the world. I was thinking how amazing it was that in a world dominated by the power of a corrupt church this one determined friar had exerted such a powerful force of reform. I marveled at how Francis had been able to establish a permanent rule and example of poverty into a church that collected and hoarded wealth. And his order is still strong and influential today.

But I wondered about the severity of the rule. Was it perhaps over zealous to ask the Brothers and Sisters to live without even the simplest comforts? Would such deprivation eventually work against itself by denying so many basic and natural human instincts, just as we see celibacy go awry in our time? Could that level of hardship eventually detract from spiritual devotion? Why did Saint Francis adopt such a severe code in the first place?

As I asked myself these questions I decided to put them to the Saint himself. Perhaps part of his spirit still looked out for his flock, just as Jesus had promised he would do. Maybe he could be contacted, especially right here near his tomb and the Franciscan center of the world.

Dear Saint Francis, why such a severe rule of order? I asked.

Then I heard his compassionate and clear response, as if he were speaking to his little sister:

> *In my time excesses, waste and overindulgence of all kinds were so deeply entrenched in the Church, while the poor went unfed, physically and spiritually. Only a stark imitation of Christ could break through it. God guided me to both preach and live poverty and service to demonstrate reform. If I lived now I might be guided differently.*

I was deeply touched by this clear explanation and felt that I understood the call to renunciation better than I had before. I sat with it gratefully and peacefully for some time that morning.

Saint Clare

After the experience with Saint Francis I wanted to learn more about Saint Clare. I had barely noticed the Basilica of Saint Clare, quite a modest church, as we walked toward the much grander Basilica of Saint Francis that morning.

On the way back through the village we again passed the many shops filled with religious art and souvenirs and cafes where tourists sat for afternoon refreshments under sun-shielding umbrellas. Just before the second entrance gate to the village, set off to one side, we located the simple church. There were far fewer visitors inside it than at the Basilica and it was sparse in comparison. A short walk and quick look around revealed one plain altar and all of its few paintings. The most famous one was the simple medieval rendering of Christ on the cross, said to be the very same Christ that commanded Francis to "rebuild my church." We stood in front of it for awhile, trying to imagine how it had been for Francis to see that mouth moving and hear its voice.

It was easy to spot a sign, "Saint Clare's tomb," and the small stairway leading down beneath the church. I went straight to it.

The tomb was much smaller and even less adorned than that of Saint Francis. A narrow walkway led directly to a glass-fronted chamber. Behind the glass lay a simulated figure of Saint Clare. She was placed on a funeral platform, dressed in the traditional Franciscan brown robe, a crown of flowers on her head with her hands clasped over her chest. Candles and fresh flowers surrounded her so that even in the late afternoon darkness of the tomb she was clearly visible. The wax-like face was lifelike, sculpted into a serene expression, but obviously a manikin. I remembered turning away from such displays in the past but this place pulled me into it.

A vibratory presence captured me, a great peaceful balm surrounding the chamber. It soothed my spirit and rested my travel-tired body. I felt deeply comforted all of a sudden. It was cool in the white, marble-walled crypt and peaceful, as it had been with Saint Francis. Yet there was also a slightly different quality here that I wanted to explore. I wanted to sit right down in that presence and stay there for a long time.

But visitors filed past the glass case, peering in at the figure for a few moments and then moved along to make space for others. I couldn't linger there without holding up the line. I looked for a corner to sit, even stand, near the tomb, but there was no space. Still touched by the experience with Saint Francis and wanting to savor this tomb more fully, I decided to come back the next day, hopefully before the tourist rush. The longing to fill up with Saint Clare's presence was not yet satisfied. A spiritual hunger still lingered.

On the way back to our hotel I bought the only three "accounts" of Saint Clare I could find in the shops. There are no definitive biographies of her because the only remaining details of her 12th century life will fill three pages. The books I read were heavily padded with preaching doctrine, much of which the nun Clare may never have even thought, much less taught. But I was especially attracted by the title of one: *Clare of Assisi: Light for the Way.**

That night I read the small books about Saint Clare, to learn more than I had read already. Though factual details were meager I learned that her noble-born mother, Ortulana, was known as a pious woman who prayed frequently. As labor for her first born began Ortulana was afraid. She ran to the church, knelt before the crucifix and fervently prayed to God for help. While on her knees she distinctly heard

"Do not be afraid, woman, for you will give birth in safety to a light which will give light more clearly than light itself." Consequently the baby girl was named Clare, for light."[12]

Adored as a prayerful child by all who knew her, Clare's soul was called by God "in a very precise and personal way" (not exactly known by her biographers) by the time she was sixteen. When she heard about the preaching friar Francis, who had given up all his noble riches to serve Christ alone, in poverty, and when she actually heard him preach, she sought his counsel and support to devote her own life in the same way.

"The Father Francis encouraged her to despise the world, showing her by his living speech how dry the hope of the world was and how deceptive its beauty," says *The Legend of Saint Clare.**

> "'So she ran away from her family to follow the rule of Saint Francis when she was only eighteen years old, "fleeing from the clamor of the world, she went down to the church in the

1. *Clare of Assisi: Light for the Way.* Compiled by a group of Poor Clares of France, Belgium and Italy. France: Editions du Signe, 1991.
2. Lainiati, Sr. C. A.. *Saint Clare of Assisi.* Santa Maria: Edizioni Porziuncola, 1994.

> field and (received) the sacred tonsure from blessed Francis himself,' reported the Canonization examiners."

Within a short time other women followed her and they became the Poor Clares. Like the Franciscan Order, the order required a commitment to poverty, chastity, charity and service to Christ alone. Poor Clares was finally blessed as an Order of the Church by the Pope on Clare's deathbed.

The book told of Clare's ascetic life of prayer, fasting and charity and how she cared for her sisters as their Mother, even though many were much older than her. One was her own mother.

The relationship between Clare and Francis has been an alluring mystery since they lived. The nun biographers claim that Clare's contribution to the Franciscan revolution had been neglected. As they said:

> "Clare then is not simply a replica of Francis male Franciscan charisma; hers is not Franciscanism in the feminine mode, as has been written. Her contribution is, rather an original and indispensable one, the feminine pole of the Franciscan…For a long time eclipsed by the light of Francis, she deserves to be considered in her own right."
>
> Ibid., p. 2

> "In the fullest meaning of the word she was truly his sister Light…When everything seemed to be crashing down around Francis, she was the living example of fidelity to his primitive ideal, to pure gospel simplicity." Ibid., 29.

It is known that Francis called for her prayers to guide him when he couldn't discern whether God wanted him to pray in isolation or preach. And that he asked to be taken to her when he was dying. Long after his death she continued his mission, through prayer and example within the enclosed convent.

The reports for Clare's canonization, only three years after her death, told of the many miracles she performed—healings of serious maladies, including insanity, deafness, dropsy, fevers and restoration of the voices of two sisters who had lost them. She was even reported to cause a small piece of bread to multiply into 50 pieces to feed the sisters. She accomplished these miracles by making the sign of the cross over the patients. Once she held off a band of soldiers who were threatening to overrun all of Assisi, by walking out to meet them, showing the cross. They retreated.

The same Canonization papers testified that at her death the Sisters saw a band of angels arrive to accompany Clare to heaven.

I went into peaceful sleep that night with a better appreciation of Clare's legacy.

The next morning I re-entered the Church of Saint Clare just after sunrise. The village walkways were still fresh after being washed down. Very few people yet walked about. The sun sparkled on the outer marble walls of the church. As I walked inside it was almost empty. I went quickly down the stairs to the tomb, relieved to see no one there yet. Immediately I felt the same pervasive serenity of the day before.

Already the candles had been lit within the glass chamber, or were they kept in perpetual burning? Anyway, it wasn't the manikin I wanted to study but this wondrous feeling of peace and comfort. I looked around for a place to meditate. A second tiny stairwell leading back up to the church I hadn't noticed before was situated quite close to the figure of Saint Clare. It was roped off with a small sign, "no admittance," but I could sit on the very bottom step without disturbing the rope or sign. I sat down there, closed my eyes and surrendered to the presence I had met before.

A Great Silence gradually opened up. It settled around me like a gentle electric cloud and then started pulling me down, as if into a deep well. I let go and descended into it.

How to describe the infinite peace and nourishment that came up to meet me? Saint Clare suffused me. I sank deeper and deeper into her Presence. I could feel her utter devotion to the Divine, her absolute abandon to It and the limitless Grace that It offered. The world disappeared. All worry, fatigue and distraction fell away. There was only That and its eternal peace. I felt my body filling up with It, a gentle nourishing mist, as I grew lighter and lighter.

I rested there, filling up with "the peace that passeth all understanding."

"Yes," said Saint Clare, "This is what I live from, this fathomless and fertile Silence. This is the source of my strength and guidance. All is possible here." Then she smiled and blessed me.

I startled, as if waking from a dream. My eyes flew open. There was the figure of Saint Clare before my eyes, inert and lifeless as before, a simple effigy of the holy body it replicated. But there was no doubt in my mind that I had felt and heard the live presence of Saint Clare. I had met her directly and I would take her blessing with me forever. It felt like we knew each other, that we loved each other. I knew she had given me an experience of that Great Silence that could never be taken away and that it would continue to instruct me.

How is this possible you might ask. I have no idea. Is it measurable? Probably not, at least with the instruments for detecting fields of energy that we now possess. Was it my imagination? No. My fantasies are short lived, fleeting as the mind's endless dance, whereas this experience was much bigger than mind. It filled my body, my heart, the soul itself, with a palpable assurance of the Silence, the Source that sustains me. It transcended teachings; it was beyond the scriptures and dogmas of any religion, yet consistent with them. It lasted through the day, and through that trip. I can still touch into It right now as I write this. I get a warm, accepted, welcoming feeling.

I wanted to stay in Assisi for a month and commune with Saint Clare but we had to meet a train that very day. Anyway, I realized, I carry the presence of Saint Clare within me. We are intimates now. She and Francis are the teachers who demonstrated to me that Saints still live.

20

Back to Indonesia

I have already told how I enjoyed a continuous nourishment of spirit at Bapak's home in Indonesia before I ever visited India and Assisi. Now I want to describe a life-altering experience when I stayed there a second time many years later. Both Indonesian trips were like a furlough in heaven. And both profoundly affected my life for years to come. The second experience happened through a prayer and blessing.

After I finished graduate school my four children presented me with a graduation gift of a full month in Indonesia. I will always cherish their insightful generosity, an example of how soul allies can assist our fundamental path.

On that second stay I arrived exhausted and in heartache from a broken relationship. Again Bapak's home provided the same peaceful, electric field I had known before, a heaven space that nourished my soul and also allowed my body, mind and heart to gradually integrate and heal in rest.

I was assigned a tiny, charming room in a corner of the compound, far from kitchen or street noise. It was paradise for my beleaguered body. For over a week I just walked around the quiet compound, feeling Bapak's spiritual presence and enjoying the beauty of tropical flowers and birds. I stayed quiet, soaked in that field and let it do its work.

Gradually I began to go sane again. There were no tasks for an exhausted intellect and my body gratefully relaxed into health. The entire time was filled with deep soul healing and nourishment. In fact, it filled my spiritual bank account for several years and still nourishes me in its memory.

I said the prayer toward the end of the stay. It was an indelible moment. It happened this way: I was lying on my cot under a mosquito net, musing about painful relationships in which I had grasped repeatedly, and unsuccessfully, for love. I always had the *idea* that love would include a whole union-of body, mind, heart and soul-and that this union would include a mutual agreement to support all of those factors in both people. But I had become disillusioned about love through relationships filled with self-interest and hidden agendas.

Lying under the mosquito net I was realizing all the energy and attention I had devoted to those relationships and thinking I couldn't endure any more romantic love. Without forethought I said aloud, "Dear God, let me finish with these painful distractions. If (and this was a big if, with lots of skepticism) there is a soul mate somewhere on this planet please bring him to me. Otherwise I'd rather be alone."

As I left Indonesia that year I had never felt freer, happier or more complete within myself. When I returned to the U.S. people said I looked transformed, healthy and fifteen years younger.

I forgot about the prayer.

But exactly one month after I returned home, with no forewarning, a soul-illuminating moment happened that brought a soul mate directly in front of me.

That trip initiated the next phase of my life, during which my life work would take full shape and a soul relationship would eventually evolve that has far outdistanced anything I ever imagined about love. But as I've said, that's another book.

21

Soul Friends

Have you ever met someone you felt you knew instantly? Has anyone ever said to you, "I don't think we've met before but I feel like I know you?" Now and then a potential soul friend appears in this way, someone who might become an invaluable ally in your journey toward soul actualization.

For example, we may feel an inexplicable connection with someone. They seem to recognize us at a deep level. The vibrational resonance alone can be like a dose of lightning. It ignites the moment, as if a match had been lit to show up the possibilities of who we are, beneath the presentation of our personalities. For awhile—minutes, weeks or months—we feel seen and empowered at an essential level, and we are renewed.

In fact, a soul connection can even feel like "falling in love at first sight." The ecstatic state of oneness that comes over us in romantic love can feel like meeting a soul mate and for awhile it allows us to rise above all attachments to our conditioning and prejudices. Finally we have met "the one" for us. For a short time the beloved seems ideal, without blemish or obstacle to our devotion. We are temporarily blind to all the foibles that would ordinarily bother us.

But usually within a short period romantic love fades because it is composed mostly of projections and idealizations from both personalities. After the honeymoon they rear their troublesome heads. The character and pitfalls of romantic love have been extensively described in psychology; helpful books have been written about it. This kind of love is almost always conditional and rarely grounded in a commitment to each other's souls. In fact, many relationships never have a soul connection, even when they are as close as family, marriage, or friendship. We can love a person, even live with them for a lifetime, without ever knowing them, or being known by them, at a soul level.

Soul connections are quite different from romantic love. They aren't about chemistry, common interests, backgrounds, gender or age. They could just as well happen with someone thirty years older or younger, of another color, from another culture, or even another language. Although they don't happen every day most of us experience significant soul connections in our lives.

They aren't always positive either. Now and then we have a very strong pull to someone who seems inappropriate or unavailable to us, perhaps even unattractive. Yet we continue to feel drawn toward them. Past karmas can cause this electricity; it may signal some unfinished soul business that wants completion.

Some soul connections are reasonable, as with friends, family, students or teachers. Others are very strange; for example with a passing stranger. But the light they shine on us is valuable because soul meetings are always significant, no matter how temporary or ephemeral. Whenever souls meet, even seemingly for the "first time," they feel they somehow know each other already. They fall into rapport quickly whether they talk or not. They pick up where they left off. The shared soul resonance is based on a spiritual intimacy that evolved through a long history of love, trust, understanding and overcoming, perhaps through many lifetimes.

Even the "negative" ones provide significant teachings. They challenged us to awaken, or remember, for a few moments or longer. They remind us that human beings can actually connect at the most essential level.

When an initial soul connection matures naturally over time it can develop into a true soul friendship. It may evolve into an abiding love that goes beneath the conditioning of the world. As Laura, a very important soul friend, once said, "A soul friend loves you to the core." Soul friendship is based on evolution and destiny rather than desires of either personality; it accepts the true nature of both persons rather than demand or expect the other to fit the standard of what is proper or appropriate in the culture. It transcends these outer conditions.

Soul friends are lifetime treasures. They help us remember and empower our true selves because we understand each other at levels that would be meaningless to many. Soul friends stand together through everything—distance, illness, changing partnerships or altered interests because they are deeply committed to their own, and the other's, soul actualization.

I have been blessed with major adult soul friends in this life, including my children, my husband Fritz, my Process Partner Laura and others. They are precious to me, their value beyond measure. They bring meaning, love, creativity and joy to my life. We have lighted each other's paths through the thickets of life and helped each other remember what we're here for. For me, one soul ally is worth a hundred social friends.

In another book I hope to tell what I've learned about recognizing and cultivating adult soul relationships. But in this book I want to focus on the very special function of childhood soul friends because they give us an early model of soul friendship that can instruct us for life. They also relate directly to our soul destiny design.

Childhood Soul Friends

Childhood soul friends don't require maturity or cultivation; they are free gifts of spirit who help us keep the essence of our own beings alive. They are dependable allies who remind us of our soul track. Whether we recognized them or not at the time, they lit up our destiny design and provided lifetime spiritual strength.

In Soul Work classes I emphasize the importance of childhood soul friends because they light up our souls early. They also ameliorate the inevitable traumas of childhood. Whereas our parents and their relationship set the pattern for our adult personality relationships, childhood soul friends demonstrate the power and potential of soul relationships.

I ask students to review their early lives to find anyone who truly affirmed their souls, anyone who provided splashes of light amid the trials of growing up. Students always find one or more of these soul friends and they are amazed when they realize how deeply influenced they were by them. Even when these encounters were short-lived, just a few days or hours, they had a lifelong impact.

Often this review yields a broader perspective on the whole life. An age of therapy has conditioned us to think of ourselves as victims of childhood. This exercise helps students see that even in the midst of suffering, abuse or chaos they had been spiritually supported by someone who recognized and loved them for who they are. Sometimes it takes only a small amount of attention, love or encouragement to counteract painful things. One student said that every time she does a life review her wounds of the past diminish.

Two childhood soul friends helped me realize the worth of my own self and gave me strength to pursue my unique soul journey later on. I have often thought that if they hadn't been in my life very early I might not have found my way.

Grandma was the first. She recognized something in me from the very beginning. I was told that she took me in her arms from the first moments after my birth and she was a protector to me for the rest of her life. While I was little she always called me "my little girl."

When I was growing up on the desert cattle ranch, I lived in union with nature, in tune with the Tao. I often slept under the stars. Sun, moon, stars, mountains, rocks, cactus—all these created my grand playhouse. Little ground creatures like prairie dogs or quail and bellowing cows coming in to water in the evening were my friends. I never felt lonely in that world. It was endlessly interesting, even comforting, especially when I left the house to get away from grief.

I learned about loneliness in human company. Whenever I was around people, including my family, I felt like an alien, as if I didn't really belong. I was not abused nor unloved by my family. Mother and my stepfather were good people who did the very best they could. Still, I just never felt quite part of the family, somehow there was a miss-match. Was I adopted I wondered? I always felt myself standing outside, watching from an unconnected distance.

But when Grandma came to visit, this feeling of being an alien disappeared. There was no distance between us. We were united beyond words, interests, history or age. When Grandma was present there was absolute safety, ease, unusual knowing and peace within myself. She loved me unconditionally, with all her heart and soul. Her love was fierce and protective and it never wavered. Each memory I have of being with Grandma is luminous, loving and creative. There was never anything *wrong* with me when I was with her, even when I was sick. Memories of her love empower and renew self-trust even now.

For example, I spent a winter with her and my step-grandfather, Lefty, as I recovered from a broken arm. The most important thing about being with them was the love and respect we shared. That short time was the highlight of my childhood; it laid the most important foundations for all that became meaningful to me later on.

I savored many new experiences during that winter. Grandma and Lefty's living conditions and style were very different from anything I knew. Their tiny apartment in Glendale, California, was a sharp contrast to the wide-open desert I was used to. There was very little money; the Great Depression was still going on. We literally saved pennies to buy ice cream once a week. But I never felt poor. Rather, I felt perfectly satisfied and interested in everything.

During the day Lefty worked while Grandma and I stayed home to *keep house*, which we did together like two adults. She taught me concrete skills, like order, cleanliness, and sewing. But her interests and instruction also went far beyond house keeping. We rode the streetcar, went to church, which I had never known on the ranch, and visited museums.

Grandma was a mature and capable woman who had overcome many obstacles, such as a year-long illness, a divorce and constant poverty. Her difficulties had only made her stronger, more patient and broad-minded. She was a student of life at many levels, an astute observer of people's behavior, well read and interested in world events. We talked on equal terms about the things on my mind or hers. She was attentive to my questions, ideas and observations, as if I were a peer. She always treated me with respect and gentle care.

Grandma also encouraged my creative explorations. When I built a "playhouse/office" behind the couch, for privacy and secrecy, she respected my space and saved little notepads for me to keep there for my own. She never questioned whether my child's strategies were consistent with those of the "real" world. Independent discovery was fine with her.

I have felt Grandma's arms around me through all this life, and after her death. She was, and is, a loving, protective and wise presence. In her nineties she hand-sewed a quilt for me, in the style she had learned as a child in the 1890s. Her fingers were swollen with arthritis but she persisted with that quilt until it was finished. Then she sent it to me. Her acceptance, love, and respect are sewn into it. To this day I use that quilt as a healing cover for clients, or myself when they are really stressed. One of them often called for it when she was feeling the need for extra strength.

I always knew Grandma was on my side, in the best way. Long after childhood when I was a young woman struggling financially with four children she sent me an occasional hundred dollars from her social security pension. Later, when I was discovering soul psychology, I received a letter from Grandma with a small snapshot picture of me, one I don't remember ever seeing. I was about five months old, sitting on a pallet in the yard of our cattle ranch. Vast space spread out behind and all around me. As I looked at the picture I could see the clear unadulterated soul of that child. She is meditating, entirely focused on connecting with the Universe around her, in attunement with It and herself. The picture sits on our bureau, next to Fritz' amazingly similar baby picture, to remind us of who we are and what we're really doing here on earth.

Because of that picture I ask students in Soul Work and Inner Child Healing classes to find the earliest possible picture of themselves and bring it to class. As we look at these children together we can see, without exception, the true nature of each particular person, shining out without inhibition. We see their unique beauty, love and almost always joy, as they arrived fresh to life with such promise.

Find your earliest baby picture and study it carefully. Look beyond setting and clothes into your soul. You will be amazed at what you discover. Then believe it!

Grandma died at age 103. During her later years I once talked about her with Arny Mindell, marveling about her loyalty to me and her longevity. He said she was a healer, holding onto life as long as she could, to maintain her presence here for those she loved, to help and heal us. That thought seemed just right.

When I saw her for the last time she was well over 100, confined to bed in a nursing home. But her spirit was as potent as ever. She looked straight into my eyes, took my hand and said,

"Honey, I will know you anyplace."

I knew it was her way of telling me that even when she died we would still be together in some way. And so we are.

She still looks at me everyday now from the beautiful picture of her at ninety which sits on my altar. Her eyes penetrate to my core, affirming her love. I often speak back to her, "Grandma, I love you so much. Thank you for everything."

A surrogate grandfather, Bill Reynolds, was my other childhood soul supporter. It took me a long time to truly comprehend the impact Bill had on my life. To my child's mind he was just safe and fun. In my normal child's life of restriction and constriction he provided spaces and hours of freedom, exploration, and affirmation of the wonder of life. Much later on I became aware of what a saving angel he was to me, and still is. From the time I can remember Bill accepted and unconditionally loved me as the soul that I am.

Bill was a mountain prospector of precious metals. He became attached to our family through a mine deal with grandfather when my mother was still a child. Bill remained part of us, visiting between prospecting trips, until his death.

He was tall and very handsome, elegant even, a little like the Barrymore movie idols. Grandma said his curly hair had once been jet black but by the time I knew him it was snow white. In the mountains he wore rough prospector clothes, big lace-up boots, and a prospector's hat that covered his white curls. A mule carried his supplies. In town he dressed like a city gentleman, jacket, tasteful tie, expensive shoes, no hat, his white hair cut and combed perfectly. He drove a big Buick, stayed in the fanciest hotel in Phoenix and took me shopping at the very best stores.

Bill had traveled all over the western frontier, even Alaska, prospecting for gold and other metals. He had found, and sold, several valuable mines for healthy sums so he was financially independent.

For me Bill was a walking education. He was intelligent, well read and had known all kinds of people. He talked about wide and varied subjects intelligently. And even though he was at least fifty years older than I was, he communicated with me like an equal, just as Grandma did. He told me about science, geography and history and was the first to introduce me to a world perspective. Although he had no use for religion he was adamant about respecting the great Creative Intelligence, as he called it, behind everything. His mind was free. Somehow he had broken out of the cocoon of conditioning; I never heard a party line, on any subject, from Bill. He was the first liberated person I ever knew. Now I realize he was a very old soul who saw beyond the propaganda and fads of the time into the long curves of history.

When I was seven I was boarded out to family friends in town for the school term. It was a dark and painful time. I was insecure, away from my parents and in the care of another very different mother. School was even worse. I couldn't relate to others in my class. Since I had been raised entirely by adults, my classmates seemed like foolish children, playing silly games. They regarded me as peculiar too, not a welcome playmate. So at home and in school I felt deserted and lonely.

Bill was my rescuer. Often, without announcement, I would see his big Buick pull up along the sidewalk at school. Suddenly my world would light up like a thousand headlights. My heart lifted out of its loneliness. I ran to the car, laughing, and jumped in. Then Bill and I were off for the day.[1] That would be a day of freedom and happiness.

Our outings always began at the "ten-cent store," my favorite, full of toys, crayons, colored pencils, bright papers and gadgets. I loved it so much that Bill once said he would buy me the whole store when he sold his next mine. We browsed the aisles, putting treasures in my basket for at least an hour until we had it full with toys, paints and books. Then to the soda fountain where I could order anything I wanted, usually a chocolate sundae.

The next stop was the finest children's dress department in the most elegant store in town. Bill sat on a lounge chair while our favorite saleswoman showed me the latest dress styles. She and I would travel back and forth, from dress rack to dressing room, many times. Between each trip I came out to model a new favorite for Bill to admire. He looked at every one attentively, never seeming to tire of this little girl's fancies. When we finished that stop we carried large bags of our latest purchases. Usually I was wearing one of them. I felt like a princess.

---

1. In this time such a relationship might not be allowed, and this act would elicit strong objection, maybe even legal action and jail. "Older man drives off with little girl." Forbidden. It was a different era entirely, when it was uncommon for children to be abducted, abused or murdered.

Then back to Bill's elegant hotel room for plays I improvised on the spot. I performed all the characters, each one in a different new dress and shoes. Bill laughed and clapped, interested in each skit as if it were premiering in a real theater. He encouraged me by asking questions about the character or the setting. If he tired of these childish creations he never showed it. From his free spirit he was able to encourage my child curiosity and give me the freedom to know my own creativity. That was a great gift at a crucial stage of development when imagination and inventiveness can easily be stifled. To this day I owe part of my creativity to Bill.

When mother reprimanded or punished me in his presence Bill always said urgently,

"Don't break her spirit!"

I have thought of this phrase many times in life when things got really tough. It gave me the strength to keep my spirit from being broken.

When we were hungry after shopping we went to the finest restaurant where again, I could order anything I wanted, always some luscious and ample specialty, so different from the macaroni and beans we ate everyday at home. The linen napkins, cut glass and proper silver kept reminding me of abundance and elegance.

When it was time to go home, I put it off as long as possible with one excuse or another. Only the big bags of treasures I carried with me made it possible to say goodbye to Bill.

Those days with Bill, as princess-for-a-day, have instructed me all my life. They were paradise escapes from an otherwise drab and lonely existence. In an environment of poverty he offered an experience of abundance and a feeling that I deserved the best. Bill believed in my creativity and nobility; and he helped me to keep finding them within myself. These moments gave me formative experiences of truly being cared for and recognized for myself. They affirmed my soul.

Recently a relative sent me a small photograph of our family when I was about seven years old. Bill was there, with his hand on my shoulder. Just looking at his face lifted my spirits. The wonderful soul nourishment of our times together flooded back through me. I put the picture on my altar where I see Bill everyday now, still touching my shoulder.

Grandma and Bill continually reinforced that I was a unique, valuable and lovable person, just as I was. With everyone else in my life I learned that I needed to earn love, to meet external requirements in order to receive approval. But Bill and Grandma encouraged me to believe in my own experience and freely explore my creative talents. They paid attention to me as if I was worth paying attention to.

They also taught me the most important basic values and skills of life: love for one another, honesty, creativity, respect of self and others, cleanliness, order, independent thinking, a world perspective that included caring for all peoples, and a true respect for the Greater Order of the Universe. They both lived their values more than taught them, and I could fully absorb them at that early age, before any resistances to authority had set in. Of course I also received similar instruction from a good mother and stepfather and teachers later. But these soul friends imparted their gifts to me so deeply because they came with unconditional love and respect for who I am. Therefore I absorbed Grandma and Bill's messages more clearly than from any subsequent schools or books.

Grandma and Bill were my first soul allies. They modeled that relationship for the years to come; from their examples I knew what a soul relationship felt like. The seeds they sewed for me in childhood flowered in adulthood for their teachings drew an indelible template for the precious soul relationships that would develop later in life.

Eventually I met that quality again in adulthood when my children were born. Then it happened with certain special students. And when I met Laura and Fritz it flowered into full bloom. Just recently I experienced soul recognition and trust with a group of people. In late 2004 four of us sat together at dinner one evening. I suddenly realized that through our work together we had become a circle of soul friends. There was deep recognition and love between us and complete acceptance and support for each other and our visions. In just two hours we were able to lay out several years of future work. We named our visions, set them into the Universal flow and sealed them with out love. It felt like we had coalesced into a mighty force for making a difference.

I look forward to the time when soul friends are greatly valued and awakened soul groups will become commonplace.

22

Rafael and Sound Healing

Magical events can call lightning, and enlightenment, directly to us. So it was in our meeting with Rafael.

Fritz and I were sitting at dinner with our group in Rio Caliente, Mexico, a wilderness retreat spa outside Guadalajara.

"Did you hear it?" the woman sitting next to me asked with eyes wide.

"What?"

"Look! He's right over there."

I turned around to see a tall young man in a traditional Mexican peasant's dress—white loose muslin trousers with a poncho that hung to his knees. He stood over a table of guests who all looked up at him with a startled stare. His dark eyes flashed as he talked and gestured to them in sweeping strokes. He laughed and so did everybody else. His black hair, almost shoulder length on a long neck, waved gracefully around his face. He looked Indian—Aztec or Mayan.

These were not actually my first impressions of the man. Rather it was the feel of a current that shot out of him, irradiating everyone at the table. He was electrifying the other side of the room. Everyone there had put down forks to watch him. Spellbound, I stared at him.

There was hardly time to register these impressions before he picked up a huge tube, about five feet long, put his mouth to it and blew out a sound that I have never heard before. It was deeply earthy and at the same time somehow transcendent.

The room went quiet, all attention commanded by this eerie sound and its pulsating vibration that penetrated the entire room. He blew several more blasts, like a calling. Then he lifted the great horn and started moving it around the room.

We all watched, transfixed, as he pointed the wide round end of the instrument directly into the chest of a seated diner. He held the 12-inch circumference of the end of the horn directly over her heart. Then he blew the booming sound directly into it. Her eyes closed and her expression changed. A peaceful, settling in look came over her face.

"Who is he?" I whispered to the person next to me.

She didn't answer. All her attention was riveted to the player as he moved to another guest's chest. The sound waved forth again and again and I saw faces change. There were expressions of eager anticipation, fear, or wonder. Eating and talking had stopped. Around he went to each person at the table, sounding into their chests. Within a short time he had circulated throughout the dining room and "treated" almost everyone there. The effects were amazing.

As we watched, by now entirely captivated by this strange performance at the dinner table, I saw someone say something to the player and gesture in my direction. He looked over at me, nodded and smiled.

I involuntarily clutched the chair as I watched him moving toward me, sounding that gigantic horn repeatedly. I guessed that the woman had told him I was one of the group leaders. I felt like moving away but at the same time was fascinated with the sound, wanting to experience it directly. He came to within a few feet of my chair and then lifted the end of the horn straight into my chest. As I felt the first undulating waves of the sound penetrate my chest I simply opened my heart and ears to receive them. I closed my eyes.

My chest started to tingle, then pulsate in a gentle but powerful way. It felt like the sound was delicately feeding every part of me—skin, muscles, heart itself. And even more than my body. I was floating in a sea of vibration that seemed both ancient and immediately present. My mind clicked off. I simply accepted this experience as a gift that I could analyze later.

When he lowered the great tube from my chest the vibration didn't stop. It still felt like thousands of miniscule bees buzzing around under my clothes. The young man looked into my eyes, smiled and nodded.

Then he turned to Fritz.

"Please, *hermano* (brother), come over here," he said as he dragged a chair close to the fireplace. I was startled to hear him speak after the huge sound of the digeredoo. I was also amazed that he spoke clear English, with a musical Latin accent, because he looked like he had come straight out of the hills of this Indian land, uninfluenced by the Spanish Conquistadors or American tourists.

Fritz got up and sat in the chair by the fireplace. I could see by his expression that he too was transfixed by what he saw and heard.

The young man knelt down, straight in front of Fritz; his head bowed to the floor. It looked like he was saying a prayer but I heard no sound. I wondered if he recognized Fritz. Then he lifted a primitive rattle and started shaking it close to Fritz' body. The raspy sound was demanding. He started chanting in a style I recognized as Indian. It was a beautiful intonement, low and guttural, then rising up high and entreating and back again to soft low sounds.

The chanting went on for some time in this manner. Fritz had closed his eyes and looked very peaceful. There was a reverent feeling about the chant. When it came to an end the young man stayed there, silent, in front of Fritz for several minutes, head still bowed. I wondered what this meant. The entire dining room was still, watching.

He rose finally and took up the digeredoo. He blew several low resounding bursts into the floor and then lifted the horn above his head. He blew a series of sounds, as if calling something forth again, and then he brought out the rattle and started a heartbeat rhythm with it, hitting the side of the digeredoo. He moved closer and focused the sound into Fritz' heart as he had done with the rest of us. Fritz' eyes were still closed but he lifted his chest into the sound as it went on for a number of tones.

Now the young man lifted the horn up, above Fritz' head, and started blowing a ring of sounds around his whole body. He moved to Fritz' back and blew behind his chest. Then he sent several powerful blasts directly into the base of Fritz' spine, at the root chakra.

This riveted my attention. I tried to see what was going on. Fritz has a very clear body; his energy is full and balanced and his tissues are free from the scars of personal history. A rare occurrence. Fritz had said to me that the root chakra was the one area of his body still not completely free. Could this young man somehow sense that? I almost held my breath as I watched the sound bombarding Fritz.

When it was over Fritz sat quietly for several minutes, absorbing the experience, respecting what had been given. He looked up at the young man with appreciation and said something. The young man smiled broadly and reached down to hug Fritz who returned the embrace.

Afterwards we were formally introduced to Rafael Bejarano. He shook hands and then immediately embraced us, in a familiar, but not offensive, way.

"I'm so happy to see you!" he said, as if he were greeting us again after a long separation. I felt comfortable with him from the start, clearly a soul connection. He felt like a brother, or a companion, even though he could easily have been a grandson.

We talked with him easily despite the resumption of dinner eating and conversation. He showed Fritz the big hollow end of the digeredoo.

"See," he said, "you can look all the way through it, nothing but empty space in there." Then he laughed.

In that moment I noticed his hands. I have never seen hands like that—how to describe them? Strong, sculptured. Long thin fingers beautifully proportioned on firm sensitive palms. The hands of an artist, or a healer, I thought.

Our class was starting within a few minutes in another building. I was surprised when Fritz asked Rafael if he ever received bodywork.

"Not enough," he laughed. "Sometimes I get tight here," he rubbed the top of his shoulders. "These babies are heavy," he pointed to the two digeredoos he was carrying.

"Well, would you like to receive a Zero Balancing session?" Fritz asked. I felt happy about Fritz' offer, I knew that Rafael would become part of our evening session then.

When Fritz, Rafael and I arrived at the classroom our group was already assembled in a big circle around the room. Fritz explained that he wanted to return the favor we had all received in the dining room by giving Rafael a Zero Balancing then and there.

Several whispered "yes!" and others around the room nodded their heads and smiled.

Fritz put a massage table in the middle of the circle and invited Rafael to sit on it. Rafael removed his poncho, sandals, belt and jewelry—he wore several magical-looking objects around his neck—as if he knew exactly what to do. Then he sat easily on the table. I thought how confident he must be with himself to receive a session in front of a whole room full of people he didn't know.

Fritz asked, "How can I serve you, Rafael? What would you like from this session?"

Rafael was quiet for a few moments as if seriously investigating what he really wanted. Normally people ask for alleviation of body pain, or perhaps release of stress, maybe even clarity about a relationship. Rafael's request was startling.

"It's very hard to explain," he began. "It probably sounds crazy but I'm trying to translate this energy I know," he gestured above and all around his body, "into sounds that can heal peoples' hearts and bring peace to this world."

There was a palpable hush as we all took that in.

"Especially the children," he said "and not only the little children but the hurt children inside all of us."

This touched me deeply because over half of my therapeutic practice has been healing wounded inner children. I've so often imagined what the world would be like if there were not so many buried hurts from childhood within all of us. Surely we would treat each other more kindly, be less judgmental and less prone to hurting others. Certainly we would be happier.

"I want to be freer to express myself in my work. So however you can strengthen me for this job I'd be grateful," Rafael concluded as he looked trustingly at Fritz.

Then he lay on the table and Fritz began his own magical healing through the Zero Balancing. I saw Rafael's body relax completely into Fritz' hands. Several times he took deep releasing breaths, sure signs that the session was reaching him at a core level.

The rest of us sat completely quiet, admiring Fritz' masterful moves, watching Rafael's open acceptance of the bodywork, but also opening ourselves to the intention in the room. Two thoughts arose in my mind: this session has opened all of us and tomorrow, after Rafael's sound healing and this Zero Balancing, we will surely express ourselves more fully.

When Fritz finished the Zero Balancing he asked Rafael to stand down from the table and walk back and forth across the room a couple of times. When he walked Rafael looked taller. He walked with the grace of a dancer and the freedom of a child.

He came back to the table to face Fritz.

"Now," said Fritz, "walk into your future."

There was an energetic shift in the room, a stop in time.

Rafael turned around and stood perfectly still for a few moments, looking into the distance ahead of him. Then he took several steps in that direction, deliberate, careful steps, as his feet seemed to barely touch the floor. He stopped, still looking ahead, as if studying something only he could see. Then after a long pause he moved again, this time with easeful confidence. His arms swung ever so slightly at his side, his head balanced perfectly but freely on his long neck.

He turned and walked back to Fritz.

"Thank you, my friend," he said simply, genuinely. Then he hugged Fritz.

As I watched his simple self-assurance, with no sign of ego, I thought, this young man has already grasped his destiny; he will fulfill it all over the world. I was stunned, humbled and grateful.

Later Fritz said to me,

"Did you see how he walked into his future? Such concentration and strength! I don't think I've ever seen anyone take command of that moment the way he did."

This was the way we met Rafael, a 26-year old sound healer with an old and awakened soul, an unexpected gift in a wilderness valley of Mexico.

As Rafael was leaving that night we asked if he could return the next week for our new group. To our delight he agreed and we were happy that we would have another opportunity to appreciate him even more fully, now that we knew something about what he could do.

The next morning we both awoke with floods of dreams that had pressed us throughout the night. We tried to remember and share them but they were just a night muddle with no order or sense.

"Strange," Fritz said, "like a purification, old things washing through and out that don't matter anymore." He moved slightly and looked around, tuning into his body.

"It's interesting," he continued, "now my body feels like the hollow tube of that digeredoo, perfectly empty and clear. I feel like an open channel between heaven and earth."

He looked that way too, clear, free and glowing.

The ancient Chinese teaching that a human's function is to be a bridge between heaven and earth came to mind. For years I have been teaching how to align the energy systems of the body—meridians and chakras—so that one could become just that bridge. It felt like Rafael's sounds were accomplishing the same thing in a different way.

Rafael arrived as a carefully guarded surprise for our group the next week. We had been on a solo, silent vision quest in the desert that day, discovering inner truth for our present life and work. We had just started talking again that evening when we met in the classroom. Everyone was excited about the surprise.

We announced Rafael.

He strode into the room in the same peasant dress, carrying two digeredoos and various hand-made flutes. He set them down carefully on the floor, looked around the room at each person and then began to explain his work, as he told the following story:

"I make sounds with these instruments to heal hearts and to spread peace in the world," he said, with touching simplicity.

"This job first happened to me when I was 17 years old. I can't explain why or how it happened, it just did. A big awakening came over a friend and me as we were riding on a bus. There was suddenly a great clarity as if a veil had been lifted and I could see myself and this world very clearly. I was filled with love for everything, the animals, plants and people. An energy came with these realizations that I couldn't contain. It just grabbed me and flowed continuously through my body for many days."

Rafael stopped for a few moments and gazed into the distance.

"That was when I knew I had to do something to help heal this world. So I have traveled to many countries and studied many indigenous sounds until I found my right instrument and sound.

"So this is the sound you will hear, and feel, now," he said, "I ask that you close your eyes when the sound comes to you so that you can absorb it more surely. After you have received it you may open them again."

He picked up the unpainted digeredoo and pointed its wide mouth to the floor.

"And I ask that this sound will heal your hearts and be a benefit to all the world."

These last words were said as a prayer and we all sat quietly for a few moments, absorbing it. After our day of silence it felt like we were taking in Rafael's words at a profound level. In that state his story wasn't hard to understand nor accept; in fact, it seemed quite natural and right.

Rafael then began his performance.

He blew several booming sounds into the floor. They echoed around the room like a low potent cloud of sound. Then he lifted the huge instrument up to the level of Fritz' chest He blew that ancient tone we had heard the week before straight into the heart. I saw Fritz shiver ever so slightly as the sound penetrated. I could feel it from where I was sitting next to him. I remembered the strong effect it had the last time and wondered what would happen now.

Then Rafael came to me and pointed the horn toward my chest. I closed my eyes and tilted my head back so that the sound could reach my throat as well. I had been focused on opening my throat chakra more fully and also healing the cervical vertebrae behind it. I said an inward prayer for that healing.

When the sound vibrated through my heart I could feel it nudging into my neck as well. Then Rafael lifted the horn slightly so that it pointed straight into my throat. Could he possibly know, or see, what I needed there, I wondered. I started making micro-movements in my neck to open every cell to the sound. I could feel it penetrating deeper. Then with an inner eye I could see light creeping through the tissues and bones as the sound continued in intermittent blasts. It felt wonderful, like a warm shower after a long hike. Oh, what a blessing this was! Wonder and gratitude filled me as the song of the digeredoo danced throughout my body.

Rafael moved to the student sitting next to me. She closed her eyes and shifted her body on the cushion to receive the sound. I could see her field expand as the tones penetrated her. They also intensified the effects still going on in my body.

And so it went around the entire room, as Rafael walked slowly, stopping to blow that eerie sound into the chests of each of the thirty-six people in the group. They drank it in. Each tone layered on top of the next, amplifying it, until by the end of the circle there was a pulsating vibration in the whole room. I still felt the tingling opening in my throat, as well as a general quickening in my body.

As Rafael came back to us full circle he smiled, set the digeredoo down and remained standing, perfectly quiet, for a few moments. It felt like the healing was still going on and we sat in it, still.

Then he picked up one of the small hand-made flutes and sat down on the floor, cross-legged, in front of us.

"This is a *wapa*," he said, holding it up for us to see. It was a curious clump of sculpted clay that fit his fingers in uneven mounds. There was nothing attractive about it but its complexity drew my attention. I marveled at how his beautiful fingers nested into it just so.

"These are sounds that strike the DNA," he said, "they have the same vibration".

That statement was incomprehensible to me; I didn't even try to get my head around it. Instead I just listened as he started to blow lean, reedy sounds through the "flute".

At first they were a thin simple line. Then this line was joined by another fuller sound on top. Like the overtone singing I had heard from a Mongolian group, I thought. A sound that could have come from an ancient cave or monastery. It was beautiful in a very foreign way and it penetrated in a different manner than the digeredoo.

Intense attention persisted in the room. I noticed that there was no restlessness, no looking around, no whispering. This man was holding everyone's awareness at a peak.

The flute notes reached a crescendo of layered, very complex, sound. Then they drifted off into an almost mournful echo as Rafael elegantly set the "wapa" down on the floor.

He stood up and picked up the second digeredoo. It was the decorated instrument with many symbols in brilliant colors. Again he blew several powerful low notes into the floor in front of us. This sound was different from the first digeredoo, the same quality of tone but another register. As he lifted the instrument high above his head and blew several notes into the ceiling. the many symbols—waves, dolphins, sun, moon, stars—seemed to dance in the air.

This time he didn't move around the circle to each person but instead went straight to the middle of the room and blew sounds in each of the four directions—east, south, west, north. Every sound was crisp, forceful as if it contained a specific request for each direction. I remembered how our workshop had started with offerings to the four directions and I thought, these sounds are amplifying our beginnings and furthering wholeness for all of us.

Suddenly Rafael started to turn slowly in the center of the room as he simultaneously blew the digeredoo. I marveled at his physical strength and confidence, as he moved gracefully in a circle, all the time blowing the instrument. This digeredoo was five feet long. He held it steadily out in front of him, with one arm stretched straight while his other hand started to hit a rattle against the digeredoo in sharp, drum-like cracks.

Then I watched, transfixed, as he began to turn more and more swiftly, still blowing. I couldn't believe my eyes as he moved faster and faster until he became a whirling blur in the center of the room. The tails of his white poncho and the digeredoo both swirled straight out from his body so that finally we saw a turning light column, rather than a man. He was like a whirling dervish except that he was also playing an instrument, in perfect rhythm with the rattle, at the same time. I had never witnessed anything like this, although I had seen real dervishes several times in my life.

I glanced around the room. Several mouths were open. Wide-open eyes stared in disbelief. There were gasps. I could see that the sounds each person had received were still working and that all of us were more healed and whole than we had been before. And then on top of all that this moving image of a living, balancing connection between heaven and earth would burn deeply into our consciousness.

That was a night none of us will forget. The image of Rafael twirling swiftly in a circle, his white poncho and black hair flying out around him and the digeredoo, sounding all the while, is seared into my consciousness as a talisman of human possibility. He gave us an experience of sound healing in our bodies that touched each one of us. And we were also shown the full magnificence of a human being, aligned with his own self, doing his right work in the world, offering the kind of healing and soul empowerment that seem absolutely essential for our world.

Fritz and I were taking a van into Guadalajara and the airport early the next morning. Rafael asked for a ride. We were delighted to have more time with him and we questioned him about his work and his ideas all the way to the outskirts of town. We asked him to tell us more about just how he had learned and developed the sound. He freely shared his story with us.

"Well when I was seventeen and had that experience and knew I needed to help heal the world, I didn't know anything about how to do it at that time. I started playing around with flutes because I loved them. I became obsessed with finding new sounds and even started making instruments, like these," he held up several of his clay flutes, "trying to find sounds that I heard in my head but couldn't find in ready-made instruments.

"Everyone was worried about me because all day long I was just making these sounds. In fact, that was all I did. I couldn't return to school, it didn't make sense.

"So I began to travel everywhere, in Mexico and the United States, to find the sounds of indigenous peoples. I wanted to learn their songs and hear their prayers. Everywhere I went I tried out different instruments. I traveled, always learning and experimenting with sound, for several years.

"During my travels I also swam with the dolphins. From them I learned another vibration, different from those of the instruments. Now this vibration also comes through the sounds I make. I show my respect to those master beings through the symbols that you see here on the digeredoo," he gestured to the colorful dolphins, waves and stars that decorated the outside of one of the digeredoos.

"Then one day someone showed me a digeredoo. I was fascinated by it. I took it up and started making sounds that delighted me from the start. Soon all I did was blow it, listen to it, and feel its vibrations resonating deep within me. They felt healing and empowering."

"It was then that I decided that this was my way to help the world, by making healing sounds.

"But first I felt the need to visit the Aborigine people who first made the digeredoo. I wanted to seek the initiation and blessing of their Elders. When I went to Australia they embraced me like a lost son. They taught me, initiated me and gave me their blessing to do this work in the world."

We were approaching Rafael's stop when he finished. But before he got out of the van he pulled three objects out of his poncho. He looked at us intently and then took each of our hands.

"This is a gift from my mother," he said, "a healer, one of the most wonderful women you can imagine," he said. I could certainly get that, having experienced her son as we had.

He placed a small pair of beautifully sculpted white open hands, with tiny glittering stones within them, into our joined hands.

"These hands," he pressed them, "are the hands of a healer. They come from one healer, my mother, to you two super healers. They are white to show purity. And they contain all these precious stones, all colors, to show the rich treasure that you carry within your own hands.

"And this," he held up a small buckskin pouch and placed it in my hand, "is for you, sister Aminah. It carries strong medicine within it for your healing work. We always carry our medicine bags wherever we go because they keep us close to the magic of our ancestors.

"This one," he held up another pouch and put it carefully into Fritz' hand, "is for you, my friend, *mi hermano*, my elder. It is a medicine bag from my ancestors to you, with special treasures I've collected for a long time."

We were both deeply touched. What else could we say to this generous, loving, talented spirit than "thank you from the bottoms of our hearts."

Rafael smiled, picked up his gear, opened the door and stepped down from the van into the busy street.

"We'll see each other again," he called back as he walked briskly down the sidewalk into the crowded campo district and quickly blended into the many bodies rushing along there.

I smiled to myself. This is a rich man, I thought, he knows who he is, where he's going and what his job is on earth, and at such a young vibrant age.

23

Desert Vision Quests

It was the Great Light on the desert when I was just five years old that first showed me the radiance behind the world and within the soul. How the soul is connected and interrelated with everything—the cactus, mountains, rocks, sky, humans here and in the Other World, sun and the Great All. And in that union with All that Is, everything is all right. No, much more—wondrous, blissful, full of joy.

Of course at that time I could only experience the Oneness in my body and soul consciousness. It wasn't possible to grasp it with the child's mind nor word it to others. So growing up I didn't tell anyone of the experience. I didn't forget it either but it remained a mystery for me, one that I couldn't integrate into ordinary life.

Years later I visited soul consciousness again in the *latihan* for several years until finally I began to experience it as a known, tangible, almost definable reality. Still, it remained cloistered in the *latihan* hall. It took returning to the desert for retreats, some forty years after the child's experience, to restimulate the experience of radiance and unity in the world.

The desert is still free nature, a field of clarity within the Tao, harmonized with heaven and earth, unmanipulated by human designs. Here in the desert I can commune with that harmony, immerse myself into It and feel its Divine order within the self.

Perhaps the earth once existed in this state of perpetual harmony, what the ancient Taoists called the Tao. Lao-tzu, the Old Master father of Taoism, described it this way in the Tao Te Ching:

In harmony with the Tao,
the sky is clear and spacious,
the earth is solid and full,
all creatures flourish together
content with the way they are,
endlessly repeating themselves,
endlessly renewed.

When man interferes with the Tao,
The sky becomes filthy,
The earth becomes depleted,
The equilibrium crumbles,
Creatures become extinct.

The Master views the parts with compassion,
Because he understands the whole.
His constant practice is humility.
He doesn't glitter like a jewel
But lets himself be shaped by the Tao,
As rugged and common as a stone.[1]

In our world now, where man has interfered grandly, it is much easier in the desert to see that whole and let myself "be shaped by the Tao, as rugged and common as a stone."

I returned to the desert in the early eighties for retreat when my life was full of tangles that I needed to work through. The ten thousand things were again crowding in on me. So I went out into the desert seeking clarity about all these things, determined to sit until a path came to me.

---

1. *Tao Te Ching*. English translation by S. Mitchell. HarperPerennial, New York, 1988.

I walked away from the cabin I was sharing with friends and sat down in a shallow gully. At first my mind raced around through the tangles, unsettled and confused. I felt the discomfort of sand and rocks beneath me, the sun on my head and the tickle of a bush against my neck. But I stayed on and after awhile my mind started to calm. Within an hour or so a sense of peacefulness began to pervade my whole being.

When I got up to return to the cabin to join my friends for fun I found that I was still hungry for that state. So I sat back down to drink in more of it. The peacefulness resumed, my mind expanded out and upward. Eventually I went into a state of continuous *latihan* and soul consciousness.

I sat for six hours that day, with small breaks to walk around, until the tangles of my life had been replaced by spaciousness. By the end I knew what to do about my relationship, living situation, completion of studies and the next direction my life should take. And I felt joyful. That long period of immersion in soul consciousness outside the *latihan* had cleared the mind. But I hadn't yet re-discovered the unity with the Tao that the child had known.

This initial return to the desert set a pattern for meditation retreats from then on. Through the years Laura and I came back many times. We developed a method for our meditation. First we visited a tiny Lady of Guadalupe shrine where we placed our prayers. We stood in front of the colorful, finely crafted Mexican statue and spoke to Her as the Divine Mother. We asked for guidance in our lives. We prayed for family members and students. And we prayed for peace in the world.

Then we climbed our separate ways up the mountain behind the shrine and found a place to sit in meditation, usually on a rock with a bush for shade, to wait for Her response. One always came, though seldom in the design we had asked for.

We returned from these retreats strengthened in our spirits to continue with our therapeutic practices.

Eventually we invited others to join us in retreats. I remember the first one was to coincide with the first World Peace Meditation, Dec. 31, 1990. We sat together at 3:30 am to read the Peace Meditation, then kept silence for an hour. Afterwards we walked together across the desert beneath the starry sky until dawn. It was an inspiring time. We felt we had contributed in some way to the deep wish for peace that was spreading across the planet.

Without exception people who came to the retreats experienced a renewal of spirit. Many arrived tired and weighed down by circumstances of their lives. At first some were repelled by the stark dryness of the seemingly lifeless desert while others were intimidated by its vast and silent spaciousness. They might be afraid of rattlesnakes or annoyed by a roommate's snoring. But within a few days they were full of wonder by the richness they had discovered—the brilliant light on cactus or rocks, the night sky, a glittering bowl of heaven, the closeness, even communication with coyotes or birds. They had come to appreciation and peace within themselves and each other and they returned to their lives closer to their souls.

One day we were all floating in the healing waters of Aqua Caliente hot springs, luxuriantly soaking our bodies into deep relaxation. I was staring out into the desert mountain landscape, in peaceful nonthinking when I almost voiced the longing that I had to teach my students here. As clear as the rippling water the local spirits said to me, "Bring your people here and we will teach them."

I was so startled that I said aloud "Really?" The prospect was exhilarating but I could hardly believe it. Just as I was questioning its validity in my mind, a rush of warmth filled my body, assuring me of its truth.

At the time it seemed impossible to my rational mind that students could be persuaded to come here from all over the country. We are far from airports and there is no easy transportation. There are no entertainments and little to buy. As someone asked me one day, "What do you *do* out there?" Nevertheless, contrary to all reason, I accepted the promise of the spirits. That was the very beginning of offering classes in the desert.

And students came. They were transfixed by the desert and their experiences. They said their studies were deeper and more easily integrated here than they had experienced before. It was easier to access their soul wisdom.

And the spirits fulfilled their promise by teaching the students directly about the essence of plants, rocks and animals. We encouraged this communication by recommending that they spend time alone in the desert.

One young woman, a bodyworker and artist, went out alone into the desert to reclaim "my power" so that she could express her multifaceted talents more effectively in the world. As she walked through a canyon, a *borrego*, the rare horned sheep of this region, bounded down the mountain toward her. She was astonished because the *borrego* is people-shy. It is considered very special to even spot one at a distance.

This *borrego* stopped abruptly on a boulder, barely thirty feet above the woman, and stared straight into her eyes for at least three minutes. She said she wasn't frightened but stood utterly still. In those few minutes she said she felt the transmission of a mighty power and skill from the animal into her. The skill that has enabled the *borrego* to survive in the desert through centuries of threat—from drought, fire, animal and human predators.

That woman has since traveled, completed doctoral studies, taught and now writes. She is a strong and clear voice of higher consciousness.

Prayers we offered during our solo days in the desert were frequently answered, even beyond our original requests. For example, another woman, a spiritual director of a large ecumenical congregation, prayed to manifest a proper facility for her flock. At the time their meeting place was in an industrial complex, the rent was going up and they didn't have the funds to meet it.

Within a few months after her prayer a sponsor offered to finance a one-city-block property in a very favorable environment that had several beautiful old buildings, neglected and near ruin. Within another year the congregation had renovated and enhanced the buildings to create a magnificent temple. The congregation grows. Blessings multiply around the teachings of the world's great religions, so that students may "awaken to the One Truth known by many names." Schools for children and ministers have been established and the temple has become a center of unity and inspiration, for its city and the world.

Sometimes the local spirits appeared as Indians who had lived here centuries before. They taught us with simple clarity about living in respect, harmony and co-creation with nature. For example, an English woman learned the healing powers of the ocotillo by communing with its spirit. The ocotillo has long sharp thorns which forbid attack to its arms. After rain it produces brilliant red flowers with many luxuriant petals. Ocotillo told this woman it was a "heart protector."

In our work we teach about the Pericardium, or Heart Protector, meridian as a guardian of the heart's intelligence and love. So this student collected some of Ocotillo's flowers and made a tincture essence of them which has assisted our learning and work with the meridian. It also taught us more about the need for protecting our inner treasures. I learned much later that the Indians made a drink from Ocotillo flowers for good health.

Another woman met a former medicine man during a day alone in the desert. He showed her healing rituals he had used and introduced her to a medicinal herb. A highly skilled physical therapist, who operates two busy clinics, sat on a huge boulder for a day and received a vision of his future clinical developments, as well as the grounded strength to accomplish them.

As these experiences accumulated, the promise of a desert vision quest of modern design, evolved. Some of us had experienced the

American Indian vision quest and understood its basic principles. A very important ritual in every traditional Indian life, the vision quest was about discovering one's unique life purpose. It took place during the puberty passage from childhood to adulthood. After instruction and ritual support young men went out alone into the wilderness to fast and pray for life guidance. They took no provisions except perhaps a knife to protect themselves from mountain lions or bears. Usually the quest went on for several days until the Great Spirit, the ancestors and spirits of nature provided a vision, either waking or in a dream, that would show their special tasks in life.

The vision might not be immediately understandable to the adolescent but he would know by its impact that it was a true sign. He brought it back to the elders or medicine man for interpretation. Often his name was changed at that time to fit the vision. For example, I once met a man on a plane who looked like any other businessman in his suit and tie. He was a lawyer. As we talked I learned that he was a full blooded American Indian whose *real* name was Thundercloud. I asked him about the name. It came from his adolescent vision quest during which thunderclouds had swept up out of nowhere and roared at him for a long time. He had translated this experience as guidance for him to become a thundercloud for his people. Now he litigates for Indian tribal rights. And he roars.

Although the Indian tradition informed our way—the necessity for silence and solitude, the teachings of nature, the possibility of destiny visions—we created our own version of a soul vision quest that fit this desert environment and the needs of contemporary people. For over ten years it has evolved according to our soul guidance, practical experience and the promptings of spirits. During such a quest in 1999 I had the vision that now informs my work. It went like this:

Fritz and I were thinking about buying a new home and had found one that seemed right. But we hadn't yet made a final decision. In a vision quest I asked for clarity about our decision and chose the region of the home we were considering.

A vision came that went beyond my request.

I walked out into the vast, empty desert beyond the home and surrendered my quandary to the Great Spirit. The air was still, nothing moved. The purple-layered mountains framed a view of the desert landscape that stretched into mirage before me. My mind calmed as I shed question upon question about the home and simply surrendered to the Will of the Divine. I was immersed in the stillness and beauty, savoring each moment.

After awhile I came upon a giant ocotillo plant that had fallen over in its old age, as they do in forty or fifty years of life. Its long elegant branches lay spread out over the sand, dry and rotting. Even its roots, still partially buried in the dirt, were dried out and decomposing. Within a few years its very form and essence would blend back into the desert completely, like all things that finish life here.

For many years I have worried, like every awakening person, about the state of our world, how it will survive, in what form and how to help it live. But that day I wasn't thinking of the world at all. I was simply being with the Tao in the desert.

Suddenly a Voice said: "The old world is dead, just as this ocotillo is dead. Even though its form is still recognizable, so has the old world fallen over in death. It doesn't recognize that it is already rotting."

Then I saw a vision of many structures around the world, both material and ideological, crumbling and falling down around us. For a moment I felt a seizure of doom and panic.

I remembered another vision I had in 1974, while I was teaching and fasting at the same time. In it I saw the great skyscrapers of the cities melting down into the streets amid chaos and terror. At the end of that vision I had also seen beautiful young people emerging out of the rubble, full of new spirit and strength.

The Voice continued: "A new world is being formed. Many Beings and forces are gathering around earth to assist its birth. And right here in this place a funnel of higher force is taking shape to help the process."

Then I was shown the funnel. It looked like an iridescent downdraft from far above. Its narrow end didn't quite touch the earth but hovered near, like a mirage. It was something like a gigantic "dust devil," as we call the whirlpools of dust that are carried by the wind across the desert, except that this one remained in one place, an opalescent spiral, undulating ever so slowly.

The voice came again: "Some of you are strong enough now to help ground this force. Others will come. They will collect in this valley to serve the evolution of Higher Order."

The vision brought immense wonder, spaciousness and joy. I stood there for a long time, opening myself to absorb its message and energy. My ordinary mind, which wouldn't have believed it, was fortunately on hold.

Certainly I had received much more than clarification about buying the home.

When I returned that evening I said to Fritz, "I agree completely with your intuitive choice of this home. Let's buy it!"

So we did and have settled here, in the vicinity of the funnel.

We recognized that this home is not just for our peace and enjoyment. It can help anchor a wider vision in the world—a vision of harmony and co-creation with nature, as well as unconditional positive respect between all humans. We decided to offer a Soul Vision Quest right here near the funnel.

For over ten years we had been leading retreats in a remote area of Mexico, called Through the Growing Edge. They were designed to provide a safe environment and tools to help people claim and express their growing edges. During those years we saw people steadily grow more soul-centered, free and creative. Gradually we could discern the groups weaving a new template for society where people interacted in mutual support rather than competition, where each person's true nature and gifts were acknowledged and celebrated. Now this desert seemed to be calling us into even more expansive edges.

In 2004 Fritz and I offered our first Soul Vision retreat in the desert. On the first evening eighteen of us gathered in our living room to initiate journeys into the unknown of our own soul visions. Calling upon the spirits of nature, the local ancestral spirits and our own inner guidance system, we asked to draw closer to our wisdom and soul purposes.

From the very beginning we could feel the blessings that have come here before, and those that are being given now. Each of us were gifted, "beyond my wildest imagination" as one participant put it, throughout a soul feeding week with meditation, tai chi, bodywork, sharing and walking the labyrinth. Insight and fulfillment came, especially during the Soul Vision Quest.

On that day we spread out across the desert with many different intentions, personalities and skills, all seeking to reconnect with the truth within ourselves, and the truth available in nature.

Each questor returned that evening, having received much more than they sought, far beyond their greatest hopes. We were full of wonder and enormous gratitude for the riches we had gained. Everyone looked more healthy, content within themselves and full of love for each other and their experiences.

We shared our experiences. Each story was fascinating and unique; each held our full attention through the never-heard-before episodes. They were funny, uplifting and enlightening.

One participant, Don Berlyn, expressed so well how inadequate words were to convey what we had learned:

On Using Words As Tools To Express Thoughts, Concepts, Emotions

Communication beyond the mind....
Words are a butter knife, when you need a scalpel
A box of twelve crayons, when you need sixty-four

A sledgehammer, when you need a paintbrush
A spray can, when you need a pen
A sink, when you need a cup.

Another participant, Dawn, did put words to some of her experience. She could have been speaking for all of us:

"If I ask a question of a stone, a mountain or a plant, an animal or my own soul…If I ask from that deep stillness, the silence within, then the answer comes. Usually simple, just a few words, and often not what I expect. I do not know from which source the answers come. I do know they are of a different resonance and quality from that of my own busy chatter mind. Maybe they are all one and the same—the stone, mountain, plant, animal, my own soul, or the Divine, the Universe—maybe there is only ONE. All things are individual instruments, all interrelated in a common chord of a vast, cosmic orchestra in which each living instrument is in harmony with the whole. When we acknowledge who we are we enroll fully into life and become One with the Universe. Then we realize it is not by accident that we come to this life."

Even though most of us couldn't really word our experience in the desert, we felt we had experienced Desert Darshan, we had been "shaped by the Tao." For a time we had become One with It.

Section VIII: Healings Along the Way

Like the sculptor who chips away the stone to reveal the sculpture within it, we awaken to who we are through a long process of clearing away what we are not. Some of the obstacles to our inner truth are simply false ideas, beliefs and habits. We can recognize these and change them through understanding and will. Others are embedded much deeper in our unconscious and require unordinary means to dislodge.

This clearing process that Bapak called "purification" can take us through progressively deeper layers, from the earliest childhood woundings to ancestral imprinting and even to past karmas. Sometimes our personal clearing overlaps with world cleansing. In my experience these deeper levels can only be released with spiritual help. And anyone who pursues a serious spiritual path will encounter the opportunity to heal, time and time again.

In this section I share several healings that the ordinary mind could neither imagine nor accomplish.

24

Father's Redemption

During my soul journey I have been in touch with various ancestors through the *latihan.* I learned of their sufferings and triumphs and have lived out those effects in my own life. They have helped me and also presented their unfinished business for us to work out together.

I learned that our ancestors aren't dead at all. They simply support, or obstruct, us from another dimension. Many indigenous peoples are not only aware of their ancestors but they make a point of honoring them, praying to them and keeping in close touch for guidance and support. They realize that their ancestors give love and also need it.

Our ancestors have many gifts and blessings to bestow upon us, such as—strength, love, special talents, and a perspective free from the buffeting of earthly-life dramas and traumas. If our soul consciousness is open enough to hear they are imminently available for conversation and assistance.

Anger, hatred, resentment and lack of forgiveness hold them here, close to earth, where they are still trapped by the tractor beams of their mistakes, sins, shortcomings and unfinished business. They are trying all the time to make amends for these "sins" related to us, but they need our cooperation. We can actually help to redeem them and ourselves in the process. They expand in consciousness and potential every time we forgive, honor or love them.

Our ancestors are engaged, with us, in the future of this world. "The sins of the fathers are visited upon them" (us) through all these thousands of years. It is part of our lifework to help them and ourselves stop that transmission. I learned that it is possible to resolve some of their unfinished business and thereby free our children and ourselves. Here is one story of resolution.

Father's accidental death when I was four years old left a nagging ache in my consciousness far into adulthood. It pushed me to seek answers where there were none by ordinary means.

For example, as a young adult I visited a spiritualist church to find out about my father. It was the only time I ever went to such a service but it made a big impact on my life.

A medium picked random questions from the audience and then addressed the appropriate spirits. I had written a request to speak with my father on a piece of paper and put it in a hat. Midway in the service the medium said: "I have a man here, about 5'10", he's a bit stocky, about forty years old. He is wearing a cowboy hat."

During this description my heart started thumping.

"He wants to tell his daughter (here I stopped breathing) how very sorry he is for all the pain and deprivation caused by his death."

I was waiting eagerly for more.

"That seems to be all he wishes to say," the medium concluded.

This phenomenon was a wonderment to me. I was still an atheist then and very skeptical about life after death. Nevertheless there was a warm sensation of having been touched by someone special. I felt comforted by the contact. It was disappointing to receive such a short message, but it had been enough for then. I never returned to that church or any other medium.

Later I worked through the ordinary emotional factors that accompany a parent's death in psychotherapy. Issues such as feeling abandoned at the survival level, or thinking of myself as the odd one at school who had no "real" father. How I longed to connect with him as part of me.

I even became grateful in a way for important developments in my inner life that his premature death stimulated. For example, it brought a realization of the gifts one can harvest from a severe trauma. This awareness has helped in my work.

As I worked through his death I came to realize that no earthly father could provide the Divine love that I finally needed. Eventually I learned to call upon the Fathers in heaven, for guidance, love and comfort.

Father also gave me the ability to communicate with the dead. I believe now that the impact of his death opened a gateway between the worlds to me. Perhaps I was trying, in the innocence of childhood, to follow him, or to call him back. However it came about, I slipped through the veils to the other side at that time. Certainly I communicated directly with Father during the Great Light experience. Although I never sought nor cultivated mediumship, it happens to me quite naturally during times of crisis or great need. This faculty has helped me and others in my work.

By mid-life, after the message from the medium, lots of therapy, the *latihan* experience at my opening, and especially after processing the nightmare that revealed important guidelines for my work, I had adjusted to, and accepted, my relationship with Father at a personality level. I felt complete with him.

Except for one thing: The way his half-dead corpse reached out for me, pleading. And his imploring eyes. I just didn't feel free of that part yet.

Only this one crucial part remained, for both Father and me—unfinished soul work. It would take a long time, over fifty years, to answer Father's plea. This is how it happened.

During one trip to India to see Sai Baba with our friend Paula, I encountered the nightmare again in a startling way.

Each morning we all traveled together to Darshan. This trip required hiring a car with an Indian driver to take us the forty-five minutes to Baba's temple. Every day it was a wild ride through streets crowded by rickshaws, bicycles, cars, trucks and Sacred Cows who often just stopped in the road. Horns blared incessantly the whole way. And each morning we drove over a railroad crossing. Of course I was once again reminded of my father's death since he was hit in just such a crossing. But I noticed, with relief, that this crossing, unlike the one where my father was killed, had a barrier arm that came down to block cars as the train passed.

We had agreed that it was best not to look at the road during these frightening trips. Instead we chatted among ourselves and simply entrusted our lives to God. But one particular morning I was looking out the window as we neared the railroad tracks. As I watched, a train came rattling toward us and its loud horn sounded. The barriers to the crossing had already started coming down. I jumped in horror as the driver speeded up to make it through before they blocked our way.

I yelled, "Stop! Don't go through!" But he paid no attention.

Several cars were stopped on the road ahead of us. Our driver honked his horn repeatedly and stepped on the gas. I could see the train coming closer and closer. My heart raced wildly. A thought streaked through my mind, this was how it was for my father and now I'm going to die the same way.

By a miracle the car shot all the way over the crossing just before the barriers hit the ground and the train sped past behind us. It seemed to me it had missed us by only a few feet.

Fritz and Paula were startled and speechless but intact. I was shattered. I couldn't breathe. My body shook all over. I cried out once, then went numb. It felt like the train had hit me. That I was dying in place.

We went on to Darshan in stunned silence, I guess giving thanks for our lives. But it wasn't over for me. I felt sick. I sat throughout Darshan praying for help. I couldn't process the train incident in any ordinary way because I was too stunned to think or feel.

Paula asked afterward if she could do anything for me. I said she could give me a Process Acupressure session to see if we could work through what had happened.

That evening we went to her room to work. As she moved through the acupoints on my body, energy started opening in my diaphragm area. Then a volcanic, multi-channeled process started. My body lurched. In internal vision I started reliving Father's death. I sobbed. My body contorted in agony. For a few moments I felt like him, sprawled across the railroad tracks. I couldn't breathe. Then the childhood nightmare flooded my consciousness again—I saw the cemetery where he is buried, his arms reaching out of his grave to me, his eyes pleading for help. Then all the many experiences dealing with his loss. All of it flashed through consciousness as a fast forward movie.

Suddenly, in a lightning instant, a complete understanding came to me. It appeared as a hologram and showed me, all at once—the work I had done about Father's death, the nightmare, its horror, its constant nagging pull and how it had seeded my life work.

Then came the body-felt realization that I had not answered my father's plea. He himself, my own personal father, had desperately asked me for help. Yes, I had prayed for him but until now I had never once *got it* about his *redemption.*

Suddenly I remembered the message in the Alps: "Pray for the father's redemption."

And now here I was, at Sai Baba's ashram, sitting at a source of redemption.

The next day before Darshan I went to the front of the temple and knelt down. I prayed, "Please Baba, take my Father and Mother into your Divine grace, into redemption."

During Darshan I felt as if they were both sitting with me in the sacred field of Baba's love. A great calm radiated through my body and soul. I felt my father's spirit lifting, lifting, his depression and guilt falling away as he began to soar. For the first time I felt enormous gratitude for the exact life these parents had given me and even for the gifts of my father's death. I said to him "rest in this peace, Father. No more sorrow, no more guilt. You are free to surrender to Divine grace."

After that the old weight lifted from me as well. I felt so much freer. A lifelong drive I had, to move on, to get on with it, to get there, to get it done, started falling away.

Shortly after we returned from India I had an early morning dream. I called it "Resurrected Lee Barkdoll (my Father's name)." Here is how I recorded it in my journal:

Dream: Father's Redemption

I am at a gathering of familiar people. Someone says, "Your father is here."

Astounded, I ask, "WHERE?"

The person takes me to Lee Barkdoll who is about thirty-nine, the age when he died. He is slightly stocky and obviously a cowboy, like the pictures I had seen of him.

I feel intense relief and excitement. I stand just before him. I can feel an electric connection between us; it registers in my body. Also intense love, a lifetime longing answered, and great appreciation for seeing him. Even in the dream, my mind goes crazy with thoughts like: 'I'm sixty already and I've lost all these years, how can I ever get enough of him? How can we build a relationship now, etc., etc.'

I start to cry on the spot even though many people surround us. He is uncomfortable with that, as any cowboy would be, and looks around for help, not knowing what to do with me.

I get myself together. Then several of us sit down in a booth. I snuggle right up next to him. I feel so much love for him, sitting there in his presence at last.

He tells me his name is Sai Baba! I ask him, "How did you get that name?"

He looks deep into my eyes, penetrating me, as if to say, 'if I possibly could, I would tell you.'

He says, "I can't tell you that."

I accept and hope someday it will be revealed to me. Then I simply know, in the way you have surety in a dream, that he is in India, close to Baba.

It was so wonderful to be that near him.

I woke up right after that, still permeated with this amazing feeling of grace.

I got up and went straight into meditation to ask Baba about it. He said: *"I sent you that dream to let you know that your father is with Me and has been redeemed as you prayed. He is now one with Me, hence the name Sai Baba. He is still learning, but he is free now…and available when you need him."*

I sat for some time, in wonder and gratitude.

At last, Father was free and one of my lifelong tasks was complete.

25

Hiroshima Revisited

The brilliant light deadly cloud of the atomic bomb blast on Hiroshima went out through all available communication waves at the time. Radio and movie newsreels carried the shocking news. The solemn voice of Walter Cronkite described it on radio the day after as:

"...the most powerful weapon ever created by man. Its impact was felt as shock waves for 1500 miles away from Hiroshima where radiation killed or injured thousands of people." (2005 estimates were 100,000).

His voice also narrated behind the image we saw on movie newsreels later—that boiling column that billowed up and out into the now-famous mushroom cloud that covered the whole sky. Its repeated images in the newspaper and the cover of Life magazine burned into our psyches.

It was 1945 and I was eleven years old. I could tell something momentous, something far beyond my comprehension, had happened by the shock on my parents' faces. They seemed thoughtful, solemn and speechless. I saw tears mounting in mother's eyes. What could I say? What should I feel?

I couldn't tell if this was a good thing or a horrible one by the fragmented statements I heard at school and around town—

"The end of the war!"

"The Japs will have to surrender now."

"All of those people cremated, how could we do such a thing?"

"This will affect us for generations to come."

"No one knows what this will mean."

Of course there was elation at the prospect that the terrifying specter of war we had been living with for four years would end. But there was also an atmosphere of shame or doom or disbelief as the reports of casualties and deaths kept coming. I couldn't decipher the implications. What should I believe?

In the fifty years since then newscasters, scientists, historians and reporters of all kinds have been analyzing and debating about that event and its ongoing effects on the world. As have all of us who remember that day.

In 1998 Fritz stood in front of a class of Zero Balancing students in Tokyo. Forty doctors and healers had come from all over Japan to learn this hands-on healing method. Their faces were attentive, respectful. They were eager to learn what Fritz was teaching and demonstrating about how Zero Balancing could bring the body and consciousness back into harmony after injury and in times of stress.

Another assistant and I were helping the students learn the gentle hand manipulations Fritz was demonstrating. We communicated with them through a Japanese-American translator, Fumiko, because very few spoke English, although we saw signs that they understood a lot of what we said. We had been working together for three days, teaching mainly through our hands on each other's bodies. An amazing nonverbal rapport, respectful and loving, had developed between all of us.

As class was beginning on the fourth day I sat in front of the class with Fritz, the other assistant, Alan Hext, and Fumiko, looking out over the faces of those forty serious healers. I was in an altered state already, from the healing field we had built together in the room but also from pain in my mouth due to a tooth extraction. The pain was beginning to reach a level beyond pills that I couldn't ignore and I was afraid the tooth site was infected.

I wasn't listening to Fritz as he began the class. My eyes were just scanning the room in a spacey, pain-medicated state. I studied the beautiful faces before me. They looked so clear, so guileless, these attentive students, absorbed in learning another hands-on skill that would help them heal others.

For the first time I noticed that many of them were about my age. Suddenly I was drifting back in time, looking into the faces of the children these students had been. War children, who would have received the opposite kind of teaching from me at that age. While I had heard "evil Japs" they would have been hearing "American demons;" while the adults around me would have been shouting with joy at each Japanese casualty, these children on the other side of the world would have heard cheers of triumph at the news of American deaths. Suddenly I was transfixed with the realization that I was looking into the beautiful healer-faces of the once-enemy. Now here we were, all working together, united in common purpose.

A huge wave of sorrow/compassion/relief welled up in my chest. Tears started trickling down my face. I tried to wipe them away inconspicuously. To show such a rush of emotion/realization seemed inappropriate in the situation. I held myself together until the break when I rushed to the ladies' room and allowed a few uncontrolled sobs.

Suddenly Fumiko stood beside me, looking concerned.

"What's the matter?" she asked. I felt completely unable to describe the feeling/realization I was still experiencing. I simply shook my head.

"I notice that you've been frowning and holding your face for a couple of days," she remarked kindly.

"Well I had a complicated tooth extraction just before we came and I'm worried that it's infected now because the pain is intensifying. I don't quite know what to do about it here," I said, embarrassed, but also relieved to take attention away from the real emotion of the moment.

"Oh. Why didn't you tell me? We can probably get help for you here. There's a remarkable healer in the group who can heal at a distance. I'll ask him to work on your mouth. Which tooth was it?"

"This one," I showed her the throbbing hole where the tooth had been.

"What do you mean he can heal at a distance?" I have to admit it wasn't the kind of help I was hoping for. I was thinking more along the lines of a dentist and antibiotics. Although I had heard of such ability and I'd read a lot about Edgar Cayce's distance healings I was doubtful. In California there are all kinds of healing claims that turn into wishful imagination upon investigation.

"If he knows where the problem is he looks at it clairvoyantly to see exactly what's needed and then he goes into that place with his mind and corrects it."

"Do you think he could tell if it's infected?"

"Probably. Anyway, I'll go and ask him right now during the break so he can get started." With that she zipped out of the ladies' room into the coffee bar to find the healer.

I certainly wasn't hopeful but I was so anxious about infection and desperate for pain relief that I was grateful for any help.

When we took our seats at the front of the room after break Fumiko whispered to me, "He said he will work on the tooth."

"Which student is it?" I whispered back.

"See those two men over there who always work together? They're like brothers. The one with the light around him is the healer."

I looked out among the sea of faces to the two men she nodded toward. Could I see a light around the larger man? I wasn't sure. Certainly he had a kind face with sparkling eyes. He smiled at me as I looked at him. Our eyes met. An instantaneous feeling of well being and familiarity came over me. I suddenly felt comforted, almost as if my own wonderful dentist had said, "It will be all right. We can fix this."

As we were leaving class that day I searched out this man and told him how much I appreciated his healing attention. He spoke no English and didn't understand my words but he clearly got the meaning. He took my hands in his and his face lit up with the most beautiful warm smile—I can still see it as I write this. Again there was that sense of deep comfort and familiarity. We just stood there in a warm cocoon, looking at each other for a few moments.

That evening the class took us out to dinner to celebrate our coming together as healers from divergent cultures. The restaurant was elegant and very full. The food was superb and it came on, course after course, for several hours. Sake flowed. The Japanese etiquette says that someone other than yourself must always fill your cup. This custom became problematic for me. Just as soon as my sake cup was emptied it was instantly filled by someone sitting nearby.

During the class the Japanese students behaved toward us with the utmost quiet respect, their faces almost impassive, as they had been taught in school to regard the Teacher. They rarely spoke and almost never asked questions. Now at this dinner we were still treated like royalty by the students and servers but there was an atmosphere of friendship and family. Spontaneous gaiety arose around the table. Everyone talked at once. Students addressed us in Japanese as if we could understand every word they said. We answered back in English as if they understood. Mime gestures instructed us how to eat with our hands. Laughter boomed, hands clapped shoulders. Several times during the dinner the healer and I met eyes and nodded and each time that sense of comfort washed over me.

At the beginning of the dinner I hadn't imagined how I could possibly get through several hours in a restaurant full of noise, food and sake, with the pain in my mouth. But hours later when we left, laughing, hugging and quite tipsy, I felt much better than I had in days and the pain had lessened.

The next morning I awoke to realize that the pain was about seventy-five percent diminished. I felt a wave of relief, not only from less pain but also from the fear of infection. "Whatever he's doing must be working, he must be healing me," I thought with great appreciation.

At class I asked Fumiko to tell the healer that I was certainly better and to find out what he was seeing at the tooth site. I saw him nodding and smiling across the room.

When Fumiko came back she reported, "He says there is no infection, just tissue trauma from the extraction. He is working on it and will continue. It will heal completely."

In the days that followed the tooth did heal completely and I had no more discomfort from it as we traveled around Japan.

Each day for the remainder of the class I went to the healer to express my appreciation, which I asked Fumiko to translate into Japanese. There wasn't much need for that actually since he and I seemed to have a clear telepathic contact.

"He says you and he were very close in a past life," Fumiko reported.

That remark amazed, and deeply touched, me. How did he see that? How did he experience it? How much did he know about it? All questions I couldn't hope to have answered in the circumstances. They would have to remain a mystery. But that one statement made me want to fully appreciate the soul connection between us. No telling what other gifts could be exchanged in that soul resonance.

I estimated that this healer was just a little younger than me. When I asked Fumiko, she found out that he was in fact about seven years my junior. I was still absorbing the realization of how far we had come in the last fifty years, from terror and killing to practicing healing together. I became curious about how this man had discovered his abilities as a healer and how he had advanced them. I asked Fumiko.

"He's from Hiroshima," she said. "And so is his friend. They're two old souls, bonded by what happened to them in Hiroshima. Because of their experiences there as children they decided to become healers. That one," she indicated my tooth healer "is a very great soul."

My eyes filled with tears. He would have been four years old when that deadly light blast altered everything in his life. Yes, I thought, he is a very great soul. A world healer.

When the class finished, many students crowded around to say goodbye. Probably we would never see them again after this profound time. In just a few days we had transcended our early conditioning from family and culture to unite in common purpose, that of relieving suffering in the world. Our hearts had been blended in that. Now we would resume our regular practices, in separate cultures, with many different client complaints. But I think all of us will cherish that experience together, when we were able to transmit our love, one to another, hands to bodies, beneath everything we had learned or lived before.

The healer and I found each other readily. We stood face to face, two mature adults, looking at each other from the eyes of bewildered children trained to hate each other, and also from love that had transcended those terrifying years of world insanity. He took both my hands in his. We looked at each other for long moments, wordlessly saying all that passed between our hearts. There was only peace between us. Those moments are still healing me, him and our war-scarred cultures.

I have never seen nor heard of this healer again. I can't even remember his name. But when I think of him now I can still see his smiling face, feel the loving care that emanated from him and know that his soul is an abiding healing presence in the world.

Six years after that memorable healing experience in Tokyo I stood before eight young Japanese counselors and psychologists and five American bodyworkers. It was the first evening of a Basic Acupressure class at Esalen Institute. The healing would continue.

26

World Peace

The setting was idyllic, Esalen Institute, one of the forefront alternative learning institutes in the world, in Big Sur California. It was summer, the optimum season. We were ready for our class and happy to be there.

Esalen sits high above the Pacific, a Shangra-la-fantasy-world rolled out like a magic carpet right up to the edge of the cliffs from where you can see the vast ocean waves stretching out to the horizon and hear their rhythmic crashing against the rocks far below. It is a global world, removed from the ordinary day-to-day life of any culture, where students from around the globe have been discovering the edges of human consciousness for forty years.

Three of us had met to teach the first Basic Acupressure class ever offered there. We were full of enthusiasm and great expectations. Susan Grant, the co-teacher, Jim Mutch, our assistant, and I were excited about the possibility of making this valuable work available to more people in the world.

We had heard that we would have eight Japanese students. This prospect was particularly interesting to us since the seeds of our work originated in Japan. A contemporary Japanese master-healer, Jiro Murai, had developed it from the centuries-long tradition of Chinese medicine. How appropriate that the gift he gave to America after World War II should be returned to Japan, Americanized with our practitioner experiences.

Susan and I had prepared with care, coordinating our teaching talents. Our pre-class notes were filled with great ideas about how to get the complex information and practice transmitted in only five days. And we were adding a new element. We planned to share fruits of the class by asking the students to bring guests into class on the last day. The students would offer acupressure sessions to anyone who wanted them from the greater community. It was a big order but we were accomplished teachers; we knew we could do it.

Halt!

On the first evening we sat before eight young Japanese counselors and psychologists and five American professionals, becoming bodyworkers. The Japanese were jet-lagged but attentive, the Americans eager to get on with the learning.

We introduced ourselves around the circle with the request for students to tell about their work and why they wanted the class. Within five minutes we realized that the Japanese did not speak, nor understand, much English. None of us spoke Japanese. They had no translator. It also became clear that the Americans wanted information and achievement; they were here to advance their bodywork skills.

A gospel song line jumped into my head, with a slight revision: "Nobody knows the trouble I'm in, nobody knows but Jesus." I thought, exactly! Only Jesus could help with this.

Susan and I quickly realized our lesson plan was useless. But how could we teach both groups effectively so that all would return home satisfied? This would be a grand exercise in fast learning and creatively. We scrapped the lesson plan, prayed for the unimaginable and opened up to the flow of the Tao.

The first job was to find common ground and unity. It couldn't be done through language. Fortunately, we could count on expert help from our assistant Jim, a loving and compassionate practitioner who had assisted Fritz and me many times in other classes at Esalen.

And we were teaching with the perfect tool—touch. So we tentatively hung onto one piece of the agenda: we would still ask each student to bring a guest from the community on the last day, if giving a full session seemed possible. It was a big IF. But we could always scratch the idea if it didn't seem doable by the end.

We had another possible resource, esoteric but worth opening up to. Since the ancient form of acupressure we are teaching was formulated by Jiro Murai in Japan, perhaps the Japanese would unconsciously resonate with an instinctive/intuitive/experiential pattern already laid down in their culture through centuries.

So we began. Touching. Finding acupoints on each other's bodies...laughing at the awkwardness, for both Japanese and Americans, of finding such points as the *tail bone* and *pubic bone.* Trading words between the languages for our names brought repeated laughter—thank you, good morning, yes, no, good, and *Point Eleven.* Before the end of the week "Point Eleven," which we also call "Excess Baggage" because of its particularly tense point location at the juncture of the shoulder and neck, had traveled throughout the institute. It turned out the Japanese were practicing it on as many bodies as possible.

Smiles of pleasure, helping hands, sighs of relaxation, pats for "well done," ummms and ahhhs—these interactions replaced language much quicker than we could have imagined.

By the end of the first day all of us had relaxed our pre-conceived notions of what the class should be. Susan, Jim and I simply opened up to what was possible within the reality at hand. The Americans also seemed willing to give up their professional ambitions to accept the richness of learning about another people. And it looked like the Japanese were letting go of any anxiety about being students in a foreign environment, through a foreign language, with foreign customs, cuisine, and people.

We had all entered a space of acceptance together. It was to become profound.

And so the week progressed, each day richer than the last. More closeness and lightness developed. We began to experience unity in the profound satisfaction of facilitating a state of safety and healing for one another. It was much deeper than language could have accomplished.

In the middle of the week Monge, a big, handsome, black-belt Karate achiever, summed up the language reality for us:

"We are communicating through our hearts," he said in mime, pointing from his heart to ours.

On the second day an American doctor sampled our class. He was "shopping," trying to decide which class of the rich menu at Esalen that week he would settle into. He looked bewildered but somewhat interested. On the third day he came again and stayed awhile longer.

At the dinner table he sat with us and asked the questions not possible in class about the work.

"Does this help musculo-skeletal problems?"

"Yes, but it also goes deeper into the system, even into the viscera."

He looked puzzled. We tried to explain about energy movement in the body, its pervasive effects throughout all the systems. I thought we were probably speaking an alien language to him. However he soon showed up in our class for good. He seemed fascinated by the process going on, between bodies, between people and in the general group atmosphere. We found out later that he is the director of a medical program at a prestigious hospital.

On the third day Susan brought help that enhanced our experiences. She invited the director of our Japanese students' program, Mr. Murakami, who had brought twenty Japanese students to Esalen. He spoke English and offered to stay with us for an hour to translate.

Mr. Murakami helped us enormously by relaying some of the key concepts we had not been able to get across. His students also had the opportunity to ask questions and make comments.

After he had heard some of our explanations Mr. Murakami said that what we were teaching reminded him of an ancient saying in Japanese—Hei Sei. He quickly wrote two Japanese characters on the board that conveyed this saying. He translated:

"Hei means inner peace. Sei means something like outer world accomplished, or achieved."

We stared at these characters while all of us, Japanese and Americans alike, let his message sink in.

It was stunning. Maybe the esoteric factor was working. This mixed group, on the third day, was communicating at a deeper level than our original lesson plan anticipated.

Those characters remained on the board for the remainder of the week and at the end I brought them home.

Mr. Murakami cleared up another puzzle for us. I had been wearing a white kimono-like jacket that has bold black Japanese characters on the back. I wear it often. I had tried many times to find out what the characters meant without success. I bought it in Koyasan, an ancient temple town in Japan during our teaching trip there in 1998. In Koyasan no one spoke enough English to tell me the meaning and since then it seemed people who knew Japanese characters couldn't decipher them either.

The Japanese students had been pointing to the jacket with what looked like unusual interest. It sounded like they were asking me what it meant, or why I wore it. I couldn't tell. But I was eager to find out from Mr. Murakami for all of us.

"Ohhh," he said, tracing the characters on my back as he said them in Japanese.

"It is a shirt worn by esoteric Buddhists. The characters mean 'The Divine is always with you.'"

Then we all said "Ohhh!"

On the fourth day the Japanese students invited the whole Esalen community to a tea ceremony on the lawn. We eagerly joined their brightly-costumed group there. Now the Japanese became our teachers from their own context.

The program began with a few words from Mr. Murakami.

"We wish to express our gratitude for the hospitality and learning we have experienced here at Esalen and give back some of that wealth.

We will show you how we perform the tea ceremony and ask you to participate. We will also demonstrate some martial arts and origami."

The Japanese students were dressed in full costume for their functions. For example, the swordswoman appeared in the long black robes of the Ninja. She stood up tall, for her swift sword-wielding demonstration. Her eyes looked as concentrated and otherworldly as any I had seen in Ninja movies.

Japanese instruments were laid out ceremoniously on the lawn. The hand-made tea bowls they had brought from Japan. Brilliantly colored papers for origami, the art of folding small paper into birds.

Each guest was served tea and shown how to turn the bowl three times before and after drinking. The demonstrations were awe-inspiring. We were transfixed by how creatively they could give us an experience of these ancient customs, when we didn't understand Japanese or the lineages of their practices.

The Americans were impressed. The Japanese were happy that their gifts had been accepted with appreciation and respect. We were settling into a space of mutual respect and sharing that was deeply satisfying.

By the end of the fourth day Susan and I realized we had all reached a state of learning and healing that far outstripped our agenda, even our visions for the work. A bonding between every member of the class had happened that we never could have anticipated. There were no outsiders nor insiders, no longer Japanese and Americans nor even men and women. We were simply one human organism, supporting each other's many talents and charms. I saw that beyond language, culture or belief systems, we all share the common bond of being ordinary humans.

Too quickly our time together was coming to a close. We wanted more but also were grateful that every member seemed completely satisfied with what they had experienced.

But the beyond-all was still to come.

We had decided to risk the gift session for guests and prepared the students accordingly. The session was scheduled for Friday morning before class, and it was optional. There was space for only eight tables in our classroom so only eight people could work. All eight Japanese wanted to bring a guest and try their skills. That left the Americans free but we invited them to come as a support team for the Japanese if they wished.

By the time I arrived very early to the classroom Jim had already prepared the room. It was clean and clear and all the tables were lined up in perfect symmetry. It looked and felt wonderful for our big experiment.

We waited.

At the appointed time the Japanese started arriving, guests in hand. The Americans also arrived. They respectfully stood beside the tables, ready to assist if needed.

I saw with relief, and just a bit of anxiety (what if our offering didn't work?), that one of the girls had brought Mr. Murakami, their Director.

I gave a very short welcome to the guests, which the Director translated. I pointed to the two characters on the board and said that we hoped to offer them an experience of Hei Sei through this acupressure session.

The guests lay on the tables and the givers took their places beside them, hands poised.

Susan guided the givers through the acupressure protocol. Japanese translation wasn't possible or relevant because of the technical terms so the Director just relaxed into the experience.

The session took about twenty minutes. Miraculously all the students performed it beautifully. When they needed help, which was seldom, Jim and I were there as well as American buddies beside them.

About twelve minutes into the session I became aware of an amazing feeling in the room. How to describe it? It was deeply quiet, serene, spacious, peaceful. The phrase "the peace that passes all understanding" came to mind.

I have experienced this before, I thought, and then it came to me: Tokyo!

The healers all together.

Yes! This IS Hei Sei! We are living it all together right now. We are at peace within ourselves, and our group is "accomplished," at peace.

This is truly a moment of world peace, I thought.

Again that overwhelming feeling of gratitude/compassion flooded over me, as it had that day in Tokyo. Tears welled up. I looked across the room and met the eyes of one of the Americans, a beautiful and sensitive young man who had been one of the most ardent students in the beginning. His eyes were also filled with tears. We exchanged a deep knowing and appreciation for this moment.

At precisely that same minute the doctor walked in, almost at the end of the guest session. I could see that he was registering the amazing spaciousness in the room. His face looked stunned. He backed up a tiny step. Then he sat down on the floor and watched the end of the session.

I would have lingered in that space for a long time but the work was finished and the guests needed to be off to their own classes. They arose from the tables, some smiling broadly, some looking dazed, and all looking lighter.

Mr. Murakami sat up.

"What an amazing experience," he said, "I felt energy in my crown center, my heart and all the way to my feet! Who would have believed you could teach them to do this in only five days! Especially her," he gestured to his giver, a charming and bright young woman we had all come to adore. Everyone laughed. She looked utterly delighted with herself.

Rather than jumping up to leave though, Mr. Murakami said he wanted to know from others what they had experienced, He would translate. Then he went around the room, to all eight guests, asking for their feedback.

"I felt good inside. Very relaxed."

"It was very strong. I feel more awake now."

"I felt all my energy centers and then I felt myself."

"I felt very peaceful inside."

And so on around the room. As a teacher I was feeling better every minute. I caught the doctor's expression. He was looking on with great interest, even wonder.

"I believe we have just experienced a moment of world peace," I said, "let us send this blessing we have received out to the whole world."

Everyone stood utterly still for a moment.

"That!" One of the Japanese students pointed to the back of my shirt. The Japanese guests turned to read the characters, which we easily remembered,

"The Divine is always with you."

Sooner than we wished it was over. We needed to pack up and the Japanese had a bus to catch right away. Still we all tarried. The Americans were hugging everyone. The Japanese, just learning this Esalen and California custom, were responding fully. They were all taking pictures with fancy cameras and saying goodbye however they could. One of the girls came up to me and threw her arms around me. She was crying.

For a second I was distressed, was something wrong? She had been one of the slowest students in the class but also the most successful at delivering the last session. No, I could see that she was crying from gratitude/overwhelm and sadness at leaving us. She repeated the hug to every last person, crying all the while. Finally one of her classmates literally pulled her away to hurry off to the bus.

As we left the classroom we saw the bus full of our Japanese friends, all of them waving vigorously at us.

We had become brothers and sisters in only five days. We were at peace within ourselves and at peace with each other.

This is the way it could happen in the world, I thought, one moment of soul lightning at a time.

Section IX: Living with Lightning: Where Do We Go From Here?

27

Full Circle

I have tried to show how lightning strokes from heaven can light up our individual souls to bring us closer to our origins. And how awakened soul consciousness can help us claim our own soul destiny design.

Now we return to the beginning—lightning in the saucer.

Surely we are living in one of the darkest periods of known history. Can we reach for guidance within the wisdom in our own souls? Do we have the faith to embrace heaven's lightning to help us not only survive, but evolve to a higher level of consciousness? Will we be strong enough to stand by and witness lightning shake and sear the world and yet discover a fragile light bulb still intact? Can we recognize the radiance behind this world in time to resurrect us from the dark? Will corpses yet arise from the graves of unconsciousness and return to life in their own divine spirits?

Predictions come along every week, on world news and through the Internet, about our chances to survive as individuals or even as a species. They range from total destruction of the planet to total salvation. But the ones I remember most clearly are those that came from my teachers.

In one of her prophetic moods Evelyn told us that all humans bent on making war here were going to be "shipped off this planet." That sounded good to us at the time even though it is reasonably unlikely, given both past history and what we're living now.

Bapak said in the 1970s that if the world survived through the 1990s it would eventually emerge into a golden age.

Sai Baba says that we have been sleeping for a thousand years but now we have an opportunity to awaken. He vowed to remain here, in his God-form, through a third incarnation, in order to "return this world to righteousness."

Then, he says, there will be one thousand years of peace.

Of course the ordinary mind can't believe in, nor even grasp, such predictions. I only offer them here as reports.

What do I think personally?

I can't reasonably assess them. But apparently my unconscious knows more about these things than my waking state does.

Therefore I conclude this book with visions and dreams.

About twenty years ago Patricia Sun, the visionary and healer we traveled with to Egypt, reported a prophetic vision of hers. I heard her tell it several times.

In the vision she saw our whole planet from space and it was dark. Then she saw a few tiny lights show up on the planetary surface. She knew, in that perception of visions, that these lights were the enlightening of individuals. Then, in rapid succession, she saw more and more lights turn on and more and more until finally the whole planet was lighted. Then a banner unfurled across the world. It read: Twenty Years. Patricia has been a faithful facilitator for this enlightening process during all those years.

About the same time I had the following vision:

I saw our planet moving through space steadily. It was approaching a Dimension in space very different from the realm it had been traveling through. I could see that a transition into this new Dimension was inevitable; it could not be avoided nor forestalled. I also knew that the Dimension itself was very beautiful, expansive and positive, and that our planet would be much better off within It. But as we got closer to this Dimension huge waves of turbulence arose in space. The transition itself was harrowing. I saw great tall skyscrapers melting down into the streets as people ran away from the debris, screaming in terror. All structures of the city were coming apart, crashing down into rubble. In 2001 I recalled this vision and realized that I had already seen what I was watching on television after 9/11.

Then, rising out of the rubble, I saw beautiful young people emerging. Their faces were shining; they were inspired and full of readiness to embrace that beautiful and expansive new Dimension.

The vision foretold that a clearing of our entire planet would inevitably occur because there were many factors of a lower vibration then active that could not exist within that other Dimension. I wondered then if it was possible for this clearing to be just like cleaning house, or whether it would take over like wild fire, burning up the dross. It seemed up to us whether we would choose a voluntary and reasonable means of entering the new Dimension, or give in to the lowest common vibration and experience an involuntary and violent transition.

Despite the massive destruction in the vision I had an uplifting feeling from it. The young people at the end were majestic, clean and fresh.

In the autumn of 2000 Fritz and I led a class in India where students from several countries met Indian healers to study with us. It was a uniquely enlightening time because we were all serious professionals who were working on ourselves diligently and learning from each other at all levels. After the class we went to Sai Baba's ashram together where the learning increased exponentially.

Shortly after we came home I had the following dream, which I quote from my journal:

Oct. 29, 2000—Dream: Baby Whose Consciousness Wants to Live

Fritz and I are getting back from India to teach a class. A woman I don't know joins us. She looks interested and has an intellectual manner but she is thin, almost wizened-looking. I think, she is highly educated and thinks she knows all the answers. She comes up to me and hands me a tiny box. A baby is inside. She says, "He's sick. His ears are infected and he needs medicine and care."

I ask her about the baby, what he has exactly and how long he has been sick. She says, "He has been in the hospital for some time where I have been seeing him but now he has been sent home and I'm too tired to take care of him."

I say," Do you mean you want to give your baby away?"

She looks me in the eye and says, "Yes. I can't care for him anymore. I have to live for myself now. You take him. You have a mother's heart." And she walks away.

I hold the tiny box with the baby close to my body, trying to give it warmth while I find medical help. Then a violent process of struggle and agony starts within me. I can tell it's about assuming responsibility for this baby as well as the horror of a mother actually voluntarily giving him away. That was the worst part—choosing her own development over the responsibility for her baby. I writhe around and finally scream at the top of my lungs for help. I appeal to several "helpers" (not Subud) but they all look helpless in the face of what I'm going through.

With a scrap of witness I realize people may think I'm going crazy and if they institutionalize me how can I care for the baby? I search pictures on the wall to find a focus point or center. Only one, the picture of a witch/crone, brings any strength or anchor. Finally I call straight out, "God, help me!" The process quiets down.

I'm still holding the baby. He badly needs medical attention for I feel he is close to death. I go to a hospital and simply barge in. Everyone looks at me in horror and pushes me out. I cry out, "This baby is about to die! Please help me!" One arrogant young doctor simply looks at me and pushes me away. As he does one of his needles sticks into me. I say, incensed,

"Take that needle out of me!"

But he still looks at me as if I'm nobody. Once again, feeling the baby's life slipping away I scream out,

"GOD HELP ME, GOD HELP US ALL! IF THIS BEING WANTS CONSCIOUSNESS IT SHOULD LIVE. Otherwise I will surrender and let it go but (I repeat it again) IF THIS BEING WANTS CONSCIOUSNESS IT SHOULD BE GIVEN THE CHANCE TO LIVE!"

The hospital staff still scoffs at me as if I am crazy. But then one young doctor looks around at me with interest. He lays down his instruments and walks over to me. He asks about the problem. I tell him. He says,

"Well, there's an experiment that has been done with running x (he said the name in the dream but I didn't get what it was...some kind of pure liquid) through the entire system which will clear up anything. I'll try it with this baby."

He hooks the baby up to a kind of distilling machine and runs this clear liquid through his body as I watch. Very quickly the baby becomes clear and the doctor says,

"That's it. He's well. He'll be fine." I look at this young man with awe and say,

"God bless you forever. You have saved the baby." I am overjoyed.

I woke up almost breathless. I said to myself you've got to remember this dream. No, write it down! So I jumped up to dress but instead started racking with sobs. I cried for a long time as if my heart were breaking.

Trying to get myself together I dressed and walked outside, still crying. I repeated "Please God, help us; what is this about?"

"The world," said my inner voice.

Then I became painfully aware of how trivial our issues usually are, how much time we waste on just normal everyday life stuff while the world is potentially perishing before our very eyes.

The next dream occurred the last of July, 2001 while Fritz and I were teaching at Esalen. It had been a wonderful week, with perfect weather and attuned students. We were having the best of times. Nothing was disturbing me.

On the morning of July 29 I awakened in a cold sweat, terrified by the following dream:

7/29/01 dream—A Monster with Headless Legs

A big class is over but people are still coming to me with their problems. I keep working because I'm doing excellent work and I feel happy about being able to help.

A mother with her child comes up. She is desperate for help. Even though the class is over I say, "OK, I'll work with you and your child," and I begin.

Then I hear and feel some huge Thing coming. I quickly push the mother and child away, saying, "Something is coming that we can't handle with this work. Run as fast as you can!" Then I run in another direction to divert the Thing from them.

But I realize I can't possibly outrun this Thing. I think, what can I do? I run for an elevator but realize I can't get into it before the Thing reaches me. I back into a niche in the wall and grow still to hide. Just then I can see the Thing for the first time. It is actually two huge legs, about fifteen feet tall. They move like great machines. It has no body nor head. I think, since it has no eyes maybe I can hide here. But I know it will find me and I'm terrified.

I wake up, shaking with fear.

I processed this dream at a personal level with some success but the meaning I gleaned didn't take the terror away. On September 11, 2001 I saw on television the devastation and terror that a huge headless monster could cause in the world. And the uselessness of our former ways of psychologically processing "problems."

After September 11 the Process Acupressure teachers and I designed a swift shock/stress body protocol that practitioners took into ground zero to offer the rescue workers there. They found that direct, caring bodywork did more than any words could to soothe the horrendous effects of that monster.

Shortly thereafter I had the following dream:

Birth of a Bodhisatva

A woman is giving birth. An expert has been called in to help her but I see that both women are stuck in the process. I go to them and stretch my arms around both their pelvises. Just as the going gets rough the mother starts to cave in as her past unfinished business arises from the pressures of childbirth. She is sobbing about her childhood, her mother's negligence, etc. Just at that time her husband walks by and calls out, "I love you." But she seems not to hear him and continues to cry about her hurt inner child.

I grasp her more firmly around the pelvis, look into her eyes directly and call out with emphatic energy, "None of that matters! Only Love matters!"

At the same time I begin to feel the vibratory presence of the child within her. It is a gigantic energy that almost causes me to faint with wonder. I see spinning planets and the galaxies within it. I know then the child is a Bodhisatva, coming to this world at a very important time to help. And I know that it is imperative to get through the birth. I start saying over and over, "Om mane padme Om," the Buddhist chant, calling for spiritual help.

I wake up gasping and trembling with the gigantic energy of the child. It is so strong that it wakes Fritz out of a sound sleep. "What's the matter?" he asks urgently.

"No words possible," I answer, "let me give it to you." And I put my arms around him, confident that he can feel the vibration. He says after awhile, "That's really big."

And finally, just as I was finishing this book, struggling with its concluding remarks about individual and world survival I had the following early morning dream.

Dream: Two Luminous Beings

I travel up a mountain where I meet a young man who resembles an old soul friend. He had a chaotic past and is still needing help.

We proceed together up the mountain and after overcoming various obstacles, including getting wet in ditches, we are suddenly joined by two huge luminous beings. One is a king-like figure, obviously in charge, the other, his helper. They are arranging various things in the world by magical means. I ask what they are doing. The response is holographic; I can hear, see and feel it all at once.

"It is now time for beauty, equality and harmony on earth. We are assisting that."

As the message is given I am shown a picture of an ordered, clean, beautiful, natural world. When the concept "harmony" is transmitted I can feel how wonderful that would be for the people. I realize this assistance is coming from a very high level.

I exclaim, "Thank God!"

Both beings lift their heads toward heaven and say,

"Yes!" implying great obedience and allegiance to their work for God.

The helper is struggling with the chaotic effect this world has on him; he has a headache. With great trepidation I say,

"If I may offer, I can give you a form of acupressure that might help. Could I try?"

He looks surprised but says, "go ahead."

Then he lies down and I start working on his body of light, an amazing experience. Gradually he smiles, looks relieved, gets up and says to the king figure:

"That's good."

I ask about the headache. He says it's gone. Then he says to me, as he gestures toward my young male companion:

"Take good care of him."

I get a feeling that the young man will be needed to help them later on.

Then they disappear.

Later in meditation I sought the message of the dream and asked if I could attune to the frequency of the light beings and talk with them. The answer was swift: *"Yes, if you're succinct."*

"May I have a general interpretation of the dream then," I asked.

"The dream is to assure you of higher purpose and consciousness at work on earth now. We are two of many beings arranging and assisting this world to come back into harmony with the Great Creative. We move with

instructions and blessings from the Great Source of Intelligence (God in your language.)

"You were told long ago to hold a higher perspective but you continue to try to fit in here for acceptance. Useless endeavor. Your help with the headache showed that the acupressure work you do is applicable even to the light bodies of higher beings, hence extremely valuable here. You also have the capacity to attune to higher frequencies which is shown in the fact that you could even see, and help, us in the dream."

"Do you have advice for me?"

"Go straight ahead with attunement and then non-attachment. Stay with this. Forget and detach from what other people will think. Get clear what you're doing—to understand what IS and how to help here with real purpose. Stay attuned to the Tao—God's will. Trust your connection and directions. Work at that level."

I have done the best I can to carry out their advice and in this book, to show how important it is to pay attention to soul lightning in our lives. All of us experience it in many different forms because it is always available from the radiance behind the world. It is not easy to recognize these gifts, and take them in fully, because so often, as the light beings reminded me, we are more concerned with fitting in. We may fear that we will be considered oddballs or even crazy if we acknowledge those strange out-of-the-ordinary experiences. We live in a society that hardly supports them.

That is one of the reasons I felt it was so important to write this book because it has become clearer and clearer to me in my lifetime that soul lightning moments bring us closer to the truth of our own souls. Each of us carries the light, and our own unique purpose, within us. We arrived here with them; their expression will bring us the inner joy of being true to ourselves. We have a responsibility to truly stand in that light and bring it to others.

With my heart and soul I encourage you to trust, and to act upon, your own gifts of spirit.

About the Author

Aminah Raheem, Ph.D. is a transpersonal psychologist, *Diplomate of Process Work,* and *Zero Balancer.* As a body/mind therapist, she originated *Process and Basic Acupressure,* psycho-spiritual approaches that work through the body's energy systems to assist conscious development and the realization of soul purpose.

In her long career as a teacher, therapist and author, Dr. Raheem has taught thousands in the helping professions to work with a compassionate, client-centered approach to the whole person. She taught at the Institute for Transpersonal Psychology in Palo Alto, California, for ten years where she observed and worked with the process of personal transformation. She now teaches body/mind/soul consciousness work internationally, through the International Alliance for Healthcare Educators. (See www.iahe.com)

Dr. Raheem's pioneering book, *Soul Return: Integrating Body, Psyche and Spirit,* still stands at the forefront of defining the relationship of body and soul. *Network* magazine described it as, "A brilliantly clear explanation of the role that spirituality plays in psychology. Expertly blending a wide background in Western psychology with a broad and sympathetic understanding of Eastern spiritual traditions, Aminah Raheem presents a scientific and well-reasoned survey of the role that factors like love, wisdom, service and enlightenment play in optimal health."

Dr. Raheem has also written many workbooks which articulate specific implementation of her work.

As the founder and president of *Soul Lightening International,* a non-profit foundation dedicated to soul awakening for the health and well being of individuals and our planet, Dr. Raheem is spreading a vision of harmonic co-existence between humans and nature and helping to chart a course for individual and global soul consciousness.

For more information about her workshops, consulting, or books, please contact: www.processacupressure.com or www.iahe.com.

Bibliography

The American Heritage Dictionary. New York: Houghton, Mifflin, 1983.

Bennett.J.G. *Concerning Subud,* published around 1959. (Out of print.)

Brinkley. D. *Saved by the Light.* New York: HarperCollins, Publishers, 1994.

Bucke.R.M., M.D. *Cosmic Consciousness.* New York: E.P. Dutton and Company, 1969.

Cornell, J. *Amma: Portrait of a Living Sage.* An imprint of Harper Collins Publishers, 2001.

Clare of Assisi: Light for the Way. Compiled by A group of Poor Clares of France, Belgium and Italy Editions du Signe, 1991.

Devi, Sri M.A. *The Awakening of Universal Motherhood.* Kerela, India: Mata Amritanandamayi Mission Trust, 2002.

Goodman, M. *The Mystery of Mother Meera.* San Francisco: Harper, 1998.

Lainiati, Sr. C. A. *Saint Clare of Assisi.* Santa Maria: Edizioni Porziuncola, 1994.

Longcroft, H. *The History of Subud.* Houston: Al-Baz Publishing, Inc., 1993.

Needleman, J. *The New Religions.* New York: E.P. Dutton & Co., Inc., 1970.

Raheem, A. *Soul Return: Integrating Body, Psyche and Spirit.* Palm Beach Gardens, Florida: Upledger Institute Publications, 2000.

Rofe, H. *The Path of Subud.* Berkeley: Undiscovered Worlds Press, 1959. (out of print)

Smith, F. F., M.D. *The Alchemy of Touch.* Santa Fe: Redwing Publications, 2005.

Tao Te Ching. Translated by S. Mitchell. New York: HarperPerennial, 1988.

Wilhelm, R. *The Secret of the Golden Flower.* New York: Harcourt Brace Jovanovich, 1962.

978-0-595-34811-4
0-595-34811-4